Revolutionary Days

Princess Julia Grant Cantacuzene, 1907

My Life Here and There

The Lakeside Classics

REVOLUTIONARY DAYS

Including passages from
My Life Here and There
1876–1917

By
Princess Julia Cantacuzene
Countess Speransky, née Grant

EDITED BY
TERENCE EMMONS

The Lakeside Press

R.R. DONNELLEY & SONS COMPANY

CHICAGO

December, 1999

PUBLISHERS' PREFACE

IT WAS EXACTLY one hundred years ago, in 1899, that the author of this year's Lakeside Classic embarked upon the adventure of her life. That summer, Julia Dent Grant, granddaughter of the famous general and ex-president, married a Russian prince and sailed off to live among the aristocracy in Imperial Russia. She and her family escaped in 1918 from the Russian Revolution and returned to the United States. Princess Cantacuzene then wrote her memoirs of one of this century's pivotal events.

It is interesting to note this book's Chicago connection. Both of Julia's parents were from Illinois. Her mother's sister was wealthy Chicago society leader Bertha Honoré (Mrs. Potter) Palmer. Julia met her prince while traveling in Europe with her aunt and uncle, visited Chicago on trips back to the United States, and, upon her permanent return, was mentored by Mrs. Palmer.

Coincidentally, 1899 was also a milestone in the history of our company. The founder and a prominent civic leader, Richard Robert Donnelley, died in April of 1899. Leadership passed to his son, Thomas Elliott Donnelley, who led the company for the next half-century. It was T.E. who, in 1903, started The Lakeside Classics series. These books were intended to typify simplicity and elegance in book design and demonstrate the latest in manufacturing methods.

Each year since then, a new title in the series has been issued as a holiday gift.

Revolutionary Days is the ninety-seventh book in The Lakeside Classics series. We continue to honor T.E.'s original concept, employing the latest commercial techniques to manufacture the book. For more information about this volume, please refer to the Colophon at the back of the book.

Our historical editor for this edition was Terence Emmons, Ph.D., who teaches Russian history at Stanford University. Professor Emmons is the editor of a multivolume, annotated bibliography of Russian émigré memoirs; the author of a book on Russians in San Francisco; and the editor and translator for a book that details the diary of a professor at a Moscow university. Professor Emmons wrote our Historical Introduction and edited and annotated the text.

* * * *

When R.R. Donnelley died one hundred years ago, the company faced significant challenges. The same is true today.

Although print continues to be a vigorous and healthy business, we know we must be vigilant to assure the right combination of people, plans, and resources to meet the expectations of our customers and shareholders. We are emphasizing four business areas that will create future profitable growth.

First, we look to transform print to meet our customers' needs for speed, targeting, and flexibility in the products and services we offer. Second, we continue to build an integrated production system of value-added services, from premedia (the stages before printing plates are made) through final distribution of products.

We also are concentrating on using our current capabilities in ways that are highly valued by our customers, such as consolidating and reconfiguring our logistics business so we can offer customers better, faster, and more economical ways to get their products to consumers. Finally, we are extending our capabilities through acquisition and expansion to leverage value-creating opportunities.

In this Preface, we will focus on the last point: how we extended our capabilities in 1999 to meet the needs of our customers, shareholders, and employees.

Early in 1999, we broadened our range of direct-mail capabilities when we purchased Communicolor, a major direct-mail marketing group. This acquisition significantly enhances our capabilities to produce a wide array of direct-mail products. We are now well positioned to assist direct marketers in improving their response rates through increasing levels of personalization and product differentiation, all provided by one source.

We recognize that the southeast United States is a growing market. Two acquisitions in 1999 were based on our decision to serve this region more effectively. Each acquisition addresses a different market segment. For example, the financial printing unit of

Cadmus Communications, with service centers in Baltimore, Charlotte, Raleigh, and Richmond, offers entry to the Southeast's financial centers. The rapid growth of this region, including the emergence of some of the largest banks in the United States, provides great opportunities in financial printing. The purchase included a print-on-demand and fulfillment center in Charlotte, enabling us to offer these popular services more efficiently in the Southeast.

Late last year, when we purchased GTE Directories' St. Petersburg, Florida, telephone directory printing plant, we added print/bind, logistics, and accelerated delivery throughout the region for telecommunications publishers. The agreement included a long-term contract to print certain GTE directories, as well.

In addition to adding new print capabilities, the company added other value-added services, including Internet-related services. During the past few years, customers have sought aggressively to extend their brands into new channels. R.R. Donnelley responded by forming the eSolutions[sm] business unit, which helps customers utilize the Internet and other electronic media to achieve brand extension. The eSolutions group creates large-scale Web sites, consults on Internet strategy, and develops Internet-based marketing programs. It enables our customers to acquire new customers, retain existing customers, and increase the lifetime value of customers.

South America also continues to provide us with

excellent opportunities for growth. Through Editorial Lord Cochrane, which is 78 percent owned by R.R. Donnelley, we made a number of moves to strengthen our position there. For example, Donnelley Cochrane Brasil Ltda. expanded into the telecommunications market by establishing its first dedicated directory plant in Brazil near São Paulo. This facility complements the company's existing directory capacity in Santiago, Chile.

We entered the book market in South America by acquiring São Paulo-based Hamburg Gráfica Editora, the largest independent book manufacturer in Brazil. Among its customers are many of South America's leading publishing houses in the elementary school, high school, trade, and professional book markets.

In Argentina, our Cochrane S.A. took full ownership of Atlántida Cochrane S.A., when it purchased the remaining 50 percent of that company. Renamed Donnelley Cochrane Argentina, the company focuses on printing high-quality magazines, inserts, and catalogs for domestic markets, including Brazil, Paraguay, and Uruguay.

Our Central and Eastern Europe operations print magazines and catalogs for Poland, the Czech Republic, Russia, Ukraine, and Germany, as well as telephone directories primarily for Poland, the Czech Republic, and Greece. To add to these capabilities, we are investing $100 million in our operations in Poland over the next three years. Specifically, we acquired 100 percent ownership of Donnelley Polish-

American Printing Company, a Kraków-based joint venture formed in 1993, and we are expanding our existing facility in Kraków, making it the largest and most advanced printing operation in the region. That plant celebrated its fifth anniversary this year. We also plan another printing plant in Kraków, with startup date to be determined.

Our current success is demonstrated in the performance measurements where we excel: customer relationships and integrated solutions, technology, and financial metrics such as margins, cash flow, debt capacity to finance growth, and return on investment. Our future success is dependent on maintaining our lead in delivering value-added products and services.

* * * *

This year, we welcomed Joseph B. Anderson, Jr., to our Board of Directors. Mr. Anderson is president and CEO of Chivas Products Ltd., a manufacturer of components for the automotive industry. Prior to that, he was general director of a business unit for General Motors Corporation. A decorated military officer, Mr. Anderson served two tours of duty in Vietnam and taught at West Point.

We wish you and your families good health and good wishes for the new year.

THE PUBLISHERS

December 1999

CONTENTS

List of Illustrations & Maps xv
Historical Introduction xvii

I. Childhood Impressions 3
II. My Grandfather's Illness and Death . 17
III. In Vienna and My Debut at Court . . 29
IV. Going Home 39
V. Months of Travel 45
VI. The Russian Home 57
VII. First Social Impressions 73
VIII. The Japanese War 91
IX. The 1905 Revolution 115
X. Calm Before the Storm 137
XI. The Knell of Autocracy 151
XII. First Days of War and Then Retreat . 165
XIII. Life in Petrograd 191
XIV. The "Occult" Party 203
XV. The Murder of Rasputin 211
XVI. The Revolution 223
XVII. The Provisional Government . . . 249
XVIII. The Arrest of the Empress 253
XIX. Aftermath of the Revolution . . . 265
XX. Kiev 289
XXI. Kerensky and Bolsheviki 301
XXII. The Rise of the Bolsheviki 315
XXIII. Kornilov and Kerensky 345
XXIV. The Bolshevik Uprising 363
XXV. Our Escape from Kiev 379
XXVI. The Crimea 397

xiv   Contents

XXVII.   Petrograd Under the Bolsheviki . . . 411
XXVIII. Last Days in Russia 427
Index   435
List of The Lakeside Classics 443

ILLUSTRATIONS & MAPS

Julia Cantacuzene, 1907. . . . . . Frontispiece
Witte and Stolypin. xxxiii
Kolchak, Rodzianko, and Kornilov xxxiv
Michael Cantacuzene. lvii
Julia Cantacuzene lviii
Frederick and Ida Honoré Grant 13
Ulysses S. Grant and family 14
Ulysses S. Grant. 21
Frederick and Ida Honoré Grant 22
Potter and Bertha Honoré Palmer 49
Michael Cantacuzene. 50
Cantacuzene wedding 53
Women's Pavilion, Columbian Exposition . 54
Bouromka Castle 59
Servants at Bouromka 60
Russian Imperial Family. 77
Dowager Empress Marie 78
Frederick Grant, baby Michael, and Julia . . 111
Julia Cantacuzene 112
Barricades in St. Petersburg 121
Julia Cantacuzene 122
Cantacuzene children. 141
Frederick Grant 142
Anna Vyrubova 145
Grigory Rasputin 146
Chevalier Guards 153
The Imperial palace, Tsarskoe Selo 154
Empress Alexandra and Anna Vyrubova . . 167

War workers in Petrograd   168
Visiting wounded soldiers   179
Red Cross train   180
Alexander Kerensky   197
Fourth Duma   198
Russian general staff   229
Soviets in the Tauride Palace   230
Nevsky Prospect, St. Petersburg   281
Julia Cantacuzene   282
Riverfront in Kiev   291
Kiev street   292
Women's Battalion of Death   297
May Day 1917, Winter Palace Square . . .   298
Empress Alexandra, Emperor Nicholas II . .   325
Map: Europe, 1888-1917   326
Map: St. Petersburg, 1899-1917   328
St. Petersburg postcard   329
Bertha Honoré Palmer   330
Ida Honoré Grant   331
Poster: October 1905 Manifesto   332
Poster: Moscow Uprising   333
Nicholas II leading troops   334
Nicholas Nikolaevich   335
"Freedom Loan"   336
Nicholas Nikolaevich   337
Battle of Lemberg   338
"Tsar Announces Declaration of War" . . .   339
Julia Cantacuzene   340
Cantacuzene villa on the Black Sea   399
Elizabeth Cantacuzene   400

HISTORICAL INTRODUCTION

O N 25 September 1899, the ultra-swanky commune of Newport, Rhode Island, "summer stronghold of the first families of the East,"[1] witnessed a wedding that was just about as aristocratic as the American republic afforded. The bride, the beautiful twenty-three-year-old Julia Grant, daughter of Brigadier General Frederick Dent Grant and niece of the formidable socialite who hosted the event, Mrs. Potter Palmer, had been born in the White House in 1876, toward the end of her grandfather's, Ulysses S. Grant's, second term.

The groom, one year Julia's senior, was a dapper Russian prince, Michael Cantacuzene, graduate of the Imperial Alexandrine Lycée in St. Petersburg, cavalry officer of the Imperial Russian Army—decked out for the occasion in his parade whites with red and silver trim, glossy high black boots, and, on his head, a golden helmet surmounted by an Imperial eagle. Prince Michael, whose full title was Prince Cantacuzene, Count Speransky, was not a prince of the ruling Romanov line, but his credentials were perhaps even more impressive: He was the direct descendant of the fourteenth-century Byzantine emperor John Cantacuzene (d. 1383) and the great-grandson of Russia's great statesman, Count Michael Speransky (1772-1839).

---

[1] Ishbel Ross, *Silhouette in Diamonds. The Life of Mrs. Potter Palmer* (New York: Arno Press, 1975), p. 127.

The following day, the young couple was en route to Russia, where Julia would spend most of the next eighteen years, raising three children (with the help of numerous domestics) and moving in the highest aristocratic circles around the court in St. Petersburg, with respites on the Cantacuzene estate of Bouromka in the Ukrainian province of Poltava, in the family villa near Yalta in the Crimea, and occasionally in the capitals and watering holes of Europe, while her husband made a brilliant military career for himself. And then "came the revolution." The core of the memoirs presented here, somewhat abridged, covers the Russian years in the life of "Princess Cantacuzene, Countess Speransky, née Grant." As chance would have it, they were fateful years for Russia.

Julia was not the first Grant to visit Russia. Shortly after his graduation from West Point in 1871, her father, Frederick Dent Grant (1850-1912),[2] accompanied General Sherman on a European tour as his aide-de-

---

[2] Julia Grant's father, U.S. Grant's eldest son, had a remarkable career, which began and ended (with the rank of major general) in the U.S. Army but also included stints as a civil engineer, businessman, New York police commissioner, and diplomat. He made a large number of acquaintances internationally among rulers and statesmen when he accompanied his parents on their world tour in 1877; these contacts later smoothed Julia's way in the beau monde of Russia and Europe. Frederick Dent Grant's military career encapsulated a sizable chunk of the history of American Manifest Destiny and imperialism, from Indian campaigns in the West to the Spanish-American War and the military administration of the Philippines and Puerto Rico. His biography has yet to be written.

camp. From the Near-Eastern leg of the tour, he entered Russia through the extreme south, where he was the guest of Grand Duke Michael Nikolaevich, viceroy of the Caucasus, and then journeyed north across the country to Moscow by carriage, and finally by rail to St. Petersburg, where he was a guest in the palace of the grand duke's wife.

Nor was Julia a provincial American at the time of her marriage. In 1888, her father had been appointed American minister to Austria, so for five years young Julia Grant lived amidst the Austro-Hungarian aristocracy and the international diplomatic corps in Vienna, went to a Viennese finishing school, learned to speak impeccable Viennese German, had a debut at court, was introduced to Emperor Franz Joseph (who was her father's frequent hunting companion) and to the empress, and danced innumerable evenings away at Viennese balls, with music sometimes provided by Strauss himself. On the way to Vienna, the Grants had been received at the court in London by Queen Victoria.

Julia Grant met her future husband, as she recounts in her memoirs, in Rome at the tail-end of a combined grand tour and convalescence journey arranged by her Aunt Bertha for her husband, Potter Palmer, in 1898. Julia, adopted as a kind of surrogate daughter by her aunt, who only had sons of her own, was invited along.

In 1870, Potter Palmer, a wealthy Chicago businessman, builder of the landmark Palmer House, had married the much younger Bertha Honoré, the daughter of another Chicago businessman, Henry Hamilton Honoré and sister of Julia's mother, Ida Marie. By the 1890s, Aunt Bertha ("Cissie") Palmer was a formidable figure in American and European high society. She had served as Chairman of the Board of Lady Managers of the World's Columbian Exposition in Chicago in 1893. She was active in Democratic politics. She shopped for clothes and jewels in London and Paris. She and her husband had attended the coronation of Tsar Nicholas II in Moscow in 1896, where she had met both the Tsarina Alexandra and the Queen of Greece.

In Rome, where the Palmer party spent considerable time at the beginning and toward the end of their long tour, they circulated at their accustomed level, going to tea with the Queen Mother of Italy, attending a mass celebrated by the Pope; and Julia, a tall, strikingly handsome young woman, fell in with a group of young diplomats, whom she describes in her memoirs as the *jeunesse dorée* (gilded youth) of the diplomatic corps. Among them was one Prince Michael Cantacuzene, who was temporarily assigned to the Russian embassy in Rome while recuperating from a horse-show accident. Within a week after the Palmer party relocated to Cannes on the way home, the prince showed up there; two days later Julia and the prince were engaged, and during the month left before she had to sail for home, the respective parents' consents had been gotten and a wedding scheduled for September in the United States. In the meantime, Cantacuzene would return to Russia for summer maneuvers.

In her memoirs, Julia skimps on the details of their courtship, which was whirlwind by any standards, but especially the Victorian. Besides her fiancé's good qualities, Julia recognized that she saw in this marriage a means of regaining the kind of social life she had clearly enjoyed in Vienna and missed after the termination of her father's diplomatic career. (Without wealth, her father had reentered the army and was currently posted to the Philippines.) And there was an air of adventure to the prospect that appealed to her nature as well. By her own admission, she knew nothing of the country she was about to adopt.

As Julia's temporary guardian, Aunt Bertha could easily have squelched the affair simply by catching an earlier steamer home. Instead, she seems to have taken an active part in persuading Julia's parents to give their consent. It is not unlikely that having a prince in the family was an idea that flattered her social ambitions. Julia's widowed grandmother, Julia Dent Grant, was said to have had misgivings about a second international marriage in the family, since her daughter Ellen (Nellie) and her children were living with her after a British marriage had failed.

We have no information about the reaction from Michael's side of the family, except Julia's report that consent was forthcoming and that her lack of dowry was no impediment. However, it was not likely to be a matter of indifference to Michael's mother, the Princess Elizabeth. (Michael's father, Prince Michael Rodi-onovich, had died in 1894.)

The Cantacuzene story is part of the history of Russia's southward expansion into Ottoman territory. The Cantacuzenes were not a particularly wealthy family by Russian aristocratic standards. The Russian line of Cantacuzenes—there was also a prominent Rumanian line during modern times—had begun with Michael's great-grandfather, Rodion Matveevich (d. 1774), who entered Russian service under Catherine the Great (reigned 1762-1796), created a regiment of Wallachian Hussars, obtained the rank of colonel of the Russian Army, and was granted princely title in keeping with the Russian practice of accepting foreign nobility into Russian service with a transfer of titles. Since the ancestral homeland of the Cantacuzenes—the Danubian principalities—was not in the end annexed by Russia (except for Bessarabia, the northern part of Moldavia), the Russian princes Cantacuzene possessed no great estates.[3] The estate of Bouromka in Poltava had come, along with the title of count, from the Speransky side of Michael's family. (Michael's father had received authorization to bear the Speransky name and titles in 1872 from his maternal grandmother, Count Speransky's daughter; this

[3]At one point in these memoirs, Julia Cantacuzene calls the family name "Greek." This is accurate enough if understood as a synonym for "non-Latin Byzantine," rather than in the modern ethnic-national sense.

was a common practice when a title would otherwise expire for lack of male issue.) Princess Elizabeth (1848-1923), née Sicard, whose ancestor, a French Huguenot, had also immigrated to Russia under Catherine II, owned, with her children, considerable real estate, including some landed holdings in addition to the large estate of Bouromka with its chateau worthy of the Loire Valley, apartments in St. Petersburg, a villa in the Crimea, and an apartment in Paris; but most of these were cash-flow liabilities rather than assets. With two younger brothers and a sister as coheirs (the Russian nobility as a rule did not practice primogeniture or any other form of unified inheritance), Prince Michael's pursuit of a military career was not a hobby.

****

The Russia to which the new Princess Cantacuzene was introduced at the end of the nineteenth century was the last of the great continental old régimes, a centralized absolute monarchy. Like the Austro-Hungarian and Ottoman Empires, Russia was a multinational empire.

Russia's social and economic landscapes at the end of the nineteenth century also in many ways more closely resembled those of a premodern old order than those of the other great powers of Europe. Russia's loss of the Crimean War to Britain and France in 1856 had diminished its international status. Russia remained predominantly agrarian with more than four-fifths of its 130 million inhabitants living in villages as peasants, occupied with agriculture, much of it not far above subsistence level. According to the first national census of 1897, about four-fifths of the peasants were still illiterate.

The nobles, less than 1 percent of the total population, still owned most of the private land in the country, still had preferential access to the higher levels of the educational system (including university preparatory secondary schools), and still enjoyed a near-monopoly in higher levels of the state bureaucracy and the officers' corps. Landed nobles dominated the *zemstvos*, the institutions of limited local self-government introduced in the reforms of the 1860s, which had included the abolition of serfdom.

What passed for a business class in late-nineteenth-century Russia was still rather small in numbers, given the low level of urban and industrial development, and with a few notable exceptions, was socially conservative. Russian polite society, therefore, tended to be a largely noble enterprise, populated by wealthy estate owners, government bureaucrats, and the military elite.

But things were changing fast by the turn of the century. As usual in Russian history, much of the initiative for change came from the state. In one way or another, the Russian state had been engaged in spurts of defensive modernization[4] at least since the sixteenth

[4]Cyril H. Black, *The Dynamics of Modernization: a Study in Comparative History* (New York: Harper & Row, 1966).

century, when it had become heavily involved with European powers to the west. The classic episode in the long history of Russia's defensive modernization, or "westernization," was the reign of Peter the Great at the beginning of the eighteenth century (1682-1725). With Peter came the introduction into Russia of large chunks of Western secular culture and technology, all for the immediate purpose of increasing Russia's military capacity to elevate it into the ranks of the great European powers. With a gigantic army of conscripted serfs and the rudimentary fiscal-industrial base required to support it that issued from the Petrine reforms, Russia emerged from the Napoleonic Wars of the early nineteenth century as the preeminent power in Europe. Defeat by the British and French in the Crimean War at mid-century precipitated another spurt of modernizing reforms, which continued, with interruptions and setbacks, until the outbreak of the Great War in 1914. Following the abolition of serfdom in 1861, the Russian state became deeply involved in promoting, under the direction of Minister of Finance Serge Witte, the further development of a heavy-industrial plant and the growth of railroads throughout the country.

Commensurately heavy investment in education was made by the state over the second half of the nineteenth century. Reforms of the 1860s had also laid the foundation of a modern system of jurisprudence, with courts, trials, and lawyers, and a modicum of self-government in towns and provinces.

Russia entered the industrial age late, and in a distinctive way. Unlike Britain and the earlier industrializing countries of western and central Europe, it was not private capitalists nor private banks that provided the initiative and capital for Russia's industrial takeoff, but the state. Under Finance Minister Serge Witte, the state by the 1890s had elaborated a fiscal strategy that allowed Russia to go on the gold standard. With a solid, convertible currency and guarantees provided by the state, both foreign capital and entrepreneurs rushed into Russia's industrialization project.

Russia's industrialization takeoff yielded several notable economic, social, and political results. The rate of industrial growth achieved in the 1890s, on a small initial base, of course, was the highest in the world (8 percent), but it was very lopsided growth, which concentrated on production of heavy industrial plant, rails, and rolling stock, and very little in the way of consumer products; in short, it was not stimulated by an internal market, and it did not do much to stimulate such a market, at least for the time being. Coming late and guided by the state, the industrial spurt borrowed the latest technology from the West and tended toward vast monopolies in the several branches of industry and toward gigantism. Concentration of industry in a few centers, in a few very large factories with huge labor forces, was characteristic of Russian industry in this takeoff period. Many of the largest concentrations of plant and proletariat were in the country's administrative centers, beginning with

St. Petersburg, which had the largest industrial labor force of any city in the country and a couple of the biggest factories in the world.

Another characteristic of Russia's industrial takeoff was that it did not produce a dynamic and politically aggressive business elite. Instead, the boards of directors of the new types of industrial enterprise tended to be populated by government bureaucrats, civil and military, and by foreigners.

The Russian autocracy engaged repeatedly in modernizing reforms, in all areas but one: It would not entertain proposals to limit its own authority. It avoided not only constitutions or merely consultative assemblies, but even a proper ministerial system of government. There was no political development to keep pace with the spread of education and the socioeconomic developments that were products of the autocracy's own modernizing policies.

The story of the revolutions of 1917 in Russia begins in the upheaval of the reform era of the 1860s, when the state itself began dismantling the old order by abolishing serfdom. A constitutional-reformist movement, focused on achieving representative government, civil and political rights, and a revolutionary-socialist movement were present from the start, but mostly went their separate ways. The constitutionalist movement (sometimes called the "liberal" movement) was gotten underway by nobles who had been mobilized by the government to participate in preparing the serf-emancipation project but had then been shunted aside by the bureaucracy. They carried their goal of representative government over into the *zemstvo* institutions of limited self-administration that were set up in 1864 in rural Russia. There they nurtured the idea of "crowning the *zemstvo* edifice" with a parliament in St. Petersburg. This was rebuffed, with some reprisals by the government in the mid-1860s, and remained mostly dormant until the end of the century.

The revolutionary socialist movement was essentially a student-based movement (largely populated, of course, by the sons and daughters of nobles). Inspired by the radical left by revolutions occurring in 1848 in Europe, young Russian radicals made their first serious attempts to organize for revolutionary action in the 1860s. They anticipated that the government's conservative reform, which often left the peasants with less land than they had worked for themselves before emancipation, would spark widespread peasant unrest, providing the fuel for a revolutionary transformation. This failed to happen, and when, more than a decade later, populist university youth took their message to the people in the villages, they were rebuffed.[5] Some veterans of this movement who had managed to escape arrest or had been released by the authorities then proceeded out of frustration to ter-

---

[5]As many as 3,000 activists, mostly university students and student-age youth of both sexes, participated in the "going to the people" movement of 1873-74, or nearly half the total number of students in the empire.

rorist acts against the state, eventually focusing on target number one, the tsar. On 1 March 1881, they succeeded in assassinating Alexander II.

The revolutionaries failed in their strategy—the new tsar, Alexander III, instead of capitulating to "The People's Will" (the deliberately ambiguous name of the terrorist organization) and summoning a constituent assembly where the people would decide on its own form of government (presumably a socialist form), mopped up the remnants of the terrorist organization and set out on a path of reaction.

At the end of the nineteenth century, and with Nicholas II crowned as tsar, Russia was on the eve of a period of intense political activity among the opponents of autocracy. But the political opposition consisted of officers without troops. The far left, on the eve of consolidating into "parties," remained merely groups of intellectuals without mass followings. Although there had been some significant labor unrest in the biggest factory centers, this activity soon subsided. There had been no truly significant peasant disturbances since the reform epoch of the 1860s.

Internationally, Russia was on its way to an alliance system with France and Britain, directed against the alliance of the German and Austro-Hungarian empires. These respective arrangements caused a regional Balkan conflict in 1914 to explode into a world war.

In the age of imperialism, Russia's efforts to maintain and enhance her status among the great powers involved her in the race for colonies and spheres of influence. This led to expansion eastward, along the lines of least resistance, into a region that had not been staked out by the more powerful European powers, but one that led to conflict with Japan, whose power Russian statesmen had egregiously underestimated, culminating in the Russo-Japanese War of 1904-05.

When the European war came in August 1914, Russia was caught halfway through a rearmament program, a situation, many scholars agree, that pushed Germany to respond to Russian mobilization with a declaration of war at that time.

* * * *

Barely a month before Julia Cantacuzene arrived in her adopted country and almost two decades after the assassination of Alexander II, a new wave of terrorism commenced in Russia: In August 1899, a student shot Nicholas Bogolepov, the minister of education, in the wake of a series of student disturbances set off by the implementation of some reactionary policies aimed at curtailing student gatherings. In April 1902, another student assassinated the minister of interior, Dmitri Sipiagin. In July 1904, his successor, Viacheslav Pleve (von Plehve) was blown up by a terrorist's bomb. By early 1905, it was the turn of a grand duke, Serge Aleksandrovich, governor general of Moscow and the tsar's uncle. During the revolutionary upheaval of 1905-06, acts of coordinated political terrorism were submerged into a general wave of violence but reemerged later, so that by 1914, planned acts of terror against government officials had claimed hundreds of lives. The most sensational case before the coming of the world war was the assassination of Prime Minister Peter Stolypin in September 1911. Most of these acts were the work of a small group of fanatics. However, the opposition, from liberals leftward, avoided outright condemnation of them, and thereby implicitly recognized terrorism as a legitimate form of leverage for political change. It was against this backdrop of real and threatened violence that the drama of Russian politics unfolded. It was a situation that could only deepen the already engrained mistrust by the ruler and his officials of the motives of the opposition, including its most moderate elements.

Stimulated by recent labor activity, a Marxist Social Democratic Labor Party (SD) had proclaimed its existence in a secret meeting in Minsk as early as 1898. By the end of 1902, the populist Socialist Revolutionary Party (SR) proclaimed its existence. (The SRs' "Combat Organization" organized the high-level assassinations of 1902-05.)

In 1902, some *zemstvo* constitutionalists and professional people set up a Russian-language periodical in Germany called *Liberation*, which aimed to unite a broad coalition in pressing for constitutional reform. Insofar as the revolutionary Left also subscribed, in theory at least, to the notion that autocracy would have to be overthrown and that a "bourgeois" régime of political and even civil liberties installed before preparations for a socialist order could be made, grounds existed for a kind of united front from moderate constitutionalists to revolutionary socialists for the purpose of achieving constitutional reform.

The Union of Liberation, organized by the moderates, mobilized the widest possible range of Russia's nascent civil society, from the socialist-oriented intelligentsia on the left to the noble *zemstvo* men on the right. It avoided a detailed ideological program and, by early 1905, had done a great deal to organize demands for constitutional reform.

By November 1904, the Union had engineered the passing of constitutionalist resolutions by an unprecedented semipublic national congress of *zemstvo* men, and by the end of the year, it was organizing the professions for pursuit of political goals: Unions of engineers, doctors, lawyers, and teachers sprang up.

And then, at the beginning of January 1905, came the surrender of Port Arthur, with the taking of many Russian prisoners and the final destruction of Russia's Pacific fleet. Twenty days later, on "Bloody Sunday," peaceful working-class petitioners in the city of St. Petersburg were dispersed by gunfire — with several hundred killed and wounded.

Under the stimulus of this political activity, the inability of the régime to conduct the war, as well as the mounting urban and rural violence at home, even traditionally conservative Russian industrialists and the provincial noble organizations had been at least partially mobilized into the opposition.

Count Sergei Witte   *Premier Peter Stolypin*

Courtesy Hoover Institution, Stanford University

Admiral Alexander Kolchak

President of the Duma
Michael Vladimirovich Rodzianko

General Lavr Kornilov

The story of the revolution of 1905 from this point on is one of ever broader circles of the population entering the opposition. Demands for fundamental political reforms were made, against the background of a growing mass movement of labor unrest in the cities and peasant disturbances in the countryside. By the spring of 1905, reports of mutinies in the army and navy began to come in.

The culmination of the liberation movement came with the massive strike activity in October 1905, which by the end of the month had led to the country's first general strike, with virtually all of industry, the communications and service sectors, the professions, the schools, and even many government offices shut down.

Faced with the nearly unanimous opposition of civil society, a working-class movement, and an unprecedented level of peasant disorders in the countryside; demoralized by the humiliation of defeat in the war with Japan (terminated in August by a negotiated peace at the Portsmouth Conference sponsored by President Theodore Roosevelt); and unsure of his ability to respond with force, due to the recent mutinies and the rail strikes that had prevented the return of troops from the Far East, Nicholas II finally promised in the Imperial Manifesto, which was issued on 30 October (17 old style), to introduce civil and political liberties and to summon a legislative assembly elected on a broad franchise.

When the tsar, under duress from his father's

cousin, the Grand Duke Nicholas Nikolaevich, and Count Witte, signed the Manifesto, he did not grant the constituent assembly or the universal suffrage demanded by the "liberation movement." But the promise to give real legislative authority to the Duma (the parliament) and to expand the suffrage to the intelligentsia and the working class was sufficient to break up the opposition. The opposition, always fragile, had recently been showing signs of coming unstuck over the radicalization of the revolution.[6] The general strike was called off, and the various groups of the opposition proceeded to form political parties for the purpose of contesting the promised parliamentary elections, with the exception of some elements of the urban far left and their working-class followings, such as the St. Petersburg Soviet (council), a committee of workers from various factories. Then, in early December, the government arrested the St. Petersburg Soviet, which was agitating for another general strike. At the very end of the year, an attempted uprising in Moscow was put down by force with considerable bloodshed. For all practical purposes, this action spelled the end of the urban revolution of 1905. Restoring order in the countryside took longer. By early 1907, the countryside had quieted down as well.

[6]The tsar disliked Count Witte but had to rely on him in the crisis as the most capable man in the government at the time. Later, when it became clear that the Duma régime had not installed social peace, Nicholas blamed Witte for talking him into signing the October Manifesto.

With the situation more or less under control, the government rather grudgingly set about making good on the October promises, drawing up an electoral law and scheduling the first national elections for spring of 1906. The first national legislature met in May 1906. It had real authority, including the right to initiate new legislation, and no law could be passed without its approval, although the tsar had the right of absolute veto. An upper house, equal to the Duma, was packed with conservatives, partly crown appointees and partly representatives of mostly conservative institutions. Once it became clear that the Duma majority was not going to be loyalist, Tsar Nicholas grew resentful of the concessions he had made in 1905.

After a series of confrontations between government and the first two Dumas (both were dismissed by the tsar after a couple of months in session, as allowed by the Fundamental Laws of 1906), the new prime minister, Peter Stolypin, drastically restricted the suffrage system to produce a more cooperative Duma. But even the new Duma, with an Octobrist majority, which represented the most moderate elements of the defunct United Front, failed to produce a pro-government majority on major issues. Stolypin had lost the confidence of the tsar long before he fell to the assassin's bullet in 1911.

The issue of social stability in post-1905 Russia has been much debated. The Stolypin agrarian reform, a grandiose undertaking designed to forge a class of efficient farmers with consolidated land plots out of the traditional peasantry, was hardly underway by the time war intervened. In the short run, it probably produced more unrest than stability. On the industrial labor front, the prospect of forming trade unions with real negotiating power undercut the revolutionary parties' inroads among the working class, but the government's inept policies toward the unions had led to a resumption of serious strike activity and increasing politicization of the working-class movement by 1912. The social context on the eve of the world war was, in sum, unsettled, but by no means out of control.

The question is often asked whether Russia could have avoided revolution had the war not intervened. There can be no definitive answer to such a question, of course, but it is important in any case to distinguish between the two revolutions of 1917: the one that overthrew autocracy ("the February Revolution") and the one that installed the Bolsheviks in power ("the October Revolution"). It is very likely that, with or without a war, a final showdown with autocracy was in order. However, it is hard to imagine the seizure of power by the Bolsheviks in the autumn of 1917 without conditions arising directly from the war.

Russia's entry into the war in August 1914 was met at first by a patriotic rally. The working-class strike movement then underway broke off, and the peasants were lying low, allowing their sons to be mobilized. Among the political parties, there was considerable enthusiasm. The majority in the Duma had actually criticized the government for pusillanimity in having allowed Austria to annex Bosnia-Herzegovina in 1908. In a special session of the Duma, all parties but the SDs and the Laborite faction voted war credits, and then accepted the proroguing (adjournment) of the Duma. Even among the socialist parties there was willingness to postpone the political struggle. Most of them accepted a war for purely defensive purposes. Only the Bolsheviks, a few Mensheviks, and the SR Left adopted an outright "defeatist" stand, calling for the transformation of the imperialist war into an international class war or even for the defeat of Russia as a means of getting rid of the autocracy.

Presented with this opportunity, the régime proceeded to squander it. The government used the war as an excuse for getting rid of the Duma: Until 1917, the Duma was summoned rarely, and only to vote credits of one kind or another in support of the war effort. In mid-1915, after Russia had suffered the first massive territorial loss of the war, all her Polish territories, the tsar dismissed the Grand Duke Nicholas Nikolaevich as supreme army commander and took over this role himself, moving to field headquarters near the front, at Mogilev. This was one of his biggest mistakes: He only got in the way, exposing himself to criticism for military failures that could have rested with the generals. Moreover, leaving for the front, Nicholas in effect left the Empress Alexandra in charge in the capital. Alexandra was a fanatical promoter of the idea of restoring full autocratic powers, and her state of mind could not be called stable in the best of conditions. It is at this point that the role of the infamous Rasputin became significant. This amateur holy man had been around for some time, but his ascendancy over the empress (to a much lesser degree over Nicholas, but he humored his wife) had begun only after Stolypin's death and was especially strong in the first two years of the war up to the time of his death in December 1916.

Rasputin's influence was real, although the empress may have been using him to further schemes of her own, especially in ministerial appointments. Rasputin's influence on the Imperial family arose from his apparent ability to stop the hemophiliac bleeding of their only son and heir to the throne; and for the empress, and perhaps others at court, he represented the people, Holy Russia, from which they felt themselves progressively isolated.

By 1916, the political situation was catastrophic, with the emperor getting in the way at the front and the empress and Rasputin misdirecting home affairs; Boris Stürmer, an incompetent if sympathetic old man, was made prime minister in February; Alexander Protopopov, who was probably certifiably insane, was made minister of interior in September. The situation became so fantastic that rumors circulated that the empress, of German origin, was a German agent (shades of the French Revolution!).

Under these circumstances, the initial support in the Duma and society soon fell away. By September 1915, the Duma majority had combined in an opposition bloc, called the Progressive Bloc, which publicly issued a reform program calling for restoration of civil rights, amnesty to political prisoners, and a "government of public confidence."

In this atmosphere, the Duma was reconvened briefly in November 1916, when Paul Miliukov delivered a famous speech denouncing the government, with innuendoes of treason. Even the representative of the extreme Right, Vladimir Purishkevich, gave an impassioned speech demanding the removal of Rasputin from the capital. The government sacrificed Stürmer but would not yield to the Progressive Bloc and went on ignoring the Duma. By now the idea was widespread that the government was going to let the country go to ruin and open it to German invasion. Even members of their immediate family began to abandon the emperor and empress.

At one time or another during the war, Russia had 15 million men under arms. Half of them became casualties, about 1.3 million killed, and the rest wounded or taken prisoner. After the big defeats of 1915, there was some improvement in what had been a serious supply situation. One more big offensive, the Brusilov offensive, mounted on the weaker Austrian front in July 1916, turned out to be long, inconclusive, and tremendously expensive in terms of human life and demoralization in the ranks. By the end of 1916, large-scale disaffection began to show up in the army, the result of the meat-grinder effect of the war, and was deepened by the general lack of enthusiasm for the war all along on the part of the peasants in uniform, for whom pan-Slav projects and democratic alliances meant nothing. By now, the anti-war propaganda of the extreme left was beginning to reach the troops. Rank-and-file patriotism might have developed were Russia winning the war, but it was losing it.

The same winter of 1916 saw the appearance of acute food shortages in the large cities and the beginnings of runaway inflation for the first time since the war began. This was the beginning of the general economic collapse that would continue through the revolution and civil war.

No one planned the February Revolution of 1917. It all began in Petrograd[7] on 8 March (23 February old style), when working-class women demonstrating for bread on International Women's Day and a lockout of some 30,000 workers in the Putilov munitions works sparked widespread strikes in the capital. What transformed this labor unrest, nothing new in itself, into a revolution was the mutiny of the Petrograd garrison and the response of the Progressive Bloc leaders.

The strikes and demonstrations of 8 March had approached the proportions of a general strike in the capital within a few days. During these days the military governor general of Petrograd did nothing, hoping the whole thing would blow over; he was fearful

[7]At the beginning of the war, the capital's name was changed from the German (actually, Dutch) "Sankt-Peterburg" to the slavicized "Petrograd."

for the loyalty of the garrison troops, of whom there were about 160,000 in town. (Petrograd was the collecting point for the shipping of fresh troops to the northern front, which was not far off.) By this time political demands had been added to the demand for food: peace and "down with autocracy." On the third day he finally took action, having received a telegram from the tsar demanding immediate suppression of the disorder. On that day, 11 March, troops fired on the crowd in several places, and the Duma, sitting in one of its rare sessions, was dissolved.

Then began the revolution: On the evening of the eleventh, the first signs of mutiny, refusal to act against the crowd, appeared in the garrisons, and widespread rebellion broke out by the following morning. By the afternoon of the twelfth, most of the garrison troops had mutinied, some with their officers, some over their officers' dead bodies, and were fraternizing with the strikers. The Duma opposition refused to disperse and appointed a thirteen-man temporary committee for restoration of order in the capital. That evening the government ministers resigned. The same day the Petrograd Soviet of Workers' Deputies (the soldiers' deputies were soon added) met in the same parliament building where the Duma committee had sat.

At this point, the Duma committee decided to form a provisional government. One of its first acts was to arrest the government ministers and incarcerate them in the Peter-Paul Fortress. Meanwhile, when the tsar heard of the government's arrest, he tried to order troops from the front to pacify the capital, but the generals, who had by this time been persuaded by the Duma men that Nicholas's removal had become a prerequisite to the restoration of order and successful pursuit of the war, refused his order. When he learned of this, Nicholas abdicated, on 15 March, at first in favor of his son with his brother Michael as regent, and then, when he realized this would mean separation from his son, in favor of Michael. At that moment, the Russian monarchy disappeared, because Michael refused the crown a few days later after the Duma men told him they could not guarantee his personal safety on the throne. The provisional government publicly announced its existence the next day.

The provisional government was so called because it was to rule only until a constituent assembly could be convened to decide the constitutional fate of the country. The source of its authority was dubious: It could not nor did it wish to claim the authority of the Duma, because it was dominated by figures from the left of the Duma. And it lacked power, in the sense that it could not control either the army or the working-class crowd in the capital. This situation caused the provisional government to enter into a sort of governing agreement with the Petrograd Soviet, which came to be known as "dual power."

In fact, anything like unified state authority disappeared along with the monarchy. Many centers of power, largely uncoordinated, sprang up to fill the vacuum: not only soviets, but factory committees, soldiers' committees, revitalized town councils and *zemstvos*, and so on.

For the liberals, the autocracy had been overthrown and a democratic order installed; the Soviets had issued a declaration of man and the citizen; and the provisional government had immediately passed a series of progressive acts: amnesty for political prisoners, abolition of capitalist punishment, the right to strike and organize. The Finnish constitution was restored, and Poland was declared free (a technicality since Poland, at the time, was occupied by the Central Powers).

The process of disintegration in the army, which was already well advanced by February, was greatly accelerated by the collapse of the monarchy and, there is little doubt, by the Petrograd Soviet's notorious "Order No. 1," which called for democratization in the army: Henceforth, soldiers and officers were to be equals except in combat, elected committees of soldiers would take charge of the weapons, and so on. The provisional government was forced by the terms of its agreement with the Soviet to respect Order No. 1 and to maintain only a "defensist" stance in the war—no annexations or indemnities as war aims.

Under the mounting pressure for an end to the war among the peasants in uniform and for land distribution by the peasants at large, there occurred the rapid leftward drift in the revolution, culminating in the Bolshevik coup d'état on 7 November (25 October, old style). We see the paralysis, first, of the liberals, and

then of the moderate socialists, led by Alexander
Kerensky (an SR who had, in fact, participated in the
very first provisional government without his party's
endorsement). From mid-July to November, Kerensky was premier. In the beginning, he was the fair-
haired boy of the revolution. But this reputation
waned rapidly under the onslaught of reality.

The crucial factor was the war: Both the liberals
and the moderate socialists were afraid to take Russia
out of the war for fear the result would be anarchy,
collapse of the Allied cause, probably counterrevolution; and the war continued to deepen the economic
crisis and to radicalize the masses. And yet it was not
in the end the concrete policies of the succeeding provisional governments that swept them away so much
as their very attempt to intervene and exercise control over an ineluctably deteriorating situation.

The Bolsheviks, after Vladimir Ilich Lenin's return
in April from European exile, were the only leftist
party to identify themselves with the popular aspira-
tions for an end to the war and the distribution of
land, and the political solution that would presumably yield them: "all power to the soviets," that is, creation of a "soviet government."

The first provisional government fell apart over the
issue of war aims. Miliukov, its foreign minister, sent a
note on 1 May to the Allies reconfirming the war aims
of the tsarist government, which included annexation
of Constantinople and the straits. Publication of this
note set off a crisis, including armed demonstrations

in the capital. Miliukov and the war minister, the left-Octobrist Alexander Guchkov, resigned. There followed the formation of the first coalition government with six "minister-socialists" brought in to share the onus of responsibility.

The first coalition government, in fact a government dominated by the moderate socialist leadership using coalition as a fig leaf, essentially continued the policies of the first provisional government. Staying in the war was given a more democratic, revolutionary rationale; there was an underlying fear that pulling out would stimulate a counterrevolution, that is, a march on Petrograd organized by the generals, who had gone along with the revolution in the first place as a way of revitalizing the war effort. Kerensky even managed to launch an offensive on the weaker southwestern front (Galicia), the "second Brusilov offensive" of early July, to reinforce the image of the new Russia as a "nation in arms." But, by the middle of the month, it had turned into a rout.

The failure of the Brusilov offensive precipitated the second major crisis of the coalition government, the "July Days," street demonstrations and garrison mutiny on 15-17 July in Petrograd that came close to a takeover by the Bolsheviks, whose slogans animated the crowds. It was averted only by the rallying to the government of several military units and the publication of documents that appeared to compromise the Bolsheviks as recipients of German money.

The July Days spelled the end of coalitions. There

followed four months of government by Kerensky, essentially a holding operation. The government became increasingly isolated from popular movements and came under increasing pressure, from left and right, to "do something."

The next phase of the revolution opens with the attempt by the generals to take over in Petrograd and restore order in the rear so as to be able to get on with the war at the front. Long awaited on the left, this "Thermidor"[8] came in early September in the form of the Kornilov affair. General Lavr Kornilov, commander in chief, a republican and supporter of the February Revolution, attempted to move on Petrograd and clean out the soviets, prop up the provisional government, and get on with the war. He was encouraged in this plan by Kerensky, who felt his control over affairs slipping away. The attempt failed disastrously: Troops sent by rail against "the revolution" were met by agitators from the capital, got out of their commanders' control, and never made it to the capital. Kerensky got cold feet, denounced Kornilov as a traitor, and ordered his arrest.

The failure of the Kornilov affair demonstrated the impossibility of a "right-wing" military solution to the political crisis, but at the time it only augmented fear of "counterrevolution," and as a result—a classic case of unintended consequences—it further radicalized

---

[8]An allusion to the events in 1794, which brought the downfall of the Jacobins and ended the radical phase of the French Revolution.

the mood in the capital and, to some extent, around the country. This was the final great impetus to the leftward wave that led directly to the Bolshevik seizure of power in early November. In the army, the officer corps now lost all semblance of control over the troops; the Russian army definitively collapsed.

The great beneficiaries were the Bolsheviks. Even before the Kornilov affair, they were free to organize and agitate again (their leaders had been temporarily under arrest or in hiding in the wake of the German gold scandal at the end of the July Days)—the soviets wanted all the help they could get in combating "counterrevolution." And so they, but also Kerensky, pursued a policy of "no enemies to the left." This was his fatal error. On 7 October, Leon Trotsky, after Lenin the most important Bolshevik in the October Revolution, was elected chairman of the Petrograd Soviet; shortly thereafter, the Soviet authorized formation of a military revolutionary committee for coordinating defense of the capital against the counterrevolution, and Trotsky was put in charge. The Bolsheviks now had the instruments of physical force needed for seizure of power.

The soviet leaders organized a "democratic conference" in the wake of the Kornilov affair; it met on 27 September, with only the socialist end of the spectrum involved, but it was unable to come up with any solutions. At this point, Kerensky set up a new cabinet of his own choosing, proclaimed Russia a republic, and scheduled elections to the constituent assembly for 24 November. The soviets did not accept the legitimacy of the Kerensky coup but agreed to convene an interim representative body to consider and give sanction to the new government's acts. This was the state conference, or "preparliament," formed from delegates to the recent Democratic Conference. It opened on 20 October.

The Bolsheviks, led by Trotsky, denounced the preparliament and walked out. It was left in fear and trembling; it was clear the Bolsheviks would soon make their move. This was no secret, and the Bolshevik Central Committee on 23 October passed a formal resolution "to proceed to armed insurrection." A little later, when it became clear that they would enjoy a majority in the second all-Russian Congress of Soviets, due to convene on 7 November (25 October old style), they coordinated their action with the opening of the congress so that they could appear to take power in the name of "soviet democracy" (whence the word "soviet" in "Soviet Union").

The Bolsheviks presented the congress of soviets with a fait accompli. The "October Revolution" was a nearly bloodless affair in Petrograd. Kerensky had fled, disguised as a woman; there were pockets of resistance from military-school cadets, and a few other acts of violence. A fair number of army officers fell victim to soldiers' revenge or apprehensions. There was considerably more violence in other cities, where the news from Petrograd provoked preparations on both sides.

Once in power in the capital and other major cities of European Russia, the Bolsheviks did not relinquish it. At first, other socialists participated in the institutions of the new "soviet" government, and although the Bolsheviks moved quickly to confiscate private bank accounts and urban real estate, they tolerated other socialist parties and even allowed a non-Bolshevik press to exist. This honeymoon of sorts lasted until early 1918. Then they dispersed the constituent assembly—which had finally convened on 18 January with less than 25 percent Bolsheviks—after only twenty-four hours. There followed a prolonged civil war.

Geographically, the civil war was a struggle between the heartland and the periphery, with the several opponents mustering forces in the borderlands and the Bolsheviks holed up for a time in the territory of the old Muscovite state, a mere fraction of European Russia. The civil war, fought with more or less organized armies, was punctuated by popular rebellions, mostly consisting of peasants who had been ruined and outraged by the armed requisitioning of their life's bread by both sides. After the Bolsheviks' victory in the civil war by the end of 1920, these rebellions continued for more than a year, now directed exclusively against Bolshevik rule.

All of this the Bolsheviks survived. In the process, the government of soviets was then transformed into a Bolshevik-Party dictatorship that tolerated the existence of no other political parties, no independent press, liberally terrorizing its real and imagined enemies. Sustained at first in their willingness to take and hold power by belief that their action in Russia would set off a European-wide, if not world-wide, socialist revolution, the Bolsheviks, once victorious and accustomed to power, had become convinced by the mid-1920s they could build "socialism in one country." This idea—pushed aggressively by Joseph Stalin, who emerged in the span of just a few years following the death of Lenin in 1924 as the supreme leader— entailed the vast and brutal industrialization campaigns and the collectivization of agriculture that commenced in the late 1920s. But that is another story.

* * * *

The excerpts we present here were commenced shortly after Julia Cantacuzene's arrival with her husband in the United States following their flight from Soviet Russia through Finland and Sweden at the beginning of 1918. They had sent their children ahead, via the trans-Siberian railway, in the summer of 1917. Begun as articles for *The Saturday Evening Post* at the invitation of its publisher, they soon emerged as books: the first, *Revolutionary Days. Recollections of Romanoffs and Bolsheviki, 1914-1917*, was published in Boston by the firm of Small, Maynard & Company in 1919 (the author's "Word to the Reader" was dated January 1919), and by the London publishers, Chapman & Hall, Ltd., the following year. In short order there appeared a second volume of memoirs, these devoted to Julia's Russian experiences before the years of war and revolution, as well as her pre-Russian youth, *My Life Here and There*, published by Charles Scribner's Sons of New York; this good-sized tome of 322 pages had been sent off to the publisher no later than May 1921. In between these two volumes of memoirs, a series of vignettes of Russian life interspersed with chapters on the Russian civil war ("Denikin's Army," "Kolchak," etc.), first published in *The Saturday Evening Post*, had been brought out by Charles Scribner's Sons in 1920.

The Cantacuzenes arrived in this country in 1918 with only the clothes on their backs and such valuables as Julia had been able to sew into the linings of her clothing and of the few trunks containing them. They had been forced to abandon such property as had not already been confiscated—a house and rental apartments in Petrograd, her husband's interest in the Cantacuzene estates in several provinces, a villa in the Crimea—and most of their liquid assets on leaving Russia. They were not typically destitute Russian refugees, of course, and they had numerous connections and some well-heeled relatives in America, especially Mrs. Palmer, who died within a few months of their arrival. She left her niece some real estate—but Julia, as a mother of three and with a husband in poor health (he had been gravely wounded early in the world war) and a very responsible person in such matters, at once practical-minded and independent, must have been seriously preoccupied with the family's financial situation. It also is reasonably clear that her unprecedented, and essentially unrepeated, burst of literary activity in 1918-21 was undertaken to improve that situation.

The memoirs of Julia Cantacuzene are not only interesting, they are of considerable value to historians of the Russian Revolution as well. Her Russian life coincided almost precisely with the crisis period of the Russian autocracy and the revolution that brought it to an end.

Written shortly after the experiences they record, the memoirs shed light on such matters as attitudes toward the autocracy and the Imperial family among the high aristocracy and in court circles, documenting the progressive isolation of the rulers. Increasingly, the autocracy came to be viewed in these circles not as a guarantor, but as a threat to the preservation of a way of life. Particularly striking is the author's affirmation of considerable support in her milieu for the boldest reformers among tsarist statesmen, such as Witte and Stolypin; for liberal politicians, such as Miliukov; and even for the February Revolution of 1917 with its initial promise of transforming Russia into a law-abiding constitutional monarchy.

Julia Cantacuzene was an eyewitness to some of the most dramatic events of the Russian Revolution, including the "July Days" and the "Kornilov affair" in Petrograd, the two most dramatic confrontations in the unfolding of the revolution between the abdication of the tsar in March and the Bolshevik seizure of power at the beginning of November. She witnessed the immediate aftermath of "October" in Kiev and the reverberations of the revolution from early 1917 until the end of the year in the Crimea.

Her comments on the Kornilov affair show that the understanding in her circles of Kornilov's motives and of Kerensky's behavior in that confusing episode were realistic and well-informed. Much the same story that she recounts from her discussions with numerous military and political figures has emerged from the best historical scholarship on the subject.

Julia's detailed descriptions of rail travel in Russia at various times during the revolution are unforgettable, and their accuracy is wholly confirmed by diverse other memoirs.

The Cantacuzenes understandably remained intensely involved in Russian affairs for some time after their arrival in the United States in early 1918. During the civil war that raged in Russia from 1918 to 1920, the political fate of the country still very much hung in the balance.

In addition to her memoirs, Julia wrote several pieces in support of the anti-Bolshevik efforts in the civil war,[9] and Michael, the demobilized major general, soon became interested in the cause of Admiral Alexander Vasilevich Kolchak, who as "Supreme

---

[9]These pieces, first published in *The Saturday Evening Post*, were collected in her book *Russian People: Revolutionary Recollections* (New York: Charles Scribner's Sons, 1920).

Ruler" was gathering forces in Siberia for an invasion of Bolshevik territory from the east. Michael traveled to join Kolchak at Omsk in western Siberia in mid-1919. Within a few months of his arrival, the retreat eastward began. At the end of 1919, Michael was sent back to the United States from Irkutsk to gather support for Kolchak, but he never returned to Russia: Shortly after his arrival in the United States, the Kolchak régime fell and Kolchak was executed.

After that, the Cantacuzenes settled in Florida where Michael, who took American citizenship early, was for some time involved in the ranching and orange grove businesses of the Palmer family. When the Palmer First National Bank was organized in Sarasota in the mid-1920s, he became its vice president. In 1934, Julia divorced Michael, who then later married Jeanette Draper, a fellow Palmer employee. He retired in 1954 and died the following year.

Following her divorce, Julia moved to Washington, D.C., where she was a prominent figure in society. For some years she was a travel advisor for *The Saturday Evening Post* and also occasionally wrote for the *Ladies' Home Journal.* Her home was a perennial gathering place for Russian émigrés. Although she experienced serious vision problems beginning at age seventy and was later blind for almost a decade, she eventually regained partial sight and remained socially active. She died at home on 4 October 1975, at the age of ninety-nine.

The Cantacuzenes' oldest child, Michael, born in

Prince Michael Cantacuzene,
after immigration to the United States

Courtesy Rodion Cantacuzene

Princess Julia Cantacuzene, 1966
Courtesy AP/Wide World Photos

St. Petersburg in 1900, graduated from Harvard in 1921. He worked as a stock broker in New York for some time, and then also as a real-estate broker in Chicago. Michael was an accomplished equestrian and field-trial shooting expert. He married Clarissa Curtis of Boston in 1921 immediately upon graduation from Harvard. They had two children, Irina and Rodion. They divorced in 1935; Michael died on Christmas Day 1972.

The oldest daughter of Michael and Julia, Barbara (Bertha), born in St. Petersburg in 1904, married a Kentuckian, Bruce Smith, in 1926, with whom she had one son, Bruce Michael Smith. They divorced in 1933, and she married William Siebern in 1934. She died in 1991.

The third child, Zinaida (Ida), born in St. Petersburg in 1908, married Sir John Coldbrook Hanbury-Williams in Washington in 1928. They then settled in England and had three children, Barbara, Elizabeth Frances, and John Michael Anthony. She died in 1984.

Julia's mother-in-law, Princess Elizabeth, stayed on for some time in the Crimea and left Russia through Odessa with the evacuating French forces in April 1919. She then lived with her third son, Serge, in Mozambique, and died there on 3 May 1923. Serge, born in 1884, graduate of the Imperial Corps of Pages and former diplomat, eventually moved to France and died in Amblainville near Paris in 1953. He and his wife, of Hungarian-Russian nobility, had two children. The Princess Elizabeth's only other surviving child,

Princess Daria (b. 1878), was married to Count Theodore Nieroth. She died in France in 1944.

* * * *

Julia Cantacuzene's assessments of the people and events she recounts should not be accepted as perfectly objective, of course. Her special viewpoint of developments was always refracted by her milieu. The author's belief that the Bolsheviks were simply German agents was at best a caricature of reality, but her views on the subject reflect a widespread conviction that was itself a historical "fact" of the time. She tends to idealize the motives and abilities of the Grand Duke Nicholas Nikolaevich, whose longtime subordinate and protégé her husband was. And so on.

But all memoirs are by nature subjective. What counts is the ability of the author to convey articulately her perspective on events to the reader and, by the same token, to persuade the reader that this perspective is representative of a historically significant social milieu. In this, Julia Cantacuzene surely succeeded.

TERENCE EMMONS

Stanford University
April 1999

Revolutionary Days

I

Childhood Impressions

IT IS FROM the many tellings of my favorite story in very early youth that I learned of a brave and handsome boy[1] who, when he was twelve or thirteen, ran away from school three times. The first time he went to his father[2] on the battlefield. The latter promptly returned him to his teachers; so a second time he joined the soldiers of his father's army and was found among them by a staff officer, who brought him to the general's camp. There the boy was reprimanded and again sent to his studies, only to leave them and reach the army a third time, just before Vicksburg. Finally, the father, won by his son's intense sportiness and his adoration for the general himself, kept this young soldier with him, let him fit himself into the stress and strain and hardship of the camp with a commander who lived more uncomfortably than anyone about him. A pony was found and an extra cot. At night father and son slept side by side in the general's tent; or the boy lay half-asleep, vaguely conscious of the silent man who walked up and down, pondered over maps,

[1]The author refers to her father, Frederick Dent Grant (1850–1912).
[2]The author refers to her grandfather, General Ulysses S. Grant (1822–1885).

3

planning coming battles and campaigns, and then sat down to write his orders for the morrow's action.

By day father and son rode forth for inspections, or to some point from which the general was to watch and guide the fighting. Always they were together. Seemingly this big-hearted, devoted boy was never in the way of the commander, and the latter, late in life, told with delight of the courage under fire and the cheerful acceptance of discomfort shown by his younger partner in the game of war.

By his father's side he entered Vicksburg, on the Fourth of July, 1863. From then on, he remained at the front, and when, in 1865, peace came, the boy of fifteen had two years of steady campaigning to his credit, with a fund of experience that aged him, but also was a great service through his later career. After the war, followed by a year of preparatory study, the young veteran entered West Point. Discipline at the academy was hard, doubtless, on anyone who had roamed over battlefields, and his high spirits kept this particular cadet in hot water; but his excellence in mathematics and a talent for all that concerned horses and drill, shooting, or other military work, helped him. He finally came through West Point.

As General Sherman's[3] aide-de-camp, the full-fledged second lieutenant took a trip to Europe, his first view of foreign lands, and he had the interesting

[3]William Tecumseh Sherman (1820–1891), Union general during the Civil War, succeeded Grant as general in chief of the army in 1869.

experience of being in France just after the Franco-Prussian War,[4] of visiting the Near East, and from there, going into the Caucasus, where he stayed at Tiflis with the then-viceroy—the Grand Duke Michael, son of Emperor Nicholas I[5] and younger brother of Alexander II.[6] From Tiflis his host sent my father north with one of his own aides-de-camp, who was to make the trip as a special messenger, carrying reports to the emperor. Together the two young officers hurried across Russia's vast steppes toward Moscow. My father fell in love with the mysterious beauty of the plains—plains where the only noises were the beating hoofs of troika[7] horses and the music of their bells. Then came a stay in Moscow, whence Russia's one and only railroad took them to St. Petersburg.

Here again the good-looking young officer received a warm welcome. Grand Duke Michael had warned his wife, and the Grand Duchess Olga Fedorovna

[4]The Franco-Prussian War, which was won by Prussia, led to the fall of Louis Napoleon's Third Empire and to the unification of Germany in the German Empire. The war began on 19 July 1870 and was officially terminated by the treaty signed at Frankfurt on 10 May 1871.

[5]Grand Duke Michael (Mikhail) Nikolaevich (1832–1909) was viceroy of the Caucasus from 1862 to 1881. His father, Emperor Nicholas I (Pavlovich) (1796–1855), ruled from 1825 to his death in 1855.

[6]Emperor Alexander II (Nikolaevich) (1818–1881) ruled from 1855 to 1881.

[7]Literally, "threesome," a team of three horses for pulling a carriage or sleigh, whose shaft bow typically was adorned with bells.

(born a princess of Baden)[8] received the stranger with kindly hospitality, making him at home in her palace on the quay. Her guest never forgot the delight of this visit and the charm of those who were so good to him in his youth.

Returning home in 1872, he actively fought Indians in our Far West, took part in the work of our government's surveying parties in Montana and out in the dry Arizona deserts, where he lived for a time the adventurous poetic life of the Far West.

As the next step in his career, my father became attached to the staff of General Philip H. Sheridan,[9] who was stationed in Chicago. There, in 1874, he met a very pretty young girl,[10] fresh from her graduation at the convent at Georgetown, where she had carried off first honors. Rapidly a romance developed. He was twenty-four, she twenty, when they were married in October 1874. The country home of Mr. and Mrs. Honoré was the frame of a brilliant scene. The bride's parents were among Chicago's most attractive and constructive people, while the bride and her sister were both of rare individual beauty and charm. Gen-

---

[8]Since the eighteenth century, for internal and geo-political considerations, male members of the Russian ruling house were wed as a rule to foreign princesses, generally from the smaller, especially northern German principalities and Denmark.

[9]Philip Henry Sheridan (1831–1888), Union general of the Civil War.

[10]Ida Marie Honoré (1854–1930), the daughter of a wealthy Chicago capitalist and real-estate developer, Henry Hamilton Honoré, originally from Maryland.

eral Sheridan and his whole staff in gala uniform were present, and the bridegroom was surrounded by a family group consisting of the president of the United States and many of the latter's distinguished followers and friends, all come to see the happy officer married.

Then the bridal couple went to live at the White House, from where young Colonel Grant made his long expeditions westward as before. In the capital, as in Chicago, the bride was a much-admired favorite. Two winters passed, and in June 1876, in a quiet room, its windows looking out under the great portico of the president's mansion, a first child was born, an unusually large girl, some thirteen pounds of chubby health—myself.

As first child of much-loved parents and a first grandchild of such grandparents as were Ulysses S. Grant and his wife, I was bound to be much petted. Many were the tales told me of my baptism, when I was named Julia for my Grant grandmother. I was christened in the great East Room by Doctor John P. Newman, pastor of the Methodist church, which my Grandfather Grant attended.

Then we left for the West. I recall suddenly being waked up and dressed in the night on a train that moved slowly amid shouting crowds. It stopped, and I was picked up and carried out in someone's arms from our car to a large open carriage. On the back seat were already installed Grandfather and Grandmother Grant, freshly arrived from their journey around the world, and all about us was a great sea of faces—men's and women's. Torches, quantities of them, burned, flared up, and smoked, then flickered down, throwing changing lights on faces which, to my child's imagination, looked wild with excitement. As a matter of fact, the owners were just then receiving a national hero with all the enthusiasm they could display. Every mouth was open, and hurrah after hurrah filled the air about as completely as the illuminated faces filled my horizon. "Grant! Grant! Welcome Grant!" "Hurrah for Grant!" "Hurrah! Grant! Grant!"

My grandfather sat absolutely quiet in his place amid bedlam let loose, but, for the first time, I remember the depth and power of his eyes, and how dark they seemed, though they shone. Grandmama, on the contrary, waved her hand and bowed and smiled. She was delighted and expressed her delight to her husband, to my mother, to everyone, in fact. Just as I was handed in to my mother, very frightened by the noise, the vast crowd lurched forward and seemed to be upon us. More and more panic-stricken, I hid my head on my mother's lap, and it took some encouragement to make me feel brave again.

Nearly forty years afterward, at the time of the Bolshevik[11] uprisings in Russia, I saw enormous mobs which strained everyone's nerves, and I was then as

[11]It was the Bolshevik (literally, "majoritarian") party that seized power in Russia in 1917 and laid the foundations of the USSR. The Bolsheviks' rivals, the Mensheviks ("minoritarians"), formed the other wing of the Russian Social-Democratic Labor Party, a Marxist revolutionary party first organized in 1898.

much frightened as anybody; but even in 1917, I was less routed than I felt myself to be when that great hearty American crowd shouted its welcome to my quiet grandfather at Colorado Springs on his return from his triumphant trip around the world.

After the little stay at Colorado Springs, we all traveled together to Galena,[12] and I finally overcame my fear of the crowds at every station, shouting their welcome to us, hurrahing and waving. The people would surround my window and give me flowers, or ask me for one of those which I had—"for a souvenir," they said. They made me tell them things, and then they would laugh and applaud, and I grew to feel I was very important to the party and that my small private reception was part of the general ovation to Grant.

At Galena we stayed with my grandparents, who returned to their wee cottage there where they had lived before the outbreak of the war. After four years on battlefields and eight in the White House, with their tour of European and Asiatic palaces thrown in, it spoke well for this prominent couple that they contentedly returned to their old place to settle down. We soon left them and went back to our own house in Chicago.

My father, on General Sheridan's staff, was more in Chicago and less in the Far West, and once he and my mother both went away, leaving me with my lovely

[12]Galena, Illinois, where the Grants had lived before the onset of the Civil War.

aunt—my mother's sister, Mrs. Palmer[13]—during their trip. They went to Mexico—an official visit that my grandfather made to President Diaz.[14] General Sheridan had accompanied my grandfather, and my father went as aide-de-camp to Sheridan, while there were several important civilians in the party also. Grandmama went, and all the other wives as well—a gay, clever group, round the great central figure.

When I was five, a new experience came in my small life. I heard that a brand-new baby boy had arrived in the house. My baby brother was named Ulysses, for my grandfather, and I took great delight in helping with his toilet. My mother's health was fragile, and my father, who had resigned from the army, brought us all on to New York where we went to a new house, 3 East 66 Street—a big dark house it seemed to me. I heard with great interest the grownups say it was given my grandfather by the citizens of Philadelphia.

Grandfather and my father were now going into a banking business in which one of my uncles was interested; the firm was called Grant & Ward. It was a flourishing concern, and into it my grandfather, as well

[13]Mrs. Potter Palmer (née Bertha Honoré) (1849–1918), the sister of the author's mother, Ida. Potter Palmer (1826–1902) was one of Chicago's wealthiest businessmen and real-estate developers, builder of the landmark hotel, the Palmer House. Mrs. Palmer, who cut a wide swath in the world of late-nineteenth-century American society, fashion, and women's issues, assumed the role of Julia's protectress, lavishing clothes and travel on her of a sort her own family could not provide.

[14]Porfirio Diaz (1830–1915), president and virtual dictator of Mexico almost uninterruptedly from 1877 to 1911.

as my father, cheerfully put what they had saved by careful economy from their army pay. In my grandfather's case, even the fund given him by New York City to express appreciation of his patriotic service was invested.

My mother was still delicate, and to strengthen her we moved for the winter to a pretty cottage at Morristown, New Jersey. She and my father were delighted with the place, and I remember very well how interested they were in furnishing their new home and how attractive they made it.

One evening in the spring of 1884, my father came home looking very weary, pale, and troubled. He hugged me as always and passed on with my mother to their upstairs sitting room. Her cry of surprise and distress rang out, and then loud questions and quiet replies floated to the hall below, where we children sat, frightened. When they came down, my mother's eyes were red, and she told me to go to bed quickly— so I went, wondering what had happened.

Next morning I learned. We hadn't any more money at all and were to go to live at Grandmama's, who seemed to have enough for some unknown reason, to keep her home, while we must give up ours. To me it was compensation enough for any trouble to go and visit Grandmama, but as the days passed I grew to feel the drama of the Grant & Ward failure and to see how much my father suffered from it. He went to town earlier and returned later. Our horses and carriages had been driven away the first day and sold. Every day packers came to pack and move some of our furniture. Each day my father came back to ask how nearly ready we were. I packed and unpacked my toys and little treasures in a fever of excitement and of desire to help. After a few days, perhaps a week, we had finished.

It was only years later I realized the heroism of my elders at that time. How on that first dreadful morning when my father and grandfather had reached the city, they had been sent for by my uncle, Ulysses, Jr., who was Ward's partner in the bank. How he had told them Ward had run away with all the funds and that the firm had failed. Practically all my father had was in this company, and what little was outside he turned at once into the common till to pay small investors. My grandfather, in the same position, acted likewise. His house in town, long before this, at his request, had been put in Grandmama's name by the citizens of Philadelphia, and he had given her the Elberon cottage during his presidency, so he decided she should keep those for now and take the whole family in.

It was the Grant & Ward failure that took us definitely into my grandparents' household to live. My father went on working in New York, and in his spare hours he helped my grandfather in looking up war records or documents among the latter's old papers. These were to be used for some articles my grandfather promised to a magazine, which offered him an unheard-of price, five hundred dollars, for a series of several.

*Frederick Dent Grant and
Ida Honoré Grant, Julia's parents*

My Life Here and There

*Former President Ulysses S. Grant, at Elberon, New Jersey,
surrounded by family (left to right): Julia's grandmother; her father,
Frederick; her brother, U.S. Grant; an unidentified woman;
Julia, and her mother, Ida.*

My Life Here and There

14

In the spring of 1884, my grandfather, in crossing the sidewalk from his house to his carriage one morning, had slipped on a bit of orange or banana peel, had fallen heavily, and had done his hip and leg an injury. Helped back into the house, a few days of care had prevented any serious developments, but he was left with a slight limp and a slowness of motion.

I know now how relieved and satisfied Grandfather must have been that his articles were vastly successful, were clamored for, and brought him large checks. I hear also he was being "begged" to write his memoirs in book form and had received very flattering propositions.

My father, General Porter, Mr. Drexel, and Mr. Childs[15] were always conversing about "the book." It was to be begun at once, and Grandpapa was to give his own personal record of the Civil War.

This was the state of things when I remember occasional remarks among various members of the family, or from the old servants, to the effect that he was not feeling quite well. Someone said he had taken cold and had a slight sore throat, and one scrap of gossip told us that he hadn't a cold but had felt his throat hurting when he had swallowed a small bit of peach

---

[15]Horace Porter (1837–1921) was a long-time aide and intimate of Grant in military and political life. Anthony J. Drexel (1826–1893) and George W. Childs (1829–1894) were old friends of Grant from Philadelphia. A banker and publisher, respectively, and philanthropists, they advised and handled various financial affairs for Grant after his presidency.

skin one day; probably something was on the peach skin that scratched the delicate throat tissues. The doctor who was called in said "smoker's throat" and gave a medicine to gargle with.

It seemed as if my grandfather was ever growing more quiet, and as autumn came, he occasionally mentioned that his throat was no better and must be treated after the family moved to town. Also, now and then, some member of the family would say to another that my grandfather had a headache. They attributed it to his present sedentary life, the trouble his hip gave him in walking, or the concentration needed in writing the book.

Soon, for some reason, my father gave up going to town for his work, and he became a constant inmate of my grandfather's office. I did not entirely comprehend why this change occurred but heard that with his hip injured, it was hard for the elderly author to move about after documents, maps, and books, while dictating was fatiguing his voice and throat.

II

My Grandfather's Illness and Death

EARLY THAT AUTUMN we all moved up to my grandparents' New York house. My grandfather seemed to be feeling quite unwell. Either his hip or throat or headaches were to blame.

I remember no parties that winter. At first, every morning early my grandfather went downtown to have his throat treated; then he returned and went to work on the book, dictating and writing. Many great men passed hours in the upstairs sitting room.

General Sherman was a constant guest. He talked a lot, was tall and vital, with a distinguished face. General "Black Jack" Logan[1] came often to sit, too; silent at first sometimes, then breaking into hot eloquence over some army memory, some occasion where my grandfather's genius had shone.

As the winter advanced, General Buckner,[2] from whom my grandfather had captured Fort Donelson

---

[1]John Alexander Logan (1826–1886), a Union "political general" who was a Democratic congressman from Illinois before being commissioned into the Civil War. He served with General Grant at the siege of Vicksburg. He was a senator from Illinois in the 1870s and 1880s.

[2]General Simon Bolivar Buckner (1823–1914) surrendered Fort Donelson in Tennessee to Brigadier General Ulysses S. Grant on 16 February 1862. Grant was lifted from obscurity and

in 1862, and several other opponents of old war days took the trouble to show their sympathy by joining the group in Grandmama's sitting room on one occasion or another, for a talk with their conqueror.

There were many civilians, too. Handsomest of these was Senator Roscoe Conkling[3]—tall, imposing, with fine gray curls, grizzled beard, and his head thrown well back. He was so distinguished-looking as to hold his companions somewhat in awe. I do not remember what he said—did not understand it very well—but when he talked, everyone listened and seemed greatly to enjoy it, and he often talked.

One frequent visitor frightened me dreadfully— Mark Twain, with his shaggy mane of long white hair, waving or carelessly tossed about his low brow, and his protruding eyebrows, which almost hid the deep-set eyes shining beneath them. He shook hands, always rather crushing my small, pudgy paw, and he would eye me with his whimsical expression, probably not even thinking of me as he did so. Then he would slowly drawl out some remark, in a curious, rather bored, monotone voice. Somehow, though I did not dare say it, I got the idea he was a crazy man, and I would draw close to one or another of the grown-ups when he was around. I remember once

promoted by Lincoln to major general as a result of this coup. Buckner later served a term as the governor of Kentucky (1887–1891).

[3]Roscoe Conkling (1829–1888) of New York, U.S. senator and Republican kingmaker to whom Grant had offered the chief justiceship in 1873.

the following summer at Mount McGregor he came upon me in the garden where I was playing, and as he spoke to me, I turned, saw him, and fled screaming to the cottage door, without replying. Since then I have frequently regretted, in reading his great contributions to American literature, that I had behaved so stupidly.

Others came to my grandparents' house in those days. One name, that of Jefferson Davis,[4] I remember hearing of as having given my grandfather great pleasure by coming, or by a message sent.

The winter wore on and my grandfather grew worse steadily. He remained constantly in his room. With strict orders given me to make no noise, not even to talk, and to come right out again, occasionally I was allowed in. He would never take anything to give him respite, as they had often begged him to do. Also, everyone spoke of the wonderful work he was still doing, and of his chapters, which were piling up.

Then came talk of summer plans. Someone suggested Mount McGregor, in the foothills of the Adirondacks—accessible, dry, invigorating, cool, all that was wanted—a small hotel where one took one's meals was there, it seemed with a wee cottage, just large enough to hold the family; woods of oak and pine; a great sweeping view out over the valley far away. The question was decided; moving the invalid frightened everyone, but the journey came off all right.

[4]Jefferson Davis (1808–1889), president of the Confederate States of America.

For a time the effort of the change and the air were wonderful, though the pain and difficulty in swallowing were as before, of course. An augmentation of strength came within a day or two, and my grandfather was able to be out a great deal, to wear his clothes, and stand the fatigue of dressing and undressing; he again took a large part in the family life, which was arranged around his so he should have as much company and talk as would amuse and distract him.

Soon—it may have been a day later, or two, or three—my mother came out on the balcony and called us children. "Quick, Papa wants you to come and see dear Grandpapa," she said.

We joined her, and she took us into the room where my grandfather was more or less reclining in his great chair. Grandmama was crying quietly and was seated by his side. She had in her hands a handkerchief and a small bottle, perhaps of cologne, and was dampening my grandfather's brow. His hair was longer and seemed to me more curled, while his eyes were closed in a face more drawn than usual and much whiter. Beads of perspiration stood on the broad forehead, and as I came forward, old Harrison[5] gently wiped similar drops from the back of the hand which was lying quietly on the chair arm. My father sat at the opposite side from Grandmama, and the doctor and nurse stood at the head, behind the invalid. Old Harrison had been kneeling near my father but rose, and

[5] Harrison Tyrrel was U.S. Grant's valet.

Former President Grant working on his memoirs in the last weeks of his life

Courtesy Library of Congress

Major General Frederick Dent Grant and Ida Honoré Grant

Courtesy Library of Congress

I took his place. My mother came behind me. "Kiss Grandpapa," she said, but I could not reach over and up to his cheek. I noticed once more how beautiful the hand was. I looked at my father, who nodded, and who put his arm about me. Then I stood for a moment or two, steadied by him, when my mother whispered: "We must go now." With a lump in my throat, I leaned down and kissed the beautiful hand and was led out of the room.

When nurse Louise waked us and dressed us early next morning, she told us that the general had had a bad night and that all the family had been down with him till two or three hours ago.

As we opened our nursery door and stepped into the hall, Harrison rushed across it from my parents' to my grandmother's door and knocked there, having left the first door thrown wide open. We reached the stairs, and I saw my father throw on his jacket—probably he had been asleep in shirt and trousers, ready for any emergency. He rushed out of his bedroom and passed us without seeing us at all, taking the staircase faster than I could imagine his doing. My mother was moving about rapidly, putting on her things also, and across the hall from Grandmama came a sob, and "I'm coming," in reply to Harrison's quick knock.

We children were taken over to the hotel. I was put in my chair and told as usual to eat all the things before me, but I couldn't. Breakfast dragged; then one of those serving it suddenly said: "It is all finished over there at the cottage." And when Louise contradicted, the servant continued: "Yes, yes, a telegram has just been brought over to forward from the hotel office, and the messenger said General Grant had just died."

I think this was the first time in my life I had felt heavy with sorrow. I had at times realized his suffering and patience, so admiration and pity mixed with the other sentiments that overcame me finally when I broke down. The storm passed. I dried my tears and thought; was there nothing I could do to help my father, who was in the cottage "attending to everything," it had been said.

I seemed without resources for usefulness. Then I remembered that one made wreaths for dead people. Perhaps I could make a wreath. It occurred to me that the prettiest wreath I had ever made was a flat one of oak leaves. I picked a quantity of leaves from the low sprouts of some fine trees and sat down to work. It went quickly, and in a half-hour or so the wreath of broad, shining leaves was finished and looked well, as it lay spread on a flat-rock table at hand.

The next thing was to get it to my grandfather. I ran back to the house, approaching from the rear, so the garden and nurse should both be avoided. Once on the balcony I went and looked in the window of the death chamber. My father was not there, but in the center of the room stood a coffin, a thing I had never seen before; and moving about, two men, strangers to me, were setting out a few chairs. I was recognized at once by the elder of the two men, who came to the door and inquired what I wanted.

"I've brought Grandpapa a wreath; I thought my Papa was here," I replied. He said after a little hesitation: "Sure, Miss, and your Papa is just after going up to snatch a little sleep, and I wouldn't disturb him if I were you. Suppose ye give me the wreath to lay on the general. It's a mighty fine wreath; and I think there's no harm in your coming in to help me yourself."

In I went with the undertaker, and he laid the wreath carefully in a circle on the casket. Then he left me standing there, gazing down at the familiar face under the glass, while he went off about his business of tidying up. It seemed heartbreaking that my grandfather should be so still, and dead.

Later, I was very proud because, with carloads of flowers coming by every train and florists bringing special great set pieces that filled the house with their beauty and fragrance, my wreath was the only one on the casket. Finally, it began to fade and the leaves to curl a little; but my father reassured me, "Never mind, pet, my little girl's wreath is going to be varnished so it will keep, and then it shall be buried with Grandpapa. I know he would have liked to keep it with him always."

Impossible to describe in detail what our family life was from 23 July to 8 August. I remember vast crowds of men's hatless heads and of women in black. The flowers piled up, and the resolutions of sympathy, engraved and framed, piled up, too. Letters were coming in by the basket load. Yet there was no confusion or talk. The maximum result was obtained always by my father's power of organization, his patience and self-control.

My father went down to New York with the body on the special train, draped with black, which carried the casket. My Uncle Ulysses came on to stay with and look after the family, taking us down to New York in a special car. Once in town we were all lodged at the old Fifth Avenue Hotel. Tremendous crowds circulated in the streets below our windows, and I was deeply interested in watching the people. Clothes, all black, were brought in, and each member of our party bought something necessary to complete wardrobes in need of deep crepe weeds.[6] Flags everywhere hung at half-mast, and a long continuous procession passed through the doors of New York's City Hall, to pay respect to my grandfather. For days his remains lay in state, and the crowds went solemnly by; men, women, and children, slowly moving on weary feet, waiting, looking, straining for a last glimpse at the well-known face.

The morning of 8 August came, and early our family took up its stand in the funeral carriages, ready to swing into line as soon as the great hearse should pass. Even my childish brain was awed by the immensity of the demonstration. From 23rd Street to 116th Street, a five-mile stretch of sympathetic people covered sidewalks and fences, windows and doors, and every face

[6]That is, mourning clothes. Crepe (crape): The black arm band worn in mourning.

was sad; some were even weeping. Except the crowd, I recall little of those hours spent in the funeral carriage. With both my parents and my Aunt Nelly, we were shut into intense heat and semi-darkness. Some sandwiches, the long silences, and now and then a question asked and answered; my weary body and my own wet eyes I only felt occasionally, but I remember well my father's white, set face and his hoarse voice.

At last we arrived at Riverside,[7] and the afternoon sun shone brightly down on the tiny temporary brick tomb. The services, simple and beautiful, were carried out rapidly, without a hitch, and ended with "taps." Then we drove back to our hotel with a feeling of unutterable weariness and loss.

From that time till the spring of 1889, we lived with my Grandmother Grant. All the first part of those years my father worked on the book, which my grandfather had left in manuscript to his heirs. It had to be gone over still and the proofs corrected, while endless detail work was also involved getting maps and illustrations carefully prepared.

Instead of the little office in the second-floor front, this room was switched back to its old employ of my grandmother's boudoir, and she moved again into what had been recently my grandfather's bedroom. The plain work furniture went up to the third floor and there, in a room just over the earlier office, my father carried through his daily task—saw publishers,

[7]The site of Grant's Tomb in upper Manhattan, overlooking the Hudson.

arranged their terms, and carried out in detail the instructions of the dead author. As the money came in after the first edition of the memoirs was sold, he handled all his mother's business in addition.

It was a great gratification to have the two volumes, written with such courage, while fighting death and enduring a martyrdom of suffering, fully appreciated by the public and attaining the results for which they were written.

The first check sent in by the publishers beat all records for size. It was for over $300,000!

III

In Vienna and My Debut at Court

ONE DAY in the spring of 1889, when I was nearly thirteen years old—a quiet, overgrown girl with long, heavy hair, but otherwise with no distinctive trait—my mother called us down to her room at supper time and announced that she had a great surprise to impart. We were all going to Vienna, to live there a long time! President Harrison had named my father "Envoy Extraordinary and Minister Plenipotentiary" to Austria, and we must prepare to be off very soon. My interest and excitement was intense. I wrote the new title over and over, until I knew how to spell and say it by heart. What I had heard of Austria was limited and vague, but I asked more, until I was informed that Vienna was considered one of Europe's brilliant capitals, that there were great families living there whose names were known in history back through the centuries, as those of robber barons and Holy Roman emperors. Also there were art, music, fine clothes, court functions, fancy leather goods, galleries of treasures, palaces.

We were going to land at Southampton, be in London a short time, and then go straight to Vienna, either through France or Germany, as my parents should decide at the last moment. Anyhow, we would have quite a trip, and I was elated by the prospect of this adventure.

We sailed early in March. Grandmama, with a companion, decided to come, too, and spend the summer months abroad; so our party made six.

At last, with the help of several books, the long, dull trip, which lasted about ten days, ended. We entered, after the trip by boat train to London, a huge caravansary where one got lost. Bad food, rooms that did not remember being cleaned, mud, drizzle, darkness—all contributed to our doleful feeling, as we did our round of sightseeing.

My father and mother were "commanded" to a drawing room and went, both looking very fine. I was allowed to help my mother dress. She was quite radiant in orange brocade embroidered with silver beads.

That day Queen Victoria was holding court and was gracious enough to remember my grandfather had visited her at Windsor Castle years before. The Prince of Wales, Albert Edward, Mama said, looked desperately bored, while the princess was smiling and gracious. Distinguished men, statesmen of various countries, asked to meet my father, and talked with him about the different interests of America and the currents of European politics—which gave my parents an unusual first reception in these official circles.

After our short stay we left for Vienna, direct by way of Belgium and Germany. My father was anxious to reach his post and take over the work given him to do, and his sense of duty suppressed all further stops along the way. He was sorry to disappoint us, he said, and promised to bring us back some day to see these lands we were skimming through.

In Vienna the legation carriage and footman were awaiting us, and we fell in love at first sight with the place. There was a long drive from the train to our hotel in the heart of the old city. The quarter first traversed had broad, open streets. Then we reached the Ring, with its rich public buildings and its parks, covering the space that had been the fortified walls of old Vienna. Suddenly we turned short at right angles and plunged into a tiny street, so narrow that it was almost possible to shake hands from one side to the other. And such sidewalks! Two people abreast was their utmost capacity; a third person had to walk in the street itself.

Suddenly we stopped. Our footman, whose name was Franz and who at once announced he had been with the legation many years and spoke "Engleesh easee," got down and opened the door. We all alighted before what looked a very unpromising place and went in. Franz explained that there was a newer hotel, but not so elegant, and that it was "not for Excellenzen to live in."

There was no lift, but a wide staircase, walled on each side, white, with a thick red carpet. One flight up, there were a dark landing, heavy red velvet curtains, and a door of white painted wood. This flew open, both panels, and we stood on the threshold of the apartment of kings, princes, and Excellenzen!

Enormous rooms, two of them, one in brown and

blue brocade of large design, the other furnished in red damask; lots of gold everywhere, on frames, mirrors, and carved backs of chairs. There were great chandeliers of gilt, bronze, or Bohemian glass—candelabra, clocks, and vases of elaborately worked metal stood on high mantels. A hundred people in each room would not have made a crowd. Perhaps to kings, princes, and Excellenzen this might be a normal habitation; to a simple little American girl, it looked like a palace, vast beyond belief. Our bedrooms were in proportion, but there were no baths at all, nor even toilet rooms. My father asked the price and was told a figure that proved that in Vienna space was a drug on the market. So we took the rooms.

Our first month we spent at the quaint Munsch Hotel. We grew to be comfortable and to like more and more the view of the square and the luxury of meals served in the huge salon. We even got used to the lack of baths, and a tub in our rooms seemed quite satisfactory.

Court mourning was deep for Rudolf, the crown prince, who had died just a few weeks before our arrival. Because of this, my parents had little social life at the beginning of our Austrian experience. My father had taken hold of the legation work and was handling it so that the clerks and secretaries were amazed at how much they could accomplish and how alive they were. An apartment had been found for us, with another in the same building for the legation offices, and we were to take possession early in the autumn.

My father had come home extremely pleased with the sovereign, when at his first reception by the latter he had presented his credentials. His Majesty had shown infinite cordiality; had said he was immensely glad to have my father represent the United States in Austria; had told how well he remembered receiving my grandfather at Schönbrunn[1] many years before, when during his trip around the world the latter stopped for a while in Vienna. The emperor asked my father about the last years of President Grant; asked news of Grandmama, whom he also remembered. He was all smiles and amiability, very magnetic—an example of what a man in his situation should be to win the hearts of those who approach him. He spoke no English and my father no French, but each had some knowledge of the language the other used, so though an interpreter was present, there was little to do.

We children took to the ways of the Austrians quickly and had an Austrian, Fräulein Mitzi, to teach us through the summer. In the autumn my brother entered the Theresianum, the great school founded by Maria Theresa for her nobility.

In the legation offices all went smoothly. My father liked his staff, especially his naval and military attachés (the latter was an old comrade of his West Point days), and both had charming wives; so his official family was a gay and happy group.

We had many attractive people constantly at our

[1]The country palace of the Hapsburgs near Vienna.

house, and by the time I was old enough to be presented at court, I had a number of well-disposed friends among my father's and mother's colleagues and among the *jeunesse dorée*,[2] which composed the groups of secretaries. I also had a lot of intimates among the young Austrian girls.

By this time my parents, and I also, were feeling very at home in the beautiful Austrian capital. I had learned to speak German almost as the natives.

I was only a little over sixteen years old when Mr. Cleveland was elected president, in November 1892. Soon after this, he honored my father with a charming personal letter telling the young American minister of the pleasure he had in learning of his fine work during the past four years. He said he would be glad if my father would remain on at his post under his Democratic administration. My father was greatly flattered and wrote at once to express his appreciation, but he declined the honor of continuing as minister at Vienna. He felt the position should go to a representative of the president's party. He told Mr. Cleveland, however, he would be only too glad to remain on until such time as the latter selected his successor.

It meant that we should be in Vienna until the late spring, and my parents decided I should go into society, or at least to the great court ball.

My debut was a matter of intense excitement to me. In my life it meant that changes, which a young girl ac-

[2]"Gilded youth."

complishes usually by degrees, were made at one sweep. I continued my lessons until the New Year of 1893 and wore short skirts and my hair in a pigtail, and then magically I was grown, and my hair went up, while my gowns touched the ground.

The dresses, three in number, made for me by the great Drécoll[3] himself, fitted and hung quite beautifully. My mother had excellent taste, and I was delighted.

After I dressed for the great ball, I went to show myself to my parents and with a lock of hair changed here and there or a pin added to my dress, my mother gave me a last careful inspection. Then she put on my throat a beautiful old necklace of Mexican filigree.

The scene of my presentation at the Austrian court was a handsome room in the more modern part of the palace, and its decorations in white-and-gold wood paneling, with brilliant brocade, were Empire, or later, in style. My father and his secretaries were the only men in simple evening dress and stood out, marked by this, in the throng, where most of the masculine portion rivaled the ladies in wearing splendid gold and silver lace and multicolored clothes—red, blue, green, and white.

Shortly after our entrance several men were introduced to me, and each paid me the banal little compliment the occasion demanded. All the younger ones asked me not to forget them in the ballroom later.

Suddenly we were all silent, and the three raps on

[3]One of the leading Parisian haute couture houses of the belle époque.

the floor had just been heard, announcing the solemn entry of the emperor and his court. Then we turned toward the door, where the emperor stood bowing and smiling genially, with the duchess of Cumberland on his arm. We all curtsied, and the long procession advanced into the room.

The emperor began with the senior ambassador and moved rather rapidly down the line without, however, any signs of being bored or hurried. He also left all the men and women convinced it was a pleasure for him, the emperor, to have those few words with his guests. He approached my father and mother and said in French, with a warm handshake: "How are you, Colonel Grant? Good evening, Madam. I hear your little girl is here tonight and that she is very *gentille*. I must meet her."

Immediately my parents separated a little, and as I stepped forward and curtseyed low, His Majesty held out a cordial hand, which grasped mine hard for a moment. He looked at me with a quick, pleasant glance that took in everything. In French he spoke again: "I'm glad you came to my ball, Mademoiselle, and I hope you will find it pretty and will enjoy yourself. You will, if you speak German; our people love those who speak their language and are at home among them. You have been years here with your father—have you learned to speak?"

I answered in German: "*Ja, Majestät!* I do speak German rather better than English, and I am quite at home in Vienna."

The emperor threw his head back and laughed with real amusement. "But you speak Viennese—it is quite charming! Where did you learn our patois?" And I said I had picked it up, because I found it so much prettier than North German. Whereupon His Majesty looked exceedingly pleased and amused, and went on to ask me a number of questions. Finally he said, "I am sure you will have great success, and I shall watch it with pleasure!"

Finally we moved through an archway and found ourselves in the immense ballroom of the Hapsburgs, where for centuries back they had held their court. The emperor turned and bowed to the duchess of Cumberland, the dance music struck up—such music as ears rarely hear—a Strauss waltz by an orchestra unrivaled in all Europe, for by Imperial command Strauss himself held the conductor's baton, and none but his own music was played for the dancing.

Then came supper. We were joined by a number of men, and I had a pleasant time of it; and as soon as the music played, we rushed back to waltz again, until at some signal the party was over, the royalty bowed and retired, and everyone began to push forward toward the various doors.

At last the day of departure came, and we went to the station in the old carriage, accompanied by the same Franz who had met us early one morning more than four years ago. Franz was in tears, and I was nearly so. My parents also were sad to leave what had been to them a very pleasant post. Flowers and sweets were brought to us in quantities; many Austrian friends were there to see us off, and nearly all the colleagues came in a large crowd. There was great excitement, and as we pulled out of the station, waving hats and sounds of good wishes followed us.

IV

Going Home

WE TRAVELED SLOWLY to Southampton and from there embarked for home. We were carrying back to America many agreeable memories. My parents had taken us children over much of western Europe. My father personally planned every journey so we should get all that was educational from our wandering.

When we landed in New York, we went at once to Cranston's Hotel on the Hudson, where my grandmother was stopping. She was well, seemed delighted to see us and to have the long sojourn abroad ended. My parents had made a delightful plan, which we were to carry out immediately. We were to go to Chicago and pay a lengthy visit to my mother's family. The World's Fair[1] was in full swing, and my beautiful aunt, Mrs. Palmer,[2] was president of the woman's division. At a time when American women were new to the game of civic work, they had obtained recognition in connection with the World's Fair and were on their

---

[1]The World's Columbian Exposition opened in Chicago in 1893.

[2]The author's aunt Bertha had been appointed Chairman of the Board of Lady Managers of the World's Columbian Exposition.

mettle to do their best. My aunt had accepted the presidency after some hesitation. The Woman's Building was made one of the most artistic in the White City on the Lake,[3] while the celebrations held there and at the lady president's splendid home were things the board was proud of.

When we reached Chicago in late July, the exposition was already in full swing, and my aunt, though tremendously occupied, was accustomed to her role and played it easily, gracefully, and without for an instant being flurried or even showing fatigue. She was forty-two then and radiant. Calm, amiable, quick, and capable, she managed her heavy duties with a gentle manner and sweet smile that bewitched her aides and made them doubly willing and enthusiastic. She was seconded by a number of distinguished women, too numerous to name, but who ably represented Chicago and many other cities in America. There were women who had come from abroad as well, bringing exhibitions from their far-away countries. It was a totally new departure, this woman's movement, and everyone was watching it with interest.

That summer left none but pleasant memories, both of the affections of the family circle, still complete, and of the excitement and interest of the World's

[3]"All around the Woman's Building other snowy edifices were going up ..., so that a White City rose like a mirage along the lake's south shore. It covered an area of 586 acres in Jackson Park." Ishbel Ross, *Silhouette in Diamonds. The Life of Mrs. Potter Palmer* (New York: Arno Press, 1975), p. 77.

Fair. When it was over, we left Chicago with regret, and I had discovered somehow that life at home was much better even than it had been in Vienna!

Early in October we went to New York. We were very poor, my mother told me, and it would be a painful experience, after all the comforts of our Vienna life, to settle down as modestly as we now must.

We found a tiny three-story house on West 73rd Street, and my parents took it for the winter. It was new, and though so small, somehow our furniture, which had come from Vienna, was crowded into it.

I found it did not much matter our being poor, except that one could not give big parties and that street-cars replaced the legation carriages. But others gave so many entertainments, it would have been difficult to fit any more into the season.

My father was busy with some writing, preparing a new popular edition of my grandfather's book, with annotations of his own, also with more maps and pictures than the original volumes had held. This soon had a large sale.

My brother loved the American ways and had plunged with zest into his school life at Cutlers. He was doing well in his studies and was becoming a great, tall fellow. Finally, having finished Cutler's at sixteen, the boy took one year at Columbia College and then entered West Point.

As the months flew by, my father found himself becoming intensely absorbed by the political situation, both in New York and nationally. He was associated with many of the eminent men of the day, among those the veteran Roscoe Conkling, who died soon after; Senator Root,[4] whose talents and character already placed him in the forefront of great men; Joseph Choate;[5] Senator William Evarts;[6] General Sherman; and General Porter; ex-President Harrison; President McKinley; and the political bosses Senator Platt[7] and Mark Hanna[8] passed through our parlor, dined at our table informally, or came to talk with my father about the interests of the country, state, or city and the aims and work of the Republican party.

My father's work became more and more serious, and he was obliged to stay in the city even through the summer months. My mother remained with him, keeping our house open and fairly comfortable even in hot weather. I went visiting friends in the environs, where there were many pleasant house-parties. My Aunt and Uncle Palmer had a cottage for two summers at Bar Harbor, and they took me there. After these seasons the same kind relations invited me to join them at Newport, and I made my debut in that

[4]Elihu Root (1845–1937), secretary of war from 1899–1904 and secretary of state from 1905–1909.

[5]Joseph Hodges Choate (1832–1917), prominent New York lawyer, later ambassador to the court of St. James.

[6]William Maxwell Evarts (1818–1901), former secretary of state under Hayes and Republican senator, 1885–1891.

[7]Thomas Collier Platt (1833–1901), Republican senator from New York, colleague of Roscoe Conkling.

[8]Marcus Alonzo Hanna (1837–1904), Cleveland businessman and Republican powerhouse, senator from 1897.

gay, smart resort, where I had a lot of friends already among the New York group of merrymakers. Habits then were simpler than they became later at Newport, and we were a crowd of carefree youths, who rode and picnicked, or went out crabbing and catboating, who danced and dined, as the spirit moved us.

I remember only one year with a shadow cast on our spirits, by the Spanish-American War. Already in spring, with the promise of war, my father had volunteered his services. He was in doubt as to how he would be used. For the few weeks while he waited, he prepared his uniform and kit. Our house was full of paraphernalia—saddle and harness, uniforms, arms, and such. Constantly men came and went who wanted my father to join one or another of the volunteer groups going to the front. He refused all these positions, though he helped several to organize, putting his old army experience at their service.

Then came a call that appealed to him. A hardworking infantry regiment of the National Guard, modest of pretension and comparatively poor of pocket, sent him a delegation. The members were offering themselves in a unit to our government, for service under fire. At a meeting the day before, they had chosen him as commander—would he accept? He did at once, and for a few days we lived in a turmoil of excitement, for no sooner had they volunteered than the government ordered them out to camp on Long Island, saying that they would go to the front.

Two weeks my father spent with these men. Then

he was ordered off by the war department to a train-
ing camp in the South, where through sizzling summer weather, he fought malaria and dysentery, and
trained raw young recruits. He suffered a short, sharp
attack of the prevailing malady but continued his duties till he could hardly stand and the doctors said he
was all but dying. My mother was wired for. Then,
after a week of good nursing, my father's magnificent
physique answered to her care, and he was back in
camp again. At last, late in the summer, came the
much-desired orders sending him to the front. He was
promoted to the rank of brigadier general, transferred
with the same rank to the Regular Army, and named
military commander on the island of Puerto Rico.

The time between July 1893 and September 1898
had passed very quickly, and my girlhood had been
gay. Being the only girl of my generation in our family,
I was greatly petted. My uncle and lovely aunt put all
possible pleasure into my girlhood, too, and gave me
much that our own limited means would not have offered. My aunt, slim and graceful, with hair grown sil-
very white, had kept her freshness and seemed more
beautiful than ever. She had no daughter and gave me
the affection she could have lavished on one.

Whenever the question of my marrying came up, I
found in her a true friend whose advice was easy to
follow, as it coincided with my own ideas of what was
right. I was grateful that in spite of our small means, I
was not pushed into a "brilliant match."

V

Months of Travel

IN THE EARLY AUTUMN of 1898, my mother was to join my father in Puerto Rico, where he was military commander. She did not want to take me with her for fear of the climate and the roughness of a newly conquered country. Uncle Palmer had passed a bad summer at Newport and was being sent abroad to spend the time of cold weather on the Nile. My aunt was taking her two boys along for a year's travel before they settled down to business. The Palmer family proposed to take me abroad with them, and I was perfectly enchanted when my mother accepted for me.

London seemed comfortable and agreeable to me. We did a little shopping, mostly for the men, and moved on to Paris, where we scarcely stopped, so anxious were we to reach the southern sunlight, which was to help my uncle. In Rome we lingered longer. Our invalid liked Rome so much that my aunt and I stayed there with him until the day our steamer sailed from Naples.

In Cairo we did much that was amusing. We visited the pyramids by moonlight and made various other charming excursions. It was a wonderful experience of pretty villages and bazaars, of imposing ruins, and especially of the dignified, graceful natives. We were a congenial party, all of us delighted by our trip, save my poor uncle, who was growing steadily worse.

Finally, on our return to Cairo, after the classic tour to the First Cataract and back, we sadly gave up the rest of our contemplated journey. We hurried to Rome, where my uncle remembered being comfortable and where he liked the doctors. We reached there just in time, for on our arrival the invalid took to his bed and various medical lights were called in to his aid. My aunt devoted nearly all her time to him.

Rome's gay carnival season was at its height, and we had not been there many days when old friends of my parents and aunt found us out.

I made friends with some young people, among whom were nearly all those gilded youths whom I had seen dining at the Grand Hotel in December. Lunches, dinners, soirées, and balls followed each other. We were even asked to a small afternoon reception and tea by the Queen Mother, a beautiful, graceful woman with delightful manners, who already knew my aunt and parents. We also went to a court ball, which was well done in every way and very pleasant, though not possessing the quaint historic and picturesque qualities of the Hapsburg court functions.

There were three or four young men among the diplomats I had met who were especially polite about accompanying us on these picnics, and who, besides, felt it their duty to invent other sightseeing expeditions in and about the city, visiting with us palaces or museums. One of these, a Russian, was only temporarily attached to his embassy. A soldier by profession, also a sportsman who made his mark among the elite of the Italians, both in riding and in handling the ribbons over a smart team of four horses, Prince Michael Cantacuzene was in the south recuperating from a horse-show accident. He had little if any duty on the embassy staff and seemed glad—in spite of his reputation of hating society—to run about with us, whether to balls or in more sporty occupations.

My uncle grew better, and we were soon to push on to Cannes, where with early spring the doctors said he would find the change of climate beneficial.

Several of our group spoke of coming with us to Cannes for a vacation, and each one was to write me more of his plans. They all kept their kindly promise as to this, giving me the opportunity of straightening things out so there might be no misunderstanding. All save one did this, for I had not been on the Riviera a week when, on walking into the hall of our hotel with an armful of bundles and an open box of candy, I found Cantacuzene seated in a deep chair reading. He dropped his book and came toward me. I had only just had a letter from him saying he was leaving Rome, going to Paris, having given up his proposed stop on the Riviera. His sudden apparition surprised me so much that my arms fell and the sweets and bundles scattered over the floor. When my aunt and cousins joined us, Cantacuzene was still gathering up the horrid things. The family were all very glad to see him, for he was an agreeable fellow. He explained with energy that he had been on the verge of starting for Paris when a telegram from the Grand Duke Kyril[1] had brought him to Cannes for a few days' visit and that he was spending the evening with this old comrade. We were also dining out, so we all parted, making an engagement for the next day some time.

At dinner I chanced to sit next to the grand duke himself, and by way of conversation I said to him how nice it was that he had brought Cantacuzene to the Riviera.

"I did not," said Kyril. "I was glad to see him when he appeared in my rooms this evening, but it filled me with amazement. All winter he has stuck in Rome—I don't know why—and now, when I gave him up, he came. I had to turn him out, since I was already engaged for tonight. He seems unusually capricious!"

It was evident Kyril's story and Cantacuzene's had not been compared before the telling and that some mystery surrounded the latter's actions. I was given future food for thought when a day or two later an old college friend of my cousin announced that I would be making a great mistake to tie up to any foreigner, no matter how nice he was. "Grants belong in America, and I want to argue the point seriously with you." As he spoke, he looked across the table to where the Russian sat.

"I assume you know that no foreigner wants me.

[1]Grand Duke Kyril Vladimirovich (1876–1938) was Tsar Nicholas II's first cousin (son of Alexander III's brother) and a career naval officer.

Potter Palmer　　　　　　　*Bertha Honoré Palmer*

Prince Michael Cantacuzene

My Life Here and There

You see all the girls who marry English, French, or Italians have fortunes. I'm too poor to be in danger. Besides, I don't think I should care for foreign life save as an incident such as this trip has been. I can safely promise you to keep myself free for any American who may appeal to me in time."

Whether it was the fine weather and the beauty of Cannes or the powers of eloquence that he displayed and his disregard for the European necessity of a dower, within two days from that of the luncheon, I found myself, in spite of my intentions, engaged to Prince Cantacuzene. Ours was a somewhat complicated position, for we were far away from both our immediate families, and for many days we kept the telegraph wires hot. Finally, we had official consent from all our parents, and were able, with my aunt's help, to make some plans. April was still to be spent in the south on my uncle's account; then we were to go to Paris, our party augmented by my fiancé. There the official announcement would be made, and I was to order my trousseau. On the first of June, we were to sail for the United States, while Cantacuzene returned to his country, to take up regimental service during the summer maneuvers. He was to join us in the autumn again for the wedding. We had known each other but two or three weeks before becoming engaged and had been a month together since then. Now the summer meant a long separation, and we were to see one another only shortly before our marriage.

I was called a gambler by some of my friends at this

time, but though generally a slow, careful person, on this occasion I was not at all hesitating or agitated over what seemed a risky business, perhaps, to others.

I knew nothing of Russia—even its geography and history were hazy in my mind—nothing of the society or family in which I was to take a place. Such Russians as I had met I liked, and I had found their point of view similar to my own. My fiancé knew beforehand I was quite poor, yet he had not hesitated over this fact.

The first days of September brought my fiancé, and after that a round of dinners began, given in our honor by kind friends. A few last details were discussed and settled connected with the wedding ceremonies. There were to be two of these—the Russian Orthodox and one in the tiny Episcopal chapel at Newport.

The Russian ceremony was to be performed first, and (by special dispensation) at home, the priests coming from New York and bringing all the necessary paraphernalia with them. It was a most beautiful service. The icons and tapers, the incense and the chanting made a charming effect in the quiet room. No one was invited, save our ushers and our family party.

At the American chapel, also, the wedding was a very pretty one, as simply carried out as possible, according to our wishes. Cantacuzene and I both disliked the idea of exaggeration or show. There were a few autumn flowers and leaves on the pews and a screen of feathery green about the altar. Bishop Potter, my parents' old friend, and Doctor Nevin, who had

The Cantacuzene wedding in Newport, Rhode Island

My Life Here and There

The Women's Pavilion, Columbian Exposition, Chicago, 1893

54

seen the birth and growth of our romance, divided the service between them.

My gown was the simplest possible. The veil of tulle had no flower or jewel to attach it to my hair. The one note of magnificence in the whole proceedings was my husband's uniform. He wore his regimental white cloth with red-and-silver trimmings, high black boots, and golden metal helmet, with the Imperial eagle of Russia on its top in silver, which caught the light and added its glistening note. Everyone was much excited about the groom's fine clothes, and his thoroughbred type, face, figure, and manner came in for favorable comment from all who met him for the first time that day.

I was given away by my brother in his West Point uniform. My father having been sent out to the Philippines in the early spring, I had not found him when I returned from abroad, and he had written us he expected to come back before our wedding. As summer passed, his work in Luzon and Samoa had become more arduous, and constant trouble with native chiefs made him feel that his duty was to stay there, not asking for the leave he had meant to take.

Consequently, he wrote and wired he did not want the marriage to be deferred but wished us to ask the president if, under these circumstances, the latter would not give my brother permission to leave West Point and to replace him for the occasion. This request Mr. McKinley kindly granted.

During the week of my wedding, my father was in

four battles, but from the firing-line out in the wilds a runner carried back a telegram and sent it from head-quarters, so it was put into my hands as we returned from church. My father's message of love, blessings, and congratulations was the first to reach me.

There were a great many interesting people at the wedding who had gathered for love of my parents and interest in their child, but I have little memory of any individual faces. My grandfather had come from Chicago with his four sons, and he was, at eighty, still well and strong, though cataracts were developing on both his eyes and he used a cane to prevent false steps. He and my Grandmother Grant found each other in the company, and taking each other's arms, they were wandering about talking, in the gayest spirits. They traveled back in their memory twenty-five years to the time of my parents' wedding, and all the company enjoyed their pleasures and their reminiscences. We had some anxiety for their safety, for Grandmama, too, was grown old and very heavy, and her eyesight was extremely bad. Our fears were misplaced, however, and they survived the heavy lunch and other pleasures of the day, and were photographed with our wedding party standing together.

We left Newport that afternoon, on a yacht loaned us by Mr. Walters, the kindest of friends, and we sailed the next morning for France. A few days in Paris to gather up our various trousseau trunks, and then we took the North Express bound for Russia.

VI

The Russian Home

ON THE FRONTIER of my new home country, I was keyed to the highest pitch of interest and curiosity. What was it which made everyone say I would find both the land and life so different from the same things in the West, and why should I feel so far away, as I was told I would?

At once, of course, I heard the unknown tongue, in which long sentences seemed to be spoken as if they were each one a single word. I saw strange square-built figures with broad, stolid faces, standing about. They said almost nothing, made no gestures, and they answered agitated questions with their patient, quiet voices. They were *muzhiki*,[1] wearing odd costumes and white aprons, also caps of a queer shape. They carried our baggage adroitly and seemed very strong. Officials in various uniforms, fine-looking, heavy-built men who wore their clothes smartly were most busy examining passports and baggage.

We were met at the frontier by a clever-looking old man who had been with my husband's grandfather, then with Cantacuzene's father, for years, and had become the majordomo, or the house steward, since the

---

[1] *Muzhik* (*muzhiki,* pl.): the familiar term for a male peasant.

57

death of my father-in-law. He took our tickets, baggage receipts, and passports, also all responsibility. He told us to eat the dinner he had ordered for us in the restaurant; he marched off to care for all else.

After our meal we walked about among the picturesque groups, before old Auguste came to tell us our special car had been hooked to the train going south and we must get into it. After twenty-four hours' more traveling we arrived at a tiny station, which was then the nearest to the old chateau of Bouromka,[2] and there, when we alighted, my husband's brother met us. He was a fourteen-year-old, charming, round-faced boy, with a cheerful smile and with a keen sense of humor lurking in his handsome eyes. He had brought me a large bunch of violets, and while we chatted with him, the contents of a big lunch-basket had been unpacked by the servants and laid out for our benefit. We ate with hearty appetites, for since the frontier had been crossed, we had had only such food as old Auguste could prepare in our car. It seemed a funny way to travel, to have to take so many things and people along to be comfortable. Auguste had brought bed linen and everything needed with him, and I learned this was really necessary, as soon as one left the main lines and the express trains.

My brother-in-law had arranged to perfection our

[2]The Cantacuzene estate of Bouromka (Buromka), a property from the Speransky side of the family (see Historical Introduction), was located in Poltava province in left-bank Ukraine (east of the Dnepr River).

Bouromka Castle, the Cantacuzene ancestral home

My Life Here and There

Valet and maid at Bouromka, Nikita and Lisa

Russian People

drive to Bouromka. Over the undulating steppes three relays of dapple-gray trotters, each set harnessed four abreast, dragged us in a huge, luxurious landau. Another carriage followed with Auguste and the bags, and a third carried our trunks. At the frontier of the Bouromka estate, a gala equipage, called traditionally the "golden carriage," awaited us. Hung so high from the ground that a ladder of four steps was used to climb into it, this carriage had a platform out behind, where between the springs two footmen in Cossack[3] dress stood holding to straps and looking very handsome in their blue, scarlet, and fur, with the family eagles fastened on their breasts. Cantacuzene and I sat on the main seat and my brother-in-law on a small one at our feet, with his back to the high box the coachman occupied.

All the men wished us health and happiness, and welcome to Bouromka. The superintendents of the estate met us with the traditional bread and salt on silver dishes, covered with towels embroidered by the women of the estate. They kissed my hands, while my husband embraced each of the old servitors heartily. They had seen him grow up and were his devoted friends, it seemed.

As we passed through each village, the peasants looked at me with curiosity in their smiling faces. We

---

[3]The Cossacks of late Imperial Russia were soldier-farmers of the southern regions, descendants of free frontiersmen of Orthodox faith and various ethnic backgrounds, famous for their equestrian skill and easily recognizable by their semi-military garb.

pulled up in the midst of a crowd on each public square, who offered us the traditional bread and salt and to whose health Cantacuzene drank as he thanked that particular village for its welcome.

Some had made arches of straw and flowers, tied with bunting, for us to pass under. All the people seemed to me most sympathetic. The villages were as picturesque as were the costumes, and I felt I was going to like Russian life and all it seemed to mean of tradition, good feeling, and interesting duties.

It grew dark, and we were met by two more men in Cossack dress, who were on horseback and carried flaming torches to light us on our way. Soon after this we swung into the park, and taking the main avenue at a gallop, we reached the house entrance through a mass of brilliant figures in peasant national dress. As we pulled up, a brass band began to play on the lawn, the front doors were thrown open, and ever so many people met my eyes—all apparently retainers of one kind or another—with Cantacuzene's mother, in a light gown, and the village priest, standing together as central figures.

We were fairly carried out of the carriage, and our outer coats were removed, I scarcely know how. Then we found ourselves pulled or shoved toward the princess. When our greetings were over, we moved into the ballroom, which looked enormous. It ran two stories high, and there was room in it for all the people. Here a welcoming thanksgiving service was celebrated by the village priest, or "pope," and during

that, I had time to get my breath and look around.
The service in Slavonic I could not understand at all,
of course, but I knew it was in the nature of a Te Deum
in honor of my husband's return to the old home with
his bride, and I was aware that while they listened, as
respectful devotees, to the words of the priest, most of
the retainers kept their eyes fixed on me—from curiosity, doubtless, as to what the new member of the
chateau family would represent in their lives.

The room's proportions were really imposing and
seemed the vaster because of the softly shaded lamp-
light and the rather scattered furniture. It had been a
ballroom but was now used as a general living room,
evidently, with big, soft chairs stretching out their
arms invitingly, and many books, periodicals, and
games scattered about.

A billiard table, a grand piano, a phonograph—all
offered themselves in different corners, while screens
of plants shut off spots where one might sit for cozy
conversations or a card game. There were large glass
cases with family souvenirs and relics, marble statues,
attractive-looking paintings, and a great chimney piece
of carved wood.

Most of all, I was struck by the floor in the great
open space between us and the priest. It was inlaid in
the most complicated designs, of oak foundation with
white maple, red mahogany, and bits of mother-of-
pearl, its surface brilliant with polish, rich with many
coatings of pure beeswax—a work of art such as I had
never seen in any other country. Afterward, I learned

this floor was hand made, hand laid, and hand polished for generations by patient people, who showed by their care of detail a true love of beauty and their instinct for good taste. In its way it was as splendid as the high-paneled ceiling or the chanting of the choir, which carried out perfectly their part of the service.

On a table stood a collection of icons that were to be ours and with which we were to be blessed. Some of these were ancient and rare, offered by the family or by friends; others in modern enamel or beaten bronze were donated by the house servants and the superintendents of the estates. Incense burned, voices rose in beautiful strains, and the whole scene was most touching, with a charm different from any I had ever experienced. It was a far cry from Newport, New York, and Paris to this new life just opening, and somehow, in spite of its strangeness, it attracted me more than I could express. I began at that first moment to feel a deep sympathy with the nation that created such a frame and lived in it, filling it so well.

The princess, my mother-in-law, was a Frenchwoman,[4] and her looks, gestures, attitudes, and ways were different from those of the others present. She

[4]Her maiden name was Sicard, but she was not an immigrant to Russia. According to family tradition, the first Sicard, a Huguenot, came to Russia in the reign of Catherine II in the late eighteenth century. While the family undoubtedly kept its French culture, it had probably long since converted to Russian Orthodoxy. According to the *Almanach de St-Pétersbourg: cour, monde et ville* for 1913/14, "Princesse Douairière Elisabeth Cárlovna, Contesse Speransky, née Sicard," maintained a residence at rue Murillo 4 in Paris.

was very handsome and was dressed in the latest fashion of Paris. She moved more quickly than did the Russians, and she wept from excitement. Her eyes roved about, alert to catch and correct any imperfection. She made an excellent effect and stood out in sharp contrast to the background of Bouromka life.

The service over, we remained where we were, I standing between my mother-in-law and my husband, and from the old priest down to the youngest servant-maid, everyone passed by us to be presented to me and to kiss my hand. Many of these faithful servants were very old in the family's service. Two tottering old chaps had known Speransky, who died in 1839![5] Many dated back to serfdom times, and practically all were born and brought up on the estate. My husband's old nurse waddled by, rolling in fat, with a new gold brooch on her ample breast, and when she kissed my hand, after hugging and kissing Cantacuzene, I thought her so motherly looking I kissed her with enthusiasm on both her ruddy cheeks. She gave me a comfortable hug and a smile in return, and from then on I had in "Grandmother Anna Vladimirivna,"[6] as she was called, a staunch ally.

[5]Michael Speransky (1772–1839) was one of the most important and famous statesmen of modern Russia. The son of a village priest, he rose to high office in the Russian government through sheer ability and was for a time the principal advisor of Tsar Alexander I and the second most powerful man in the state. He was given the title of Count (Graf) in 1839 for his work in codifying Russian laws.

[6]That is, Anna Vladimirovna.

Soon all the servants and I were extremely friendly, and through almost twenty years, I always saw only signs of their goodwill and understanding devotion. It was the qualities of these simple, lowly country folk that first made me fond of my new home. Afterward, as I grew to know them and their compatriots better, the same traits made me admire all classes of Russians for their utterly simple dignity, their patience, and their courage.

It took a little while to get used to the size of the old house and its complicated plan, and I was always getting lost and asking my way about. There was much I liked and much that was amusing at Bouromka. The average American housekeeper would have gone quite mad from the inconvenient arrangements. The pumping by hand of all the water for that enormous establishment; the fetching and carrying necessary; the mere fact that two men spent their entire days cleaning, filling, and lighting kerosene lamps; that we all lived with doors and windows unbolted, even open— French windows standing wide on the terraces through summer nights; that all one's treasures lay about in complete safety for years, generations even; all this seemed amazing!

Outside, the country was very beautiful, and I never could decide whether I loved the flat steppe-land best, with its splendor of harvests waving and its chocolate-colored furrowed fields so full of promise, or whether the woods and meadow stretches were more admirable in their green peacefulness, with cattle feeding and streams flowing gently by. The number of our animals and the variety of work on the estate were absorbing, and it seemed to my American mind interesting and amusing to think how self-sufficient we were, seventy versts[7] away—about forty-six miles—from post, telegraph, railroad, and electricity. Yet life was entirely civilized and comfortable, and everything moved as if by well-oiled machinery.

After two or three days the princess departed for St. Petersburg to conduct my young brother-in-law to school, and we remained on for two weeks or so through the golden magnificence of the early autumn. My husband took me over the whole of the estate, and during that first stay in the Russian country place, I grew to know much about the way of running it with its wheels within wheels. Originally it had consisted of some 30,000 desiatinas (there are about two and two-thirds acres to a desiatina). With the abolition of serfdom, half of this had been given to the liberated peasants by the emperor, and the government had paid a nominal sum to the landowner for the confiscation. Later, through three generations, various reasons led to further sacrifices of a small part of Bouromka's land, but thirteen or fourteen thousand desiatinas were still ours. Interweaving its borders with peasant commune lands, it made a fair sight and gave one the feeling that one was lord of a small kingdom, with all rights and responsibilities belonging to it.

[7]A verst (in Russian, *verstá*) is almost exactly equivalent to a kilometer (.66 mile).

The village outside our gates was very picturesque, but it gave me a heartache to see the wretchedness that reigned there and the unhealthy looks of many of the people. Situated on the green, sloping banks of a tiny lake, it was ideally pretty and showed the Russian deep-rooted instinct both for the practical and for the beautiful. Cattle and people both drank and bathed in the crystal water. Their homes, smothered in trees and gay flowers, were of a charming general effect from a distance. Close by it was different, for the thatched roofs all needed mending, were blown about terribly, and let in rain and snow. The houses themselves had usually crooked walls with tiny windows fixed in the plaster. One saw evidences of poverty, misery, filth, shiftlessness, overcrowding, and discomfort. To me it was deeply distressing to think the people who, when serving in our house or on the estate where conditions were better, showed us sunny faces and sang gaily over work, which they carried out in quick intelligence in their natural state but in their own village homes lived in such a sad, unhealthy way.

My husband's father had been dead a long time; my mother-in-law, in the hands of her superintendents during her children's minority, was exploited by these men almost as much as were the peasants, and besides, she had been away from the country place a great deal. She had done much to better the chateau and other buildings on the estate, but she was facing large annual deficits caused by overexpenditure and underproduction. The people were not considered part of her responsibility. I do not know if this situation was the same all over Russia, but I was told Bouromka was a model of prosperity and the Little Russian[8] peasants were happier and cleverer than those of the north.

For a long time it seemed difficult to understand why our people should suffer so much more than the inhabitants of other lands. By degrees I learned the influences that had been at work for centuries, and these Russians then made an even greater appeal, especially as through the years between 1900 and 1914, I was carefully watching their development.

It was the middle of November when we went up to the capital[9] from Bouromka. Heavy rains had set in, which made our ploughed fields fertile but turned our roads to quagmires. Six horses harnessed to a great berline, like a landau, could scarcely drag it through the heavy mud that oozed over our hubs, and our spending the winter in that special spot on the road was apparently among the possibilities.

The long trip in old-fashioned trains with no conveniences to me was an amusing adventure, for we had space and provisions and plenty of servants along. All this changed after some years, but I remember with interest those funny arrangements, the piles of hand baggage and the ready, helpful people, who through atavistic traits of a desire to please, doubtless, knew how to make us travel easily.

[8]That is, Ukrainian.
[9]St. Petersburg.

We were to go to the home of my mother-in-law on arriving in the capital, and she had offered us a part of her large apartment for the winter, or until such time as we found one in which to settle ourselves. She was to send her carriage to meet us at the station, and we were to have the feeling of a homecoming, she had said with much enthusiasm.

It was a drizzling morning with dirty snow covering the streets thinly. Scarcely light as yet, the place looked dull, and a very raw, icy wind swept across one's face. The carriage, through mistake or neglect, was not there, so perforce we drove across the city in a queer vehicle called a droshky, with a driver as odd as his turnout, conducting a horse which had a night's work already in his weary legs, I'm sure, from the slow way he moved.

That drive was my only bad experience in the magnificent city which I was to love so dearly as my home through many years, but it was horrid, and it seemed miles from the Warsaw station to Fontanka, where the princess lived.

When at last we were safely landed at her front door and made our way up the great staircase into her well-heated rooms, our spirits rose. The princess received us with as much excitement as in Bouromka, but with less ceremony, and I was at once introduced to my husband's sister and her husband. The former had extraordinary distinction; small and fragile, she was the quintessence of find breeding, with gentle hands, and eyes of great beauty. Her rare intelligence, wit, and sweetness were all her own. Shy as a rule and not demonstrative, she was of those of whom the French genius spoke when he said: "The most attractive women never draw attention, but always hold it."

I found her very simple and winning, and we at once adopted each other as sisters. During twenty long years, we have been that and faithful friends besides. Her husband, warm-hearted and charming, made himself my kindly comrade immediately, and I found him also most sympathetic through a long relationship. By degrees I realized the city's splendor, which thrilled me, and I even had a taste of society life almost at once.

Taken all in all, though, I had a bad time at first, for, arriving in November, by Christmas I had already spent three weeks ill in bed, while at the end of January, I went to bed again, to remain till Easter, with a grave case of typhoid. Then a slight relapse kept me ill or convalescent until the end of May.

When my brain was not more or less clouded, I felt deeply depressed by so much illness, but my young husband was a most excellent nurse, and he and his brother and sister were amiably ready to amuse me and cheer me through the slow hours of recovery.

In June we moved into our new apartment on the banks of the Neva, and though it was much smaller than the princess's home, we were enchanted to establish ourselves. We both loved the great river, which was a constantly changing picture.

My mother had come to me during my illness in the

winter, and in the summer she returned for six weeks, taking the long, fatiguing trip with much patience.

In July our first child was born, a splendid fat boy with Cantacuzene eyes of deep brown. He was lusty and healthy, and I was immensely proud of this new member of the family.

My husband had a sailor brother but fifteen months his junior, and the latter returned from the Orient about the time young Mike was born. Boris at once adopted me and the baby, of whom he greatly approved. After meeting this member of my family, I felt I truly had every reason to congratulate myself on the lovable circle my husband had given me through our marriage.

With a pretty home to look after, full of things that we liked, with a fine son and an agreeable husband, I was taking a new start in Russian life. I felt well and strong after all the care connected with my various illnesses and looked forward to seeing something of St. Petersburg's court society and to meeting the various people of world renown whom I knew largely composed it.

VII

First Social Impressions

GETTING TO KNOW people in St. Petersburg was an interesting experience. It was not like meeting a society when passing through some foreign city, with the idea that one would be moving on soon and that mutual impressions made were only of casual importance. Some of these Russians were now my relatives; all of them potentially were my friends, and I knew I must live among them through the remainder of my days. They were different from any companions of my past. I had the feeling they were much simpler and more natural. Etiquette existed, but its hand was less heavy in St. Petersburg than in Vienna.

Peter the Great[1] had established a grading of rank, and the rule was that no army officer below the rank of colonel could go to court and take his wife to palace entertainments, unless she or he were attached to the person of some member of the Imperial family. In the latter case they went officially as part of their service. An inherited title did not change this court position at all. One could be head of a princely family, yet have no

---

[1]Peter I, also known as Peter the Great, the first Russian emperor (1672–1725), reigned from 1682 until his death. It was Peter who founded the city of St. Petersburg (named after his patron saint) and moved the capital of the country there from Moscow.

court rank, though every colonel, even of humble origin, all over the empire had a right to go to the big court ball and take his wife. Birth counted historically and socially but not officially, while official bureaucratic rank, military and civil, gave one certain court rights. This was impressed on me at once by my mother-in-law, and as my husband at twenty-four was a lieutenant only, even with the prestige of his being in the Empress Dowager's own Chevalier Guards, and with all the pleasant relatives and our social position, he could not take me to court nor go himself, unless he should be ordered there on duty. He did not want to leave his regimental service, so it looked as though we would be obliged to wait for years before I should have the official right of being presented to the two empresses,[2] which was, of course, the first step to court recognition.

In the lives of several women, this had been a handicap during all their youth, I heard; but I was more fortunate, and almost at once the difficulty was cleared away from my path. First, at a small ball at the palace of the Grand Duke Vladimir, the Grand Duchess Marie, our hostess, came and took me by the hand, saying: "Come, Joy, I have been talking to the empress

[2]Maria Fedorovna (1847–1928), Dowager Empress, formerly the Princess Dagmar of Denmark, sister of Queen Alexandra of England; and Empress Alexandra Fedorovna (1872–1918), a princess of Hesse-Darmstadt, who had been raised in Kensington Palace by her grandmother, Queen Victoria. Prior to marrying Russian royalty, foreign princesses converted to Orthodoxy and were given a Russian name and patronymic, usually Fedorovna.

of you, and she says I may personally present you to her"; so I was taken up to where the young empress stood, and the grand duchess said a few kindly words and pushed me forward into the empty space kept clear about the sovereign. The latter was exceedingly quiet and timid. After two or three perfunctory questions, which I answered, she fell into her usual attitude of silent distraction, so I curtsied and wandered off. However, I had actually talked with Her Majesty, which made everyone say that I must ask for a formal audience at once, not only of the empresses but of all the grand duchesses as well. Once one had bowed before Her Majesty, to neglect these latter would be wrong, apparently.

Shortly after this came another pleasant surprise. Quite from a blue sky I received a letter from the senior lady-in-waiting of the Dowager Empress, who said the duchess of Cumberland had written asking Her Majesty to receive me kindly, as my parents had been the latter's friends in Vienna. Consequently, I found myself one morning called to an audience at the Anichkov palace, the residence of the Empress Mother. The latter showed herself as gracious as she always was.

The news of all this irregularity soon spread about. As the presentations had then been accomplished, however, I received invitations to a number of court functions, and forever after had a perfectly ideal time. Of course, my special honors raised a clamor, since a number of women similarly situated were waiting about, on the sidelines, for fate and years to bring them recognition, while I was invited everywhere and enjoying myself extremely.

I was most fortunate in several other ways. Firstly, my husband had grown up on terms of constant companionship with several of the younger grand dukes. The Grand Duchess Marie had given us a little dinner so I should know all these. That evening the duke of Edinburgh, brother of King Edward VII, had dropped in to the party, met me, and told everyone present my family history and how he had met my grandfather long ago. When he had finished, I was firmly fixed, with all my background in the minds of those present, and my road became socially easy.

Sponsored thus, and being young, full of energy, and with a great desire to please my new compatriots, I was able to take my place immediately among the gay young matrons of the Imperial capital.

It seems, however, that the younger empress, after seeing me, had said to someone that my ball gown was cut in a deep square instead of the classic court décolleté, which was straight across and off the shoulders. This little sentence was repeated and magnified until it was made into a severe criticism of me and of American manners in general. It amounted to nothing after a week, but at the time it made me more prominent and won sympathy for me. I forebore from complaining, naturally; but the fact that there were many women present with gowns as square as mine, since a grand-ducal entertainment was counted a private ball,

Emperor Nicholas II, Empress Alexandra, and the Russian Imperial family

Courtesy Hoover Institution, Stanford University

Dowager Empress Marie,
mother of Emperor Nicholas II

made the blow at a well-meaning, helpless stranger work all in my favor.

Afterward I discovered that a strained feeling existed between the women of St. Petersburg's aristocratic group and the young empress. It had developed soon after Her Majesty's arrival and grew rapidly, encouraged by the wretched plotters, whose game it was to control their empress to their own ends. Following the incident of my gown, four or five young women deliberately wore square-cut gowns to the next court ball, and when the empress's severe remarks were repeated to the town, the culprits defended themselves with some energy. Gossip and bitterness followed, all of which seemed both amazing and unnecessary, but showed how the wind blew already in 1901.

My first years in St. Petersburg, until the outbreak of the Japanese War,[3] were the most brilliant socially I saw there. The Empress Mother did not appear often, but when she did so, she took first place at court. Her conversation was as gay and agreeable as she herself was. Putting each one at his ease, she seemed most human and womanly, an inspiration to do one's best. Her manner was exactly that of her sister, the duchess of Cumberland, and I felt somehow I had always known her.

[3]The Russo-Japanese War, begun with the Japanese attack on Port Arthur (southern tip of Liaotung Peninsula) on 8 February 1904 and terminated by the Treaty of Portsmouth in August 1905, was fought entirely around Russia's maritime possessions in the Far East.

Once her kindly attitude and tact saved me in a very painful and false situation, which I owed to the German Crown Prince. The latter—I think in the season of 1902—came to St. Petersburg for a week's visit. It was at a time when the German emperor was trying to win ours over and when he was harping on the fact of his first-cousinship with our young empress—the kaiser's mother and the mother of our empress were both daughters of Queen Victoria: the princess royal and Alice of England.

The German kaiser hit on the plan of sending his eldest son, then still unmarried, out to Russia to visit the regiment of which Wilhelm II was honorary commander and to spend a week at our court. Our emperor attached to the Crown Prince three officers with a number of minor secretaries. At the head of this group was old Prince Dolgoruky, one of our emperor's "adjutant-generals," then a "general of the Imperial suite." Further, because the visitor was young and a sportsman, and because he spoke no Russian and hated to use French, my husband was chosen, together with an A.D.C. of His Majesty, as attendants.

Cantacuzene, one of the best horsemen in Russia and a keen polo player, attracted young Wilhelm. Their conversation was always in English, which Wilhelm liked and used with great facility. He and my husband got on excellently.

After his first court dinner and an afternoon official call at the German embassy, the Crown Prince unfortunately had fallen ill with a sharp case of influenza. It broke up the court ball, which was countermanded. The German embassy ball came off without him. The old Grand Duke Michael[4] did not recall his invitations either, and happily for himself the Crown Prince was able to attend.

Beyond the members of the Imperial family and their courts in attendance, there was no guest who was not of the gay, ultra-smart set of young, married dancers, with the best of the crack guard regiment's bachelor officers added for extra partners. The German embassy members all came, the only diplomats invited. Only the ambassador and Count Lüttwitz, the military attaché, were married. Countess Alvensleben was said to be an intimate friend of the German kaiser. She was old and plain, dressed atrociously, was very dry in her manner, and did everything by rule. She even arranged her hair stiffly with a green construction on top, which we disrespectful youngsters called a tennis net. She was rather easily annoyed and tried to dictate to us.

The little Lüttwitz woman was American born, but had become so German that she spoke her mother tongue with German construction of phrase, and called her husband "my man" in English! Lüttwitz was most unpopular, and we always felt sorry for his wife, but her German affectations got on the nerves of a good many of us who, like myself, tried to be nice to her at first.

[4]Grand Duke Michael Nikolaevich (1832–1909) was Nicholas II's great-uncle.

As I came into the great ballroom, Countess Lüt-twitz turned around and said to me in English: "We are just arranging the women so we can take them up and present them to our Crown Prince when he arrives with Their Majesties. Won't you come too? You are one of the best dancers, and I am sure would like to be presented to his Imperial Highness."

I promptly replied that if he danced well, I should like very much to have the Crown Prince presented to me, but I did not expect to be presented to him. "I've never been presented to any man. Our tsarevich is always introduced to ladies like any other gentleman."

"But it is not the German court etiquette, and the Crown Prince would be surprised to have things otherwise. He will not dance with you if you are not properly presented to him by Countess Alvensleben," insisted the little countess, beginning to look hot.

It struck me as supremely funny that this American woman should have reached such a mental attitude, and with a laugh I replied: "My dear countess, this isn't Berlin, this is St. Petersburg, and *our* etiquette says the gentlemen of Russia ask to be presented to us. I am told by my husband that your Crown Prince is most polite; I fancy, therefore, he will follow our customs during his visit. If not, and if in order to dance with him I have to wait in a line and be presented to him, I am quite sure I shall be content to enjoy this ball with my Russian partners. So please don't have me on your mind at all."

A number of other women joined me and we stood

as far from the entrance door as possible. We still were there, when the music struck up and in the doorway appeared all the royalties, among them the emperor's brother Michael, who was one of my favorite partners always, and a perfect dancer. He came across the room and took me out for the opening waltz. When we finished it, he invited me to be his partner for the mazurka. Then he said: "I'm going to bring our cousin and introduce him to you. You will like him, and he dances awfully well."

He went and fetched Wilhelm from the crowd at the door and brought him straight to our side of the ballroom, and introduced him quite informally to me and then to all the other women who had followed me over there. The Crown Prince showed no sign of shock at this breach of etiquette, and being, for the first time since his arrival, in young, gay company, he proved his enthusiasm and his admirable qualities as a dancer at once. He asked me to waltz and I accepted, feeling a wicked joy as we passed the corner where the ladies from Germany stood looking with stony expressions at my excellent partner and me.

Everything went swimmingly; I danced every moment until supper time, which I was to take at a little table, thus arranged by Prince Obolensky, my partner. The Crown Prince was designated to sit on the right of the Empress Mother at her table, since he was the guest of honor. Some important old lady was to be on his other hand. Prince Dolgoruky came up to us, explained the plan, and said as the Empress Mother would be placed next our host, Wilhelm must join the other lady and escort her to supper. The arrogant petulance of the young German showed for the first time. "I won't; I have already asked a partner, the princess here, and she must come with me to Her Majesty's table!" he exclaimed.

I then ventured to take part in the conversation. "Really, sir, I couldn't sup with you; firstly, because I wouldn't for the world intrude at the table of the Empress Mother; secondly, because I mustn't drop out of my own party, and here is Prince Obolensky come for me. So thank you and *au revoir*," and I moved my hand from within his arm and turned toward my waiting supper partner.

The Crown Prince seized my hand so I could not withdraw it and, turning to the old Prince Dolgoruky, said quite rudely: "I told you, I won't; either the princess comes to this table where I sit, or I won't go. Arrange it as you can."

I protested with some energy: "Really, sir, it is impossible to change the plans of our host. You are leaving and will not feel the consequences, whereas I, who belong here, will be accused of having attempted to push myself forward, and I cannot consent to that. You must excuse me."

The Crown Prince looked furious and protested again so crossly that old Prince Dolgoruky, who was an accomplished courtier, turned to me, saying: "Will you remain with His Imperial Highness while I see what can be done?"

I was seriously annoyed by my situation. I seemed helpless to handle my arrogant companion. But Prince Dolgoruky returned and said: "Will you come to this table where Her Majesty is? One of the grand duchesses has ceded you her seat."

The Crown Prince at last let my arm loose, and as we approached, the Empress Mother looked up and smiled; Wilhelm bowed low over her hand and I curtsied. She stretched me her hand, and I kissed it. Looking amused, she said to him, "Will you sit here?" and to me, "Sit just beyond."

I moved away from her chair and around the Crown Prince's, reaching the rear of the one which the empress had pointed to, when to my own and everyone's amazement, old Countess Alvensleben, appearing out of space, stepped between the table and my chair, and plumped herself down into it, saying: *"Nun also! Dass ist jetzt mein Platz!"* (Well, now, this is my place.)

The Empress Mother looked as if her merriment would get beyond control, and the Crown Prince looked as if an explosion of violent temper was to occur. I felt I should certainly cry in another moment. One of the gentlemen who was two seats from the German ambassadress rose.

"Princess, sit here," he said. "With Her Majesty's permission I can easily move to another table and you must take my place."

"Yes, sit there," the empress said, and gave the charming Russian courtier and me a radiant smile. Of course, there was some talk, but it soon died out, for Her Majesty was afterward as lovely as she had been in the sudden emergency.

Through years following this, each first of January brought us a telegram of greeting, or some souvenir, from the Crown Prince: a small painting of himself on horseback, a photograph of him with his fiancée, three or four watercolors showing the ancient uniforms his regiments had worn, a picture of his eldest son. Once when I went through Berlin, His Imperial Highness, learning I was there, called me on the telephone and invited me to "go with my wife and me to the play and to supper." I accepted, and they came to fetch me with the utmost informality, the Crown Prince descending and coming into the hotel after me and returning me later to my door. That was a quiet, pleasant little party. The Crown Prince was amiable with his wife that night, and they seemed a congenial couple. A year or so later, when they visited Russia, I had the same impression again. But, I could more readily believe in his defects than his virtues, so when the war came, I had no scruple in throwing away or turning to the wall the various souvenirs he had sent us during ten or twelve years.

The Crown Prince was to do me one more ill turn, however, which might have ended badly had it not been for Russian chivalry and intelligence. It was in the early part of February 1915 that, one day, I was asked for on the telephone by General Rauch, an old and prized friend of ours, and at that time one of the important men in the departmental command of the capital. He begged me to receive him at once and alone. I acquiesced, wondering at his strange request; and when within a few minutes he appeared, he looked more anxious and solemn than ever.

I said, "What is the secret, dear General? Can I do you any service?"

"No," he answered, "except by replying to a few questions. Were you expecting any mail from anyone abroad?"

I began to enumerate the various members of my family, who regularly wrote to me, but Rauch interrupted: "You have no correspondent in Germany?"

"No," I said.

"Can you tell me then what this is?" he asked, and he drew a large envelope from his dispatch-case. "Perhaps it is addressed to someone else?"

I took the big envelope and read the address. "I am the only Princess Cantacuzene, née Grant. It is for me and is peculiarly addressed; it says only 'St. Petersburg, via Rumania.' It has a large red seal with 'W' and the German Imperial crown. Yes, I can tell you without looking further what you will find in this, General, if you open it; it will be a portrait of the Crown Prince of Germany, or a picture of something that concerns him. He sends me some such souvenir each year, for the first of January. I had not had one this year, but I confess I thought it was because His Imperial Highness had intelligence and chivalry sufficient to realize that in wartime his remembrance would be obnoxious and, possibly, compromising. Perhaps this was sent me through the stupidity of some secretary left in charge in Berlin, who forwards these things for the Crown Prince each year and has this season used his habitual list without corrections."

Rauch examined the envelope with care. "No, this bears the stamp of the 'Fifth Army,' which is the one young Wilhelm now commands on the western front. Also, it bears the signature of his hofmarschall—marshal of his court. I'm afraid it is sent by the Crown Prince himself. What do you think you'd better do about it? The big envelope arrived this morning at the censor's and made a sensation. The matter was brought to the chief there, who rang up our department, as he knew enough to realize he mustn't accuse you lightly. I asked to handle the matter—said I would take it off his hands. I am satisfied (if you tell me you have not received or written a letter) that you are telling the truth, and I will satisfy the chief at the censor bureau. This is my end of the business, but I should like to know what you are going to do."

I said, firstly, I would make him a present of the picture, which he promptly declined; secondly, I would at once write the whole history to my husband, asking him to inform the commander-in-chief, so that if the latter ever heard the story from another source, he would not think I had tried to hide it; thirdly, I would tell Prince Orlov[5] also, so he would be in pos-

[5]Prince Vladimir Nikolaevich Orlov (1868–1927), the scion of an

session of the facts, in case Madame Vyrubova[6] had the story from her spies and tried to use it to my detriment.

Finally I said: "Dear General, if you won't accept this as a gift, to whom shall I offer it? I don't want it in the house."

And Rauch replied: "I think all your measures are wise. Suppose you ask your husband or Vlady Orlov what to do with the thing."

I asked if I could not send it back. I thought that the best way to revenge myself for the nasty trick of the arrogant Crown Prince. I felt sure he had wished to prove that, no matter what he and his armies might do to our Allied forces, his prestige in the eyes of those who had known him remained unimpaired. Or else he had done this thing to compromise my husband and myself and make trouble, simply. Either way it seemed horrid, and I was keen for paying him back.

I wrote my husband, who told the story to his chief. The latter laughed, said I had acted right, and to think no more of it. Then I told Orlov. He felt as I did—it would be fun to return the picture, and we tried to do so through one of several channels. The German censor would have prevented its reaching its destination

---

illustrious noble family, was a career army officer and a member of Nicholas II's suite.

[6]Anna Aleksandrovna Vyrubova (née Taneeva) (1884–1964), lady-in-waiting and confidante of the Empress Alexandra. Vyrubova was widely believed to be Alexandra's chief liaison with the notorious Rasputin and a sinister influence on her.

by ordinary mail; of course, none of the neutral embassies would let their couriers handle it. We learned this by consulting the American chargé d'affaires; neither could any member of the Red Cross undertake the carrying of so undesirable a packet. Evidently this picture was to be a white elephant on my hands.

My mother-in-law, who became greatly excited when she heard the tale, said I ought to tear the portrait, and then return it, writing an insulting letter, too, but my anger was cold rather than hot, and I did not feel such action would express my sentiments.

I persuaded Orlov to put the ugly thing in his safe and keep it, which he did, until the moment when I was leaving Russia. Then he returned it to me as a souvenir of one of my friends, he said, and to recommend me to Trotsky-Bronstein[7] in case we were captured by the Bolsheviki on the frontier! This did not happen, luckily, and I believe Wilhelm has sent me no more pictures of himself.

---

[7]Leon Trotsky (Lev Bronstein) (1879–1940), the leading figure, after Lenin, in the Bolshevik October revolution of 1917. He was the first Soviet commissar (minister) for foreign affairs (1917–18); during the civil war (1918–21) he was, under various designations, head of the Red Army.

VIII

The Japanese War

During these early years I spent my time exclusively between the duties of our attractive home, with its nursery, and the gay functions that made up my round of society life, intimate or official. I began to feel I was making many friends, both men and women, and I was growing Russian in my ways. I loved all I was doing and was anxious to make those whom I admired realize my sympathy and enthusiasm. They answered my expressions of understanding as if sure of my sincerity and adopted me completely within a short time.

My youth and high spirits did not prevent my seeing much that was sad in Russia. Both in the country and the city, there was a yearning spirit among the people that promised trouble in time. This was especially so toward the end of 1903.

I had all sorts of quaint trials getting our household started. I fortunately began with few theories, and such as I had were soon left behind. The family servants had traditions they considered much more important than the ideas of any newcomer, and I learned their ways more easily than they did mine. They always called everything "ours," and took vast pride and pains to make our small entertainments a success. All the servants were "our children" and as much members of the family as we ourselves. They expected us to take care of them and be interested in their personal affairs, and they were sure of our help and forgiveness when in trouble or at fault.

In all the years I was in Russia, no servant ever left us of his own accord, and only a few were dismissed—those few being some picked up accidentally, who had not the patriarchal ideas. In the house, silver, jewels, money, and other valuables were kept in drawers and cupboards that no one ever locked. It would have been an insult to do so, for never to my knowledge did anything, however unimportant, disappear.

The baby, young Mike, was common property. Old Auguste, his great-grandfather's valet, and his father's nurse, Grandmother Anna Vladimirovna, would gossip endlessly with his own nurse as to what resemblances they thought most prominent. When the boy was born, Auguste made me a gift of some strawberry preserves I had once declared excellent when I had tasted them at the princess's. Incidentally, she prized these too much to serve them often, as they were made of fruit exceptionally large and fine from Bouromka's hotbeds. At the moment I thanked Auguste without noticing more than that he had shown me a nice little attention in offering me a dainty I liked. But when the preserves were served one day, I made inquiries, only to find the old fellow had simply taken his gift from the storerooms in his charge. "The princess won't mind; she will never know; and even if she does, I will tell her it is much better to tempt your appetite in illness and when you have given us a young prince, than to feed these preserves to visitors." This was his only explanation. There was no sign of regret of having given what was not his. On the contrary, he and the princess were one, and I a sick child who had deserved the best. One might as well accept this code of morals, which had its charm.

I remember the drama each week when my mother-in-law paid her bills and scolded Auguste for a crime he never admitted until after their accounts were settled to his satisfaction. He was called thief in the process, for invariably his supply bills were enlarged, to cover extra sums he gave to my young brother-in-law,[1] thus augmenting the boy's allowance for goodies and fun at the Page Corps School.

Regularly my mother-in-law, when the last book was gone over and settled, would say: "Now, admit you have stolen at least twenty rubles for Guy."

And Auguste would tuck the money in his pocket and the books under his arm and reply, "Well, Your Highness, boys are only young a little while, and they always need a little more than they have," and would go away contentedly, while the princess, with tears in her eyes, would tell us how touching the old fellow

---

[1] Sergei Mikhailovich (Guy) Cantacuzene (1884–1953) was at the time enrolled in the Imperial Corps of Pages, one of the elite secondary schools established in the eighteenth century for sons of the nobility. One graduated from the corps with officer rank in the army.

was and how he loved Guy. Bad policies theoretically, but in practice they worked out well.

This young brother belonged to us all and had his special place always in our small home. In fact, both my brothers-in-law spent much of their free time near my tea table. Our baby was always sprawling or creeping and, later, walking and playing about the open fire in my salon at five o'clock. It became the pleasantest hour of the day—one for quiet talk and restful discussions, from which I learned more of Russia and my new compatriots than in any other way. With freezing weather outside, inside, the open blaze, singing kettle, and cozy armchairs helped any caller who dropped in to thaw his ideas. Pleasant regimental comrades, a few agreeable foreign diplomats, gradually, also some older men whom I met at dinners, came and began the intimate circle that later through the years was to grow considerably. I liked these people, and though at first my husband fought rather shy of "tea-parties," after a time he fell into the habit of coming home from his club to smoke his last afternoon pipe in his own easy chair and join in the informal talk. I heard a lot about certain regimental interests and grew to know the ideals and ways of the men who composed our organization. I scarcely had to study or even to ask questions. My education progressed rapidly.

In listening to my visitors each day, I began to catch their attitude and atmosphere, to realize what remarkable culture they had. The literature, art, and music of the country, its history and great past, made them, as well as the peasantry, what they were. It was absorbingly interesting, and I grew to love my Russians more and more.

Strangely enough, in the apparent quiet that reigned, these men showed signs of anxiety as to what was ahead of us. Often they spoke of the peasant, of his backwardness in education, yet of his cleverness— and they spoke of their own efforts to develop these dark millions. They would almost always talk of the bureaucracy with impatience and annoyance, sometimes criticizing Peter the Great for installing it, with all the general clumsiness of our governmental machinery. They complained of the difficulty each man had in obtaining action in cases when it would be an advantage all round. Of the injustice and favoritism being practiced or allowed, there was also much said. The party that wished reforms or improvements was large, and their blame of the empress's policy in isolating herself—of the undesirability of the shut-in and exclusively family life of the sovereigns, of the protection given to cover various scandalous exploitations by a group in our Far Eastern Siberian country—was extremely marked. The names of Alekseev and Bezobrazov[2] were at the time constantly circulating and

[2]Admiral Aleksei Mikhailovich Abaza (b. 1868), Admiral Evgeny Ivanovich Alekseev (1843–1909), and Alexander Mikhailovich Bezobrazov (1866–1933) were promoters of the aggressive Russian penetration of Korea that led directly to the Russo-Japanese War. Alekseev was the illegitimate son of Tsar Alexander II and therefore the great-uncle of Nicholas II.

were anathema, and when I asked what these men had done, "Stolen and exploited; everything!" would be the rejoinder. Witte's[3] figure was looming large on the horizon. He promised to be a giant in history.

As time passed, both those who praised and those who blamed Witte found material to prove their theories. The first group gave him great credit for the Portsmouth Treaty,[4] negotiated in spite of the ever-changing orders and the constant antagonism toward him at home. His friends gave him equal admiration for the manifesto[5] he dragged from the sovereign during the revolution, that of the seventeenth of October. The opponents of Witte through those years howled him down for these very things, saying the peace treaty was made just when Russia might have won the war, as Japan was worn out, and that the manifesto was a matter of cowardice on Witte's part, though he was always a liberal.

Long before these events he had made a trip across Siberia and was received everywhere with honors, which, we were told by gossips, were so great as to

---

[3]Sergei Yulevich Witte (1849–1915), an aggressively modernizing statesman, was architect, as minister of finance from 1892 to 1903, of Russian industrialization, and in 1905–1906, Russia's first prime minister.

[4]As Russian plenipotentiary at the Portsmouth (New Hampshire) Conference convened by President Theodore Roosevelt, Witte had obtained a negotiated peace with Japan on 5 September 1905.

[5]The Imperial Manifesto of 30 (17 old style) October 1905, which lay the groundwork for transforming the autocracy into a constitutional monarchy, was written by Witte.

make the sovereign jealous. The Trans-Siberian Railroad was largely a creation of Witte's, who was for economic development on the eastern outskirts of the empire, I heard. But Germany's action and certain political influences at home brought about a situation that roused Japanese suspicions. This in turn produced an atmosphere requiring but a small spark to light the war fires. His worst enemies never denied that Witte's talent kept Russia from financial disaster during the war and the revolution of 1905 or that he developed our industries as no one had until then. But it was always added that this was not Slav,[6] nor for the good of a country so essentially agricultural as ours, and that though Witte might know about foreign affairs, he did not know our own people well.

I listened and my curiosity grew, until one day I met his wife, of whom also gossip had much to say. She was a lady of vague antecedents, and I decided they were vague only because so many excited people told such extraordinary stories about her. She stood easily on her own merits—a woman of forty-five or so, of dark beauty and a dignified manner, with a most intelligent expression and a luminous smile. Her clothes, of simple cut, perfectly fitted her still fine figure. She wore few trimmings and few jewels, but those she did wear were admirable. She held herself proudly, never made an advance conversationally. Her

[6]A reference to the doctrine of Slavophilism, which emphasized Russia's, and by later extension all of the Slavic and Orthodox peoples', difference from "Europe."

response was warm enough to seem grateful, however, and her talk was both intelligent and cultured. She was Jewish by origin, though belonging to the Russian Church and attending it. She had married Witte rather late in life, and he had adopted her daughter and given the latter his name.

Madame Witte was never received at court. Little by little, however, she formed a group of friends whom she held firmly to her. I thought her magnetic when we met, and afterward watched her career and her husband's with curiosity. He overshadowed all other figures between the time I first realized how great was the drama being played in Russia and the moment when the first Duma[7] was dissolved—and she, in her way, was acting as brilliant a role as her husband's.

Witte, I think, cared socially for only a few persons, but with these his vivid conversation was very interesting. I had the opportunity of enjoying the treat of hearing him on two or three occasions. He had greatly liked the Americans during his short stay in the United States. He had met my parents and remembered a long chat with my father, while he admired my mother's beauty.

Usually at a dinner table, however, he was taciturn to a degree. Many women who were his partners thought he meant to insult them, and they said that to hear him eat his soup was agony. One person told me

[7]The Duma (an old Russian term for "deliberative council") was the lower house of the bicameral legislative system introduced in the wake of the October Manifesto (see note 5).

he had watched him pick a chicken leg and throw the
bone under the table! The great man was ugly, but
with deep, fine eyes and capable hands. He was huge
and looked strong, though he was not compactly built.
I found him rather attractive in looks as well as in what
he said. He seemed to care in society only to see his
wife surrounded and his adopted child enjoying herself. A crowd looking for benefits as his power increased gathered about them. The daughter married
a Narishkin, son of one of the empire's greatest families, and a fragile little boy was born to this young couple. To see Witte at his best, one had to see the great
man with that grandson on his lap—the great bear
then knew how to be as tender as any old nurse might
have been.

Through the period of revolution, the concessions
made to popular demands, and the meeting and dis-
solution of the first Duma, I became convinced in
spite of hot attacks on his motives that Witte sincerely
meant well and wanted to see Russia move forward.
I think he wanted to inaugurate many liberal reforms
and to cooperate with the most patriotic elements the
country could produce. Somehow, most of these did
not trust him, and whether this distrust was deserved
or not, it was fatal to the success of the work undertaken by Witte. As the best were not with him, he
joined up with the most extreme and less understanding to get his majorities; then, disillusioned or
from a desire to establish a better balance, he swung
back toward the reactionaries and tried to save the

situation by seemingly tying up with them. This see-sawing was disastrous to him, as to the prestige both of the government and the emperor. The latter forced Witte to drop out of public life, a deeply disappointed man, while Stolypin[8] took over the government.

Witte, during the final epoch of his power, seemed to lose courage. He apparently feared to make decisions or to face physical danger. He then lived in the Winter Palace by his own demand, surrounded with guards, and one had to pass several pairs of sentinels to reach Madame Witte's salon. Of course, his enemies made capital of these signs. Those who supported him still vowed he was sincere, far-seeing and patriotic, loyally devoted to the sovereign's best interests, fighting the vacillations of the emperor, the intrigues of would-be rivals, and never supported by His Majesty in critical moments. That it was this memory that made his retirement so bitter seemed certain in spite of his new title, and his great fortune.[9] Those who hated him told us it was his own fault he was not trusted and was put out. I never knew the

---

[8]Peter Arkadevich Stolypin (1862–1911), an interior ministry official and former provincial governor, succeeded to the premiership in July 1906; author of the notorious coup d'état of 16 (3) June 1907, which restricted the suffrage with the aim of producing a more tractable Duma, and principal proponent of an ambitious land reform program designed to break up communal peasant tenure and create a class of independent farmers.

[9]Witte had received a large cash reward upon his retirement from the finance ministry, and the title of count for his efforts in Portsmouth.

truth, but it seems certain he was not a man who inspired faith in his integrity of purpose.

In 1902, I found myself one evening at an official dinner, next to a large man with a strong, handsome face and rather long gray hair, which was thin on the top of his head. His noble poise and fearless, keen eyes particularly struck me. The dinner was at an embassy, and the newly arrived chief of mission, or his secretaries, had been sufficiently vague about Russian etiquette to place people according to their rank of birth instead of their official bureaucratic rights.

Several of the older men were consequently furious and criticized their host, but my neighbor, turning to me, said with a smile: "They are amusing are they not, to fuss so about where they should sit? For my part, I admit I think it is a great improvement to sit at the end of the table between two young and pretty women instead of being always up at the head with old people like myself. I'm grateful to Providence, and think this system should be encouraged."

I was equally delighted personally, for I rarely had such an interesting partner as this. Plehve[10]—for it was the minister of the interior—and I began a friendship that evening that lasted until his assassination. I knew little of his policies. Afterward, I heard he stood for all that was retrograde and severe, and I heard him blamed, too, for much that others did that was wrong. I am inclined to think if we had talked of politics, we

[10]Viacheslav Konstantinovich Plehve (1846–1904), minister of the interior, assassinated by a revolutionary terrorist.

should have disagreed often, but in the two or three seasons during which the busy man came frequently to my tea table direct from his chancellery or cabinet meetings, he never talked of his work in any instance I can recall.

Always a chatterbox, I would plunge into details of my latest ball or my baby's last achievement, while he would slowly sip his tea and listen as if to the story of a child's game, with his big, shaggy head leaning on the hand that shaded his eyes. After an hour he would get up, and with a "Thank you for a very pleasant rest," he would depart. My curiosity was intense. He knew it and was never trite. It was a strange friendship, for Plehve was older than my father. Except that I knew he had a delightfully typical old lady for a wife (since I had met her at official functions and we had exchanged calls), and that he once mentioned he had a daughter much my senior, I heard nothing of his home life or his work. His patriotism seemed great, and he carried his heavy responsibilities with a superb strength, which made no complaint, while he lived unflinchingly up to what he thought was his duty, with no fear or care for himself.

Our last conversation proved this mentality. It was late in the spring, and I was leaving for the country in a few days. Plehve had come to say good-bye, and remained until one or two other callers had departed. After a little silence he rose to make his *adieux*.

"I am sorry you are going away," he said seriously. "I have enjoyed coming here sometimes for a quiet hour very much, and I'm afraid I won't see you again."

"But I shall be back in town in the autumn, and on the contrary, I hope you will again take up this nice habit of dropping in on me often."

"If I am still alive, I will surely be among your frequent callers, but these people who think I am doing everything wrong, and who have been trying to assassinate me for some time back, are more than ever trailing me now. Probably they will get me soon."

"You are minister of the interior with the police in your department. Why don't you protect yourself?" I asked.

"It wouldn't look well, nor be well, for me to surround myself with police and show fear, would it? When I have things to do, I will go out like other men, whatever the consequences. I'm afraid there is only one way—to perform one's duty and take what comes. If I disappear, there will be someone to replace me. A pleasant summer to you, and thanks again!"

He kissed my hand and departed, with his shaggy lion's head thrown well back and his step as tranquil as ever.

Within a few weeks—I think in July[11]—Plehve was starting out for Peterhof Palace to make his weekly report to the emperor. On his way to the railroad station, a bomb was thrown at his carriage. The vehicle, coachman, horses, and the minister of the interior were blown to bits—beyond recognition. I mourned

[11]28 (15) July 1904.

his tragic end very much, for I knew that whatever his policies, he was honest and faithful, devoted to his emperor and his country, and that few had his courage and energy, as well as the unselfish spirit, which readily sacrificed his private taste for constant thankless service and threatening dangers always so perfectly realized. He was the first older man I saw much of after my marriage, and he seemed to me typical of the best in that mistaken group of ultra-retrograde officials of old Russia.

One felt great changes with each succeeding season. The Japanese war came unexpectedly. Shortly before it the great Ito[12] passed through St. Petersburg, hoping for a friendly reception and to make a loan. He was badly received by our government and pushed on to England, where he effected both a loan and soon afterward a treaty, I think.

I heard from the American ambassador that Ito had spoken to him of my grandfather; said he had heard I was married and living in St. Petersburg and had asked could the ambassador not arrange a meeting with me? Instead of telling me about it, the diplomat had taken on himself to reply that he could not do so.

I was much annoyed when my ex-compatriot told me of this speech of his to the statesman from Japan. It would have been most interesting to meet Ito, and my personal action would have neither shocked nor

---

[12]Prince Hirobumi Ito (1841–1909), the most important Japanese statesman of the age; sometime premier, foreign minister, Korean resident-general.

inconvenienced anyone, for Russians are thoroughly broadminded. Besides, if there was a strain, perhaps unavoidable in government circles, it seemed unnecessarily underscoring it to have a diplomat draw it into personal relations. I was disappointed and indignant over the matter, but it was too late to counteract a most unfortunate impression.

Soon afterward, at the first court ball of the season, my young brother-in-law was on duty as the emperor's page. Standing just behind the sovereign, he made the tour of the diplomatic circle and heard the emperor's remarks and questions to each chief of mission; also, the latter's replies. To the Japanese ambassador His Majesty took great pains to be especially gracious that evening, giving him more time than to anyone else, and there was a feeling created in the minds of all as they listened that a responsive attitude was noticeable. With their last words the emperor and Japan's representative each expressed pleasure that certain difficulties were overcome and their two empires were good friends. When he came home, my brother-in-law told us of the incident, and several other people corroborated his statement.

But the following day, to our horror, bad news spread.[13] The *Variag* was sunk, and the declaration of war followed almost instantly. My husband's regiment was not ordered to Manchuria, so I knew of the war only by hearsay. I could not yet read enough Russian

[13]The Japanese attack on Port Arthur, 8 February 1904.

to follow in the newspapers our progress at the front. I was quite ill; our eldest little girl was born a few days before the *Petropavlovsk* went down in the battle at Port Arthur. As time progressed, however, I became more and more absorbed by events in the East—Port Arthur's siege and splendid defense; the heroic fighting of our troops, always insufficiently supplied by a single-track and newly built railroad; the noble efforts of Prince Khilkov,[14] minister of transport, to keep the provision and troop trains moving, his going out and living at the point most difficult to arrange for, and his death out there from exhaustion toward the end of the work he carried through with such genius. I was also interested in Kuropatkin's[15] early prestige. When he left, he had so many icons given him, it was said he had to add an extra car to his special train. He had been chief of staff to Skobelev,[16] the brilliant figure of the Turkish War, and few doubted his capacity to carry everything before him as our generalissimo.

For many months no one in St. Petersburg talked of anything but the Manchurian news, but little by little changes occurred in the tenor of our conversations.

[14]Prince Michael Ivanovich Khilkov (1834–1909), minister of transport from 1895 to 1905.

[15]Infantry General Aleksei Nikolaevich Kuropatkin (1848–1925) was appointed head of the Manchurian Army at the beginning of the Russo-Japanese War and, in October 1904, commander in chief of Russian Armies in the Far East. He was removed from that post in March 1905 after the defeat of the Russian army at Mukden.

[16]General Michael Dmitrievich Skobelev (1843–1882), popular hero of the Russo-Turkish War of 1877–78.

There were tales of disappointments and disillusions. There also was bitterness, pity, the desire for rest and peace, and an ever-increasing anxiety; tales of battles and ships lost; tales of incompetency of the commander-in-chief and some of the other favorites; tales of confusion and sufferings among our troops; tales of officers and men under fire doing heroic work. The inefficiency of the war ministry was being proved. One heard constantly of the weight of political power in the army; how the commanders were hampered from St. Petersburg; how there was jealousy, or fear of letting the head men out at the front handle the situation and perhaps gain more power and glory than was good for them.

The second fleet was being built and was to go to Far Eastern waters. My sailor brother-in-law was leaving with it on the *Alexander III,* one of its biggest ships. He was all impatience to be off, yet he said—and other of his comrades constantly repeated the same thing— that from the work being done by incompetent hands through favoritism, and the stealing going on among contractors and those who handled the contract-making, everything about the new fleet was wrong and of secondary quality. These splendid-looking sea-monsters of our new unit were doomed to go to the bottom as soon as they were touched in battle. No one seemed to be considered punishable for these thefts or the criminal carelessness, and no inquiry was possible. The Grand Duke Alexis was among those most seriously accused. We hear that the admiral who was to take this fleet to sea came and begged the emperor on his knees not to give him the responsibility of this command, as he knew the ships were not seaworthy nor properly armed and armored. Then gossip told how our emperor had explained that the fleet as it was must go. It could not be rebuilt, and the admiral must prove his devotion and save the Imperial honor.

The emperor wanted to move out to the front himself and had many a long argument with those about him on this subject, but was persuaded not to go, since his being so far away from the capital in such grave times would strain the home situation. It was already serious and needed careful nursing. Once there was talk of the Grand Duke Nicholas Nikolaevich[17] taking over the entire command of our armies, as Kuropatkin made retreat and retreat and no advances. I heard the emperor sent for him and offered him the first place at the front. Nicholas Nikolaevich was reported to have replied he would accept in the emergency, but only on one condition: He would carry all the responsibility, but he insisted on giving military commands without advice or hampering from the capital. The emperor and his advisors could not make up their minds to such a decision, so the grand duke refused to take over the campaign. Things conse-

[17]Grand Duke Nicholas Nikolaevich (the younger) (1856–1929), first cousin of Nicholas II's father. A career soldier, he occupied many important military offices before being named commander in chief of Russian armies at the outbreak of the world war in 1914. He was married to Princess Anastasia of Montenegro (1867–1935).

quently stayed as they were, and Russia drifted to the final defeats at sea and on land. Disorders and talk of revolution meanwhile grew, and the pessimism in the capital became more and more noticeable, with constant shilly-shallying on the part of the government.

The death of my sailor brother-in-law[18] from tropical fever, contracted on the long trip to the Orient, threw us all into personal mourning, but one's soul was weighted anyhow with the general misery and danger. We women worked with one or another of the sewing groups, preparing bandages and underclothes or warm woolen garments for the soldiers. A lot of my women friends went out to Siberia with various hospital trains or Red Cross units. I personally, though I managed to be half of each day at the large workrooms organized by the Grand Duchess Maria Pavlovna, found time for nothing more, because of my two babies; one was but newly born.

In the summer of 1901, my father had arranged to get a leave from his duties in the Philippines at the same time my brother's furlough from West Point was due, and with my mother, they had taken the long journey to join me in Russia. I left young Mike with his paternal grandmother, while I, with my brother-in-law Guy and along with my maid, traveled north from Bouromka to meet my own home people. It was a most delightful reunion. In total, we spent

[18]Prince Boris Mikhailovich Cantacuzene (b. 1876), a naval lieutenant of the Imperial guard, died in Colombo, Ceylon, on 13 April 1905.

some ten days in St. Petersburg sightseeing together as a group.

I had had no time or occasion since my wedding for anything like this before, and I felt carried back to my girlhood days as we wandered through the Russian palaces, museum, and galleries filled with marvelous treasures generations of Romanovs had had offered them by vassals or had bought with singular good judgment and good luck. We visited Tsarskoe, Peterhof, and Gatchina,[19] and drove about the environs.

My father had not been in Russia since his youth. He found much of interest besides mere sightseeing. In the politics, the countryside, the capital, and the mode of life there were changes—a move forward. He thought there was much room for reform in the government's method, but he loved the patriarchal life.

From St. Petersburg to Bouromka we went by Moscow and Kiev, which I had never visited until then, and which I vastly enjoyed in such company.

It was very amusing to show my family the life of the great agricultural district of Russia, with its waving fields of wheat, its myriad workers, and all the machinery we used. That we were so far from a railroad and so dependent on ourselves for everything, yet so able, by organized effort, to supply ourselves and be comfortable, even luxurious, surprised them. The enormous space outside and in the house, the number

[19]Imperial palaces: Tsarskoe Selo was built in 1749–52; Gatchina, also near St. Petersburg, had been the residence of Emperor Paul I (1754–1801; reigned 1796–1801).

Frederick Dent Grant, with baby Michael and Julia

Courtesy Rodion Cantacuzene

Princess Julia Cantacuzene, ca. 1904
Courtesy Library of Congress

of servants and work hands in the chateau and on the estate, the beauty of the park and lake, the rolling land and forests, the richness of soil and crops, the size of our herds and the variety of our production dazed their American mentality, used to ringing a telephone or buying things ready-made. That we made the bricks, cut the timber, forged the metal, had our own plumbers, our doctors for man and beast, produced our own food; made our own linen and kitchen pottery largely; did the paneling, inlaying, or carving; also that what few things came from outside, whether books, pianos, macaroni, rice, and tea, or a few other luxuries to eat or to wear, had to be dragged by carts seventy-two versts in the good season—were facts difficult to grasp. That a telegram came fifty miles in a rider's pocket, and the mail and newspapers the same distance three or four times a week, struck them as funny. These primitive ways were doubly strange as compared with the excellent cooking and hand laundry, with the smartly dressed party at dinner, the admirable works of art, the family portraits, the 20,000 volumes of famous rare editions in the great library, and the collections of cameos, jewels, engraving, bronzes, old silver, and china; not to mention our cellar's treasures, some vintages going back to the early days of the nineteenth century.

My mother liked the house and baby best, but the men enjoyed the out-of-door life and delighted my husband and brother-in-law, who took them hither and thither over the estate. What hypnotized them was the size of the place, and when they realized that half of its land had been taken from us and given to the peasants at the emancipation of the serfs, it rather took away their breath. My father liked the old servitors and their picturesque ways, and he had occult means of communicating his good feeling to them, for during years afterward, the dear creatures were always talking of the visit of the "American general" and what he did. My mother they had seen before and saw again, but my father's one visit sank deep into their simple minds.

IX

The 1905 Revolution

IN THE SUMMER of 1903, I went abroad to the wedding of my eldest Palmer cousin in London, then spent the season on the Normandy coast with our boy, and that autumn joined my dear aunt for a motor trip through northern Italy and southern France, with the chateaux of the Loire thrown in to make our program perfect. My husband had been able to join us for the journey. Later in Paris, we were in grave anxiety over a serious case of typhoid that laid low my aunt after we returned from our wanderings. I remained with the invalid until the holidays and reached St. Petersburg only at the beginning of the season, a few weeks before the war broke out.

We had taken another motor trip in the delightful country of the north of France and into Belgium the year before, and I realized with joy how well my aunt and my husband understood each other. Uncle Palmer had died, and we had been so fond of him, it made an added bond by our sympathy with my aunt's mourning.

The summer of 1904 I spent in St. Petersburg and at Bouromka between war work and family cares. The peasants were being drawn on for mobilization, and their attitude toward the war was most curious. They were not in the least aware of what it was all about and were not especially interested. Japan was an empty name—so was Siberia, for that matter, it was so far away—and to be fighting out there did not mean to them a defense of their land. Yet they were perfectly docile. The Little Father[1] needed them; they were called, and went, unmurmuring, asking no questions. I stood on the porch of our village town hall and heard the proclamation read to a group of dignified, serious men who had bathed and put on their holiday clothes ready for departure. Round them clung their women, in gay kerchiefs and embroidered national costumes, while curly-headed children held to the hands of the protectors they were to lose so soon.

Silent and respectful, they listened to the Imperial orders, then to the voice of their priest, as he chanted a service and blessing, while the women wept and the children hid their heads against the latter's skirts, frightened. We had come down from the chateau to bid our village contingent godspeed and to bring each soldier a little medal of St. George to protect him in battle. For the first time I admired as well as liked our peasants!

The war had an excellent effect on our people. They learned to handle questions of provisioning the extra women and children, showing in this both ability and good sense. The soldiers who traveled across the empire brought back new light, with ideas of Rus-

[1] *Batiushka,* colloquial term for "father," a customary way of referring to the tsar; also used to address a priest.

sia's size that were not mythical; in certain cases, an enthusiasm for our great Far East that led to the emigration of a lot of fine people to the Siberian plains. The era of war and the miserable management of everything brought out a new spirit in many classes of Russians. The liberals—and most of the nobility I saw were in the group—felt it was high time the country should be put in order and helped forward, with education given and land reforms made. The army officers were keen to see a saner policy pursued by the government and wished the sovereign would make reforms of his own accord. These might be gifts now. We were beginning to feel that otherwise they would become concessions torn from him in the near future.

I don't think the young empress had at that time any special political influence or ambition, but her personal weight with the emperor was very great, for he was deeply in love with her. From taste, or because she was beginning to feel her unpopularity, she influenced him always more and more toward a mystical, religious, retired life, and by degrees, with one excuse or another, she got rid of all those who thought the emperor's duty was to show himself oftener and take more part in the nation's life.

Their group was reduced to a small number of attendants, among whom Mademoiselle Taneeva—soon to become by her marriage Madame Vyrubova—was beginning to appear constantly with her mistress. The empress's poor health was a good reason for seeing almost no one; this, and the fragile heir's extreme youth, were excuses for long sojourns at Tsarskoe Selo or at Peterhof. The intrigues Madame Vyrubova was always carrying on against one or another of her colleagues, who were gradually being banished, made us all angry.

Events jostled one another. One could scarcely get one's breath, with the new anxieties and excitements of the winter of 1905. There were disorders in the factory districts in Poland. At Moscow and in several other cities, real revolution was occurring. The murder of several ministers and of the Grand Duke Serge,[2] also attempts on the lives of many prominent men, added bloodshed.

Finally the crowd from the outskirts of the capital came to the Winter Palace one January Sunday[3] to see the emperor and call to him for bread. His flight to Tsarskoe—against his will, it was said—and the order given to fire on the crowd were bad signs. The Imperial guards were all sent out for this work of calming and patroling the city, and I know there was a meeting of some officers (of one regiment, at least), who questioned whether these orders were not to be disobeyed. They fell into line, however, and followed the road of military discipline. But with many the temptation to rebellion was very strong, as they realized everything had been done to make the situation acute and that the

[2]The Grand Duke Serge (Sergei) Aleksandrovich (1857–1905), uncle of Nicholas II and perennial governor general of Moscow, was assassinated by a revolutionary terrorist on 17 February 1905.
[3]The infamous "Bloody Sunday," 22 (9 old style) January 1905.

nation had been long-suffering in the hands of a blind
bureaucratic machine that, however good its intentions, was terribly out of date. Every reasonable man
and woman felt reforms were in order.

For months the pendulum swung backward and
forward. The emperor resisted the upheaval, but the
war disasters occurred, peace was signed, everyone
suffered, and at last the situation in the capital became
critical. Post and railroad service stopped, there was a
question of water and electricity doing likewise, and
no one dared prophesy what each day might bring
forth. Through the Bloody Sunday period in early
1905, my husband, with his comrades, was on duty in
the streets. He had been called to the regimental barracks on the Saturday evening and had said, if he
could, he would give me news by phone, but I was
not to try to reach him. Sunday, one of the officer's
wives who lived in an apartment in the barracks rang
me up to say our commanding general had asked her
to notify all the women that our troops were ordered
out on duty against the rioters. She could not say
where they were going, but were there further news,
she would let us hear.

Sunday night there was an informal dinner at the
Orlovs', who lived some twenty minutes' drive from
us. To get there, I had to pass the quay, across the
Palace Square, and down the Grand Morskaia. I telephoned to Princess Orlov, who told me she did not
know who would come but that all was quiet in her
neighborhood, and she was alone and anxious to have

me there for company's sake. Her husband had been on duty with the sovereign for forty-eight hours past and had accompanied the Imperial family to Tsarskoe the night before. Of course, she had not heard from him. Wouldn't I come and dine even if we were to be but two? I said I was at home with my babies, had been cut off from all rumors for twenty-four hours. Also that the streets in my quarter seemed normal, and I would make the attempt to get to her, reserving the right to turn back in case I encountered obstacles.

I ordered out my small open sleigh, with a single fast trotter and faithful, strong Dimenti, my favorite coachman, thinking this unpretentious vehicle would not attract attention, and the big man and rapid horse would make for safety. On the quay, when I started, there was no sign of life. Then suddenly, as we glided onward, we saw small fires burning, cavalry horses picketed about them, while the riders sat on the ground warming themselves. Sentinels marched up and down in the biting cold, and here and there, in porters' lodges of some palace or ministry buildings, hot coffee or soup was being served to half-frozen officers. The soldiers were more comfortable, for their arrangements were made as if at maneuvers and their portable kitchens were at work. No provision was made for the officers. Some sent home, as did my husband, for a fur robe and sandwiches with a bottle of wine, while others took turns enjoying the hospitality of friendly neighboring houses to snatch sleep. They spent their waking hours seated on the curbstone by

Barricades in St. Petersburg
Courtesy Hoover Institution, Stanford University

Princess Julia Cantacuzene

Revolutionary Days

the camp-fires. The thermometer was far below freezing, the air like crystal, and the river and the town deadly silent as I crossed them. Gold domes and spires of our churches shimmered, and the palaces looked as proud and splendid as in ordinary times, though a pall of fear and threat haunted the picture, and it seemed horribly lonesome to be the only person about. I reached my destination safely, after being stopped as I passed the cordon of troops going into the palace's protected zone and getting out of it again. We sat alone at dinner, Princess Orlov and I, and first one message, then another, came to us. It was said that a riot was taking place at the other end of the Grand Morskaia with machine guns trained on the mob. It was then reported the mob was marching out to Tsarskoe Selo to attack the Imperial family in their refuge. We were told about ten other wild rumors the frightened servants brought in from their expeditions to the tea-houses in the neighborhood or that were telephoned us by friends shut up alone and as panic-stricken as ourselves.

Three times that evening we got authentic news. Once my husband telephoned to me, mainly to say that I was crazy to be out, but incidentally he announced the quarter where he was stationed with his squadron was quiet and that they had not fired a shot nor seen any rioters in the twelve hours they had been there near the Marble Palace. I was not to be anxious, though they were ordered to spend the night. He had sent an orderly home for his fur robe and long fur coat and had thus heard of my escapade. I told him I had moved easily, was in plain tailor clothes, and using our small sleigh, and I reassured him as to the wisdom of my expedition; regaled him, also, with the sensational gossip that had reached me.

Afterward, I heard my parents had been seriously worried, as the New York papers had talked of Bloody Sunday in large print and announced the Neva was running red with blood and some 50,000 people had been butchered! As a matter of fact, I have never heard it said there had been more than 285 killed in those days of disorder.[4]

When we first reached Bouromka in the early summer, it looked and seemed about as usual. We enjoyed our stay extremely. I heard from someone of the servants the way our peasants were being won to revolution was by propaganda sheets that announced His Majesty had been captured and thrown into prison by the bureaucrats and landowners, and that he called on his peasants to come to his rescue. This seemed a most eloquent tribute to our humble peasants' loyalty to their ruler!

Late that summer I went abroad with my two chil-

---

[4]It is impossible to say where this number came from. There has never been an exact count of the casualties of Bloody Sunday. The immediately fatal casualties probably numbered closer to 150, but there were twice that many wounded, some of whom undoubtedly did not recover. See Abraham Ascher, *The Revolution of 1905. Russia in Disarray* (Stanford: Stanford University Press, 1988), pp. 90–92.

dren to see my aunt. I was glad of the rest and a change following what had been a most exciting year. Cantacuzene had his autumn leave after the maneuvers, and he joined us. We were motoring in England, when he received a telegram ordering him back at once to his regiment in St. Petersburg. From Oxford, where the wire found us, he started within an hour by direct train for the Dover boat, and I was to follow as soon as I could gather up our children and baggage and get accommodations on the North Express. A week later I made the crossing from Dover to Ostend with the two children and their old nurse. We found comfortable compartments in our *wagon de luxe,* and with nothing, as I supposed, to disturb us until the changing of trains at the Russian frontier, we settled ourselves, unpacked our bags, had dinner, and the youngsters—aged four-and-a-half and one-and-a-half years—were tucked into their berths.

After passing Liège, I was just beginning to undress, when a conductor came through the car and stopped at my compartment door. He knocked and I opened.

"Are you the lady going to St. Petersburg whose tickets I verified a little while ago?"

"I am."

"We have just heard news at Liège that the Compagnie Internationale cannot take passengers beyond the Russian frontier, as all trains are stopped there by a strike. The telegram is from Königsberg, ordering us to warn all passengers. Madam can go through to Königsberg and wait there, or get off at Berlin. I am sure, as soon as possible, service will be continued."

I felt rather dazed by the possibilities. This news meant probable danger in St. Petersburg—certainly privations of various kinds; a supply of fresh milk cut off. Little Mike and Baby Bertha were young to face all that. Yet I wanted to reach home as soon as possible, for it seemed it was there I had a first duty. If I took the children to Berlin or Königsberg, I would be tied down by them to a foreign city until life at home became entirely settled, and I neither wanted to linger in Germany, nor did I feel I ought to abandon them anywhere on the road and push on alone.

Suddenly, I had a brilliant idea. I would take our whole party back to London, pack the children off to America with my aunt, and then, being foot-loose and free, I would return to the frontier of Russia and see what could be arranged about getting through to the capital. I asked the conductor if I could get off at Aix-la-Chapelle and get my baggage from the baggage-car.

"That will be in a half-hour, madam, and I don't know; such a thing was never done before, to get off a North Express in the middle of the night and desire to open the baggage-car, which is sealed, and take out baggage that has been checked through to St. Petersburg."

I asked if he could take those trunks through to their destination.

"No, madam, but Aix is so soon."

I persuaded him that Aix was as good as Berlin to take off trunks, and that since the train's stopping completely at the Russian frontier made an unusual circumstance, the mere fact of another exception to rule was but a detail.

He went off to get the train-master and bring him to discuss our situation and my unreasonable ideas. Meanwhile I roused the tired babies and nurse and put them back into their clothes. I was convinced that to return to London was my right program. The train-master or conductor-in-chief was easy to convert, and soon we were scrambling down into the dark night from our well-warmed, cozy compartments, with our trunks and bags thrown out beside us and the North Express disappearing in the distance.

After a little I began to think I had made a grave mistake. The station was dark and deserted, the night cold, and I had not planned my next steps. I found a man to carry our hand-baggage and asked him about the nearest hotel. He showed me one across the road and said it was not good, but he thought I could get two or three rooms there. I started him, the children, the nurse, and the small baggage over. Then I went to the station-master, who arranged for our tickets to London, gave me the time of departure early next morning, and reversed my trunk-checks so our things would return to London with us. I also sent a telegram to my aunt. I was able to rejoin my little people then with everything prepared for the morrow's trip.

I did not like the looks of the hotel people, still less

the rooms' aspect; but the children were too weary
from their long day and our trip from London to go
farther. I put them in the inside room with the nurse,
who assured me the sheets of the beds had been used
and the washstand not cleaned. I was unsympathetic
and said as it was after midnight and we must rise at
five, she could let the children sleep outside the covers
on her own traveling-shawls with their little pillows
and that they need not wash until we were on the
London Express next morning.

They were all much too sleepy to care long about
discomfort, so my advice was taken and quiet soon
reigned in the temporary nursery. I had the sitting
room to myself and was very much frightened by the
noise and looks of the place we were in. It had gilt,
shoddy furniture, and mirrors; dirt everywhere; a
door that though locked, looked as if it would shake
down easily under pressure. Everything in the room
was cracked or broken as if fights were the natural
ending of the days' entertainments, and from somewhere in the house came shouts, oaths, and shuffling,
which seemed very threatening.

About daylight, things quieted down, and though a
few guests started off singing in the street, while others tumbled upstairs past my door, banging against it
by accident, no harm came to us. I had spent most of
the night awake, resting on a sofa, with my revolver on
the table by me. It was the only thing I had unpacked.

When the hour to depart came, the town was still
asleep, but a pushcart was found and our bags piled

on it and taken to the station. There the head man was most attentive and put us into our right train, politely arranging all our baggage, out of pity for our forlorn state, I think.

Once in London everything worked out for the best. My aunt said, with her sweetness of old days, she was delighted to have us back for a little and that she would take the children safely to my parents in America. The latter cabled they would gladly keep the grandchildren for me. My husband wired his consent to my proposed plan. So one morning early I parted from the little people. My aunt and the babies started for a steamer at Southampton, I for the Dover-Ostend boat to attempt again the trip home—alone this time, with baggage much reduced and one small trunk so packed that, in case trains were not running in Russia, I could arrange to travel by troika sleigh from Germany to St. Petersburg.

At Liège I was told again no trains were going through. At Berlin the news was still unchanged, but I felt encouraged, anyhow, for the American ambassador, Mr. George Meter, and his secretary, Mr. Miles, going to St. Petersburg, got on my car. I knew I would have protection and company, whatever happened. As we neared Russia, the train emptied rapidly. Finally I think there were no travelers but Mr. Meter's party, myself, a nice young man I had met casually in society in St. Petersburg, and one other stranger. At the frontier the embassy servant in uniform met the ambassador. I had been asked by my husband to bring him back a new revolver, also one for a friend of his; this besides my own. I was in grave doubt as to how to pass my purchases into a country where both arms and ammunition were recently forbidden. Mr. Meter solved the problem.

"What have you in that case?" he asked, pointing, and I answered that case held my jewels.

"Well, suppose you confide your finery to me. I can pass it by the customs, since it isn't dutiable, with a good conscience. Before handing it over, if you want to pack cartridges in your jewel-case, I don't see who can prevent it."

I did this on his hint, and when we got out to change trains, Mr. Miles politely helped carry my valuables, choosing that particular box, so my dangerous weapons actually entered Russia in another's hands.

Once the frontier was crossed, our advance was mere chance. One train had started ahead of us and had reached Gatchina without mishap, from which place the travelers had gone to St. Petersburg by sleigh. We expected to be stopped at any station and to take this same means for the final stages of our journey—so we had our rugs and bags strapped and ready. At each station, however, some official would come through the train and announce that since we were still safe, we would push on to the next town.

Triumphantly we rolled into the big station at the capital and felt we were the first to open traffic again on the full length of the route. My husband came to meet me, glad to think the children were in safety and that I had returned home for the winter in spite of the troubles, which still kept the city's inhabitants on the alert. There had been a general strike on and off for two or three weeks. Amateur volunteers had been sorting and delivering mails, and even the telegraph had not functioned for a time. Now things were quieter, but still uncertain.

When disorder had been calmed in St. Petersburg and elsewhere, and the iron discipline of Trepov[5] as dictator was relaxed, a new government established itself. It brought a notable change on the landowners' estates and to the peasants' homes; at least this was so in our province, south of Kiev, where I saw events develop. The Grand Duke Nikolai Nikolaevich was put in command of the troops in and around St. Petersburg; and though he stood for discipline and maintained it in the city, he was also just and generous, a Russian among Russians, and understood his charge and responsibility. He lived up to his duties with the same calm, intelligent grasp of the subject he showed later as commander-in-chief during the world war. He expressed confidence and showed it always.

Another figure growing popular in St. Petersburg at this time was that of Stolypin. He had been made "president of the council of ministers" and had been allowed to form a cabinet of men who were liberal.

[5]Dmitri Fedorovich Trepov (1855–1906), a former Moscow police chief with the reputation as intrepid defender of order, had been named governor general of St. Petersburg in the aftermath of Bloody Sunday and, in May 1905, assistant interior minister and head of the department of police.

After himself, the most noticeable personality in this group was Krivoshein.[6] Newly named minister of agriculture, he possessed intellect and character, knew his duties to perfection and the peasants' psychology as well. Speaking no language but Russian, even in society, this man of rugged and brusque ways made a great hit and was soon a much-invited and highly honored guest at many a great dinner, where on serious subjects he led the conversation and in frivolous ones looked on and listened in silent study of our society's queer ways. He was a very powerful person, this Krivoshein, with many natural gifts of brain, but little culture. A self-made man, reliable, loyal, and patriotic, he rapidly won general confidence. He had none of Witte's affectations and was much better liked, I think.

Stolypin also had a nature and a physique that were impressive; tall and well-bred-looking, he did not, however, seem cosmopolitan. Somehow, I thought him a little queer in full dress, though never clumsy, undignified, or shy. He was of noble birth and great culture. He was extremely interesting on many subjects, especially concerning Russia, and if one could sit and converse quietly with him at the dinner table or elsewhere he had immense charm and magnetism. I do not know of anyone in the Duma or the government who had his reputation for eloquence.

With Krivoshein's cooperation, Stolypin thought

[6]Alexander Vasilevich Krivoshein (1858–1923) was the main official in charge of implementing the land reforms of the Stolypin era. Technically, there was no "ministry of agriculture" at the time.

out and introduced the land reforms, which were to be tried in a few of our Little Russian provinces, and if found satisfactory, were to be carried out all over the Russian empire. Each peasant individually was to own and keep his land, do with it as he pleased, and get the full benefit of the work and care he put into it. The old system of land being held in common by the villagers, with the portions transferred year by year to different hands for cultivation, had produced discouragement, laziness, run-down crops—for the good-for-nothing man did as little as possible, while the sober, hard worker if he fertilized and plowed his share deeply saw the square he had improved given away in a season, his good grain sold, mixed with the other's bad, and no result to him but his own weariness. The sense of proprietorship, however, brought energy, ambition, and pride. In turn, these put the people forward so rapidly that within a few years we saw our peasant farmers owning 300 and more acres bought from their own group or from us; soon, good machinery and animals were purchased, they grew grain as fine as ours, and sold it at the same prices.

Stolypin never had the emperor's friendship. I think it was represented to His Majesty that much which was being done, though conducive to law and order and an increase of prosperity in the realm, was not exactly in line with old autocratic ideals. Therefore, the sovereign was told that he should not encourage this man's enthusiasms. Apparently, however, Stolypin took such difficulties calmly. He faced in the same way the various attacks of which he was a victim now and then in the parliament, and sometimes even from his collaborators. Danger lurked for him at every turn from the assassin. Sipiagin,[7] Plehve, and the Grand Duke Serge had been killed, and unsuccessful attempts had been made on several others. Stolypin's house was blown up and one of his daughters severely wounded, and a second effort was made without the man's temper or nerves being ruffled or his calm service to emperor and country changed.

In Kiev, finally, he met his end, through a revolver shot fired into his stomach by a young degenerate, paid for the task.[8] Stolypin remained tranquil and serene during several long days of agony, when no hope of recovery could be held out. He sent for his family and quietly prepared for death. The conduct of the sovereigns at that time was looked on with surprise, for beyond a first formal message of sympathy and another final written word of condolence, no notice was taken by them of his death. It was said by some the empress feared to have her husband either see Stolypin after the shooting or to have His Majesty

[7]Dmitri Sergeevich Sipiagin (1853–1902), minister of internal affairs, was assassinated in 1902 by a revolutionary terrorist, as in the cases of Plehve and the Grand Duke Serge Aleksandrovich, by a member of the Socialist-Revolutionary Combat Organization.

[8]Dmitri Grigorevich Bogrov (1887–1911), a young lawyer with ties to revolutionary circles who worked as a spy for the secret police, assassinated Stolypin on 14 September 1911, probably in an attempt to avoid his own murder by the Combat Organization, which had exposed his police connections. He was arrested, court-martialled, and hanged ten days after he shot Stolypin.

attend the great man's funeral; others said it was by request of the secret police that the emperor avoided all this. No one knew, but a bad impression of weakness or lack of appreciation was rather general.

Politically, through the ebb and flow of opinion, we felt Russia was moving forward and that in a few short years, the emperor would give a constitution, for it would be demanded of him by healthy elements in the nation. They sanely waited, worked for progress, and were not mere degenerates or hasty visionaries. Parties were forming of some substance in the second and third Duma, and were learning to handle themselves. Russia was growing fast. The occasional step backward or to the side was resented, though many such occurred, for a strong retrograde group was always ready to stem the tide. Of this party, the empress was supposed generally to be the protectress, and her influence with the emperor was used always in that direction. Old Goremykin was her protégé, and there were others than he behind the scenes who used Her Majesty's prestige to cover their machinations, I believe, largely without her knowledge. She chose her companions, unfortunately, from the worst people within reach, and deliberately began—by Madame Vyrubova's advice—to get rid of the decent, self-respecting, loyal people who had been about her at first. The emperor, by degrees, lived more and more strictly in his family circle, with only two or three attendants with whom the empress liked to talk. Even his aides, his secretary, and Prince Orlov, who for years had been his friend, comrade, and confidant, were being attacked. The struggle was on and was growing more and more marked at court each month.

There was criticism, rivalry, and much personal bitterness, yet evolution or even revolution (a "palace revolution") was often spoken of by those from whom I should never have expected it. It was a new atmosphere altogether in which we lived.

X

Calm Before the Storm

OUR OWN LIFE had been changing somewhat. We had made two delightful trips to America, visits long to be remembered for their happy reunions and crowding pleasures. We went in 1906 and made a beautiful trip with my lovely aunt and my favorite cousins through the American Far West. We visited Chicago and Washington, and stayed on quaint Governor's Island, where my father was in command, saw all the old friends in New York or elsewhere, and enjoyed many a country house party. When we returned to Russia, we took the children with us. "The Revolution" was over by the beginning of 1907.

Just then, Cantacuzene was named to the staff of the Grand Duke Nicholas, and a companionship of service with seven or eight years of happiness for my husband began. Born of perfect understanding on both sides, a paternal, loyal affection on the part of the splendid chief, which never wavered, and an absolute devotion and enthusiastic admiration on my husband's part, relations were always reliable and appreciative.

The grand duke, suspicious of the Germans, feared the kaiser's caresses for our ruler and country. He was anxious to get fortresses and cannon established on our western frontier, and he pressed preparations, but with little or no effect. He threw his influence into breaking up the compact[1] Wilhelm had engineered during the latter's visit to our emperor's yacht in Finnish waters. I do not think our chief ever trusted or liked Count Witte. He never said this that I know of, but it was considered a fact, and Mr. E. J. Dillon's description[2] of these years when he was Count Witte's confidential aide would seem to prove this theory.

However, at the time of the "Willy-Nicky correspondence,"[3] the grand duke loyally worked with Witte and helped the latter straighten out the political tangle and our sovereign to regain his foothold. I believe my husband's chief never took part in politics after that. He studiously avoided them and demanded the same attitude from his court; but everyone knew he stood for law, order, and liberality, and that he was pro-Russian first and, after that, pro-Ally—never pro-German. Also, it was known the Grand Duchess

[1] The notorious Björkö Treaty, signed by the Emperors Wilhelm of Germany and Nicholas of Russia during a yachting rendezvous in the Baltic on 24 July 1904, was a mutual defense pact that would have undone the Franco-Russian alliance. It was nullified at the insistence of the foreign ministers of both countries.

[2] Emil Joseph Dillon (1854–1933), Dublin-born perennial special correspondent of the *Daily Telegraph,* sometime Russian newspaper editor and professor, and confidant of Count Witte. The author refers to Dillon's book, *The Eclipse of Russia,* which was published in London and New York in 1918.

[3] *The Kaiser's Letters to the Tsar* were published in London in 1920 and were instantly dubbed "The Willy-Nicky Correspondence."

Anastasia, his wife, was a Slav princess by birth—a Montenegrin—educated in St. Petersburg and thoroughly anti-German. She had been one of the empress's intimates, only to be suddenly and rather roughly dropped. Although no one quite found out why, everyone spent much time guessing.

It required some tact and discretion to live in our court atmosphere with its various currents, but this was less difficult with Russians than it would have been elsewhere, as society was simpler among them than most other peoples, and unless one were particularly clumsy in criticizing, one was allowed to live in peace and think what one pleased.

Through those years I began to feel a great interest in politics and see a good deal of the diplomats and cabinet ministers. Mr. Izvolsky, the minister of foreign affairs, and his wife were very sympathetic, and their salon, where I often went, always seemed full of interesting people.

In November 1908, our third child was born, a golden-haired baby, the first Cantacuzene to have blue eyes. That same year a new note was introduced into our lives by our buying a pretty cottage at the great military camp of Krasnoe Selo, within an hour's driving distance of the capital. We rebuilt this home and made it very attractive with furniture and ornaments of generations ago, keeping it all in one period. We grew to love this home best of any we owned, and our life was always happy there.

In 1910, we made another trip to the United States,

which was delightful, when we spent four months with the family and old friends, filling our time with delightful excursions again. We journeyed down to Florida and fell in love with that part of America because of its sunny, turquoise sky and sea, and smiling landscapes. For Christmas in Chicago, twenty-odd of his descendants gathered round the ninety-year-old patriarch, my Grandfather Honoré.

It was pleasant to find my father in the full flush of his career, settled at Governor's Island and, having made a fine record, still active and doing well in his patriotic way. At sixty, he was hale, hearty, and still keen.

After this visit home I never again saw my father alive. Within a year he showed the first signs of the illness that was to claim him as its victim, and through the winter of 1911–12, he went on with his duties, knowing he was doomed. No realization of his danger came to my mother apparently until it was too late to let me hear, so it chanced that returning home from an official party in St. Petersburg one night, I found a cable asking me to go across the sea because my father asked for me. During the preparations for that distressing journey, another wire followed, saying that my father had died suddenly. One has to know the misery of such a departure and trip to realize what it means to be too late and to miss the last words or last smile of one who was deeply loved. Never can I forget my journey—the hideous traveling through Russian snow and over the bleak plains of East Prussia.

The landing in New York and the heartbreak of the

Cantacuzene children:
Michael, Bertha, and Ida

My Life Here and There

Major General Frederick Dent Grant

Courtesy National Archives

funeral, the touching demonstrations of admiration and love for my father by his comrades and his soldiers, by the old policemen who had served under him, and by the city of New York, won our gratitude and moved us deeply. His body was taken through the city's thoroughfares lined with vast crowds; the latter stood with heads bared, and bowed, wiping their eyes as the gun carriage passed, draped with the flag he had served since his thirteenth year in one capacity or another. We went up the Hudson, taking this devoted son past the place where his father lay, to another above it and equally beautiful, on the great river. At West Point our pilgrimage ended. There, amid his comrades of old school and army life, we deposited this son of the academy, who had been so devoted to his school and had lived by its high tradition.

My mother was broken up, her life changed in every way, and a little relaxation from the shock and strain of the preceding weeks seemed desirable. She was prevailed upon to accompany me abroad; within a few days of the funeral, we sailed for Russia.

For two years I led a life of complete retirement. The children, growing older, needed my attention and I stayed much at home. The ever-increasing circle around my tea table, where friends gathered to talk informally on all sorts of subjects, still retained its interest in my eyes, and the conversation never lagged.

I was learning much of the world at large with its political questions. It seemed to me that we had a great future and that at last the liberals more and more were moving toward an evolution of the right sort. Many men talked of a constitution. It was well known that when certain of the ministers who most insistently advocated reform went to the emperor with reports and suggestions to which His Majesty listened with sighs of deep sympathy; and also that in spite of Madame Vyrubova's efforts, certain honest courtiers held their influence. The empress was constantly ill, and she kept around her a strange crowd, who spent their time flattering her and feeding her with gossip and charlatanism. She was drifting away, living solely for her children and for her occult group of friends.

There was no doubt in anyone's mind regarding Madame Vyrubova's relations with Rasputin,[4] or of the fact that she had invented him and declared him to be a miracle-worker, thus installing him as a sort of backstairs prophet. His prayers were said to do the empress good, and also the young heir to the throne, who was an invalid. Madame Vyrubova had persuaded Her Majesty that she herself could not survive

[4]Grigory Efimovich Rasputin (Novykh) (1864 or 1865–1916), "The Holy Devil" of René Fülöp-Miller's biography of the 1920s, was a self-proclaimed prophet and faith-healer (not an ordained priest) who acquired considerable influence over the Empress Alexandra in the years just before the world war by his evident ability to stop the tsarevich's hemophiliac bleeding. This influence was widely believed to extend to the disastrous series of ministerial appointments made during the war, especially after Nicholas's move to army headquarters in mid-1915. Hatred of Rasputin was general in Russian high society. He was murdered by Prince Yusupov and a group of confederates, including a grand duke, on 30 December 1916.

Madame Anna Vyrubova in court dress

Grigory Rasputin

Revolutionary Days

being separated a day from the mistress she adored. Also, she was convincing about Rasputin. He was a simple peasant; it would please the people of Russia to know a representative of theirs stood high at court. By the pure, real faith that moved him, Rasputin had power from on high to prophesy and heal, and his intervention averted the nervous pains from which the empress had suffered since so long. The latter was brought firmly to believe all this, and the fact, continuously retold, that her son was stronger and would eventually recover perfect health by their private saint's constant intercession and watchful care, made the distraught empress a victim, yielding more and more to the foul influence of the plotters.

As she gained power and dared to show it, Madame Vyrubova made a few allies in court circles, all among the worst elements, who either feared her or hoped to share the spoils she gained. Many of us realized the wretch was doing harm but how much, no one could calculate. We saw her creeping into the intimacy of the sovereigns, but she played the fool extremely well and was never suspected of political ambitions. We discovered early in the game that she wanted to seem a figure in the court. Many people shrugged their shoulders and decided to accept punishment for ignoring the favorite's pretensions if necessary. Many would not call on her. She and I spoke when we met, but the acquaintance went no further, for to me, as to many to others, Madame Vyrubova was a repulsive creature.

As for Rasputin, I never met or saw him. Coarse, vicious, hideous he was known to be, yet he exerted an unholy fascination on any number of women who had crowded about him and composed his clientele. He drank and in general lived brutally, though without other plans than to be materially enriched or to have warmth and finery and food.

Those who had known the empress enough to realize her culture were much distressed to see her so badly advised, but there seemed nothing to prevent her being exploited. Her influence over her husband grew and grew, until by degrees he lost familiar contact with those who might have given him real enlightenment and truth.

Early in 1913, the 300th anniversary of the accession of the Romanovs to the Imperial throne was celebrated. The deeds of our Imperial family through three centuries of history were recalled in tableaux, song, and ceremony.

Never had the palace looked more magnificent, nor had the power of the ruler seemed more assured. The city of St. Petersburg was officially dressed in bunting. Two special gala fêtes were given. One, offered by the nobles of the capital to their emperor, was a ball in the "Council Hall of the Nobility."

A few nights later there was a gala performance at the opera house. This time the sovereigns were hosts to their court and to the government officials. The house had never had a grander evening.

After assisting at the week's rejoicing, the emperor,

his wife, and children retired again to Tsarskoe, and we were left with the impression of a fairy dream, which had lasted a few days and had renewed our historical loyalty for the throne and its occupants.

The next winter, 1913–14, I had laid aside my mourning finally but expected to take little part in what promised to be a gay season. Fate decreed otherwise, however, and that last winter before the war I passed in dancing. It was a last fling before the breaking down of all that had made the frame of our brilliant youth and life, and it seems as if we all instinctively felt we must eat, drink, and be merry.

That year, 1914, as usual, the sovereigns and their court spent the spring in pleasant comfort at Livadia,[5] on the coast of the Black Sea. Both the emperor and the empress were fond of this, their personal home, and with the excuse of Her Majesty's health and that of the tsarevich, they lengthened their sojourn in the south each year.

Both Madame Vyrubova and her occult partner Rasputin were growing arrogant in 1914 toward the members of the court, whenever their Imperial protectress was not watching; but in her presence they always played modest roles and represented themselves to be a pair of humble saints who spent their time in prayer. Officials were approached by them for favors, however, and in their petitions covert threats were felt.

[5]The Imperial estate on the south coast of the Crimea, near Yalta.

At the end of the spring, the sovereigns and their followers returned north, and they scarcely had time to settle for the summer in Peterhof, make preparations, and receive the president of the French Republic,[6] who was scheduled for an official visit of about a week's duration, when the murder at Sarajevo[7] suddenly startled all Europe. The menace of it touching us was not sufficiently felt, however, to cause any change of program, so the feasting and receptions, the reviews and gala theaters to honor our ally and our guest were continued, in full security that all was well. At last the visit ended, and Poincaré sailed away. Then we realized quite suddenly that we had war to face and at short notice.

[6]Raymond Poincaré (1860–1934) was president of France from 1913 to 1920. He visited Russia from 20 July to 23 July. Immediately after he left St. Petersburg, Austria delivered its ultimatum of war to Serbia.

[7]The murder of the Austrian Archduke Francis Ferdinand (1863–1914) by the Bosnian Serbian nationalist Gavrilo Princip (1894–1918) provoked the crisis that led directly to the outbreak of the First World War.

XI

The Knell of Autocracy

FOR 25 JULY 1914, Saturday evening, a gala performance of the Imperial ballet was "commanded"
in the quaint theater of our military camp at Krasnoe
Selo. Since the time of the great Peter, the guard regiments of Russian autocrats have summered here; and
this night, for the last event of the season, the pretty
playhouse and garden were illuminated and decorated
with flags, our own and the French. The latter were a
remaining tribute to our allies, who had left us a few
days previously after a lengthy visit. Satisfaction in the
past, hope for the future showed on all faces, now that
Poincaré and the brilliant René Viviani[1] were on their
homeward route across the northern sea; and we
breathed easily in the sense of relaxation from cere-
monious functions. We expected this evening to be
one of unalloyed, informal pleasure.

A few friends dined at our camp-cottage; and in
the party some diplomats, come down from town,
brought us the unexpected news—which we called
"sensational and exaggerated"—of an agitated stock
exchange, an anxious foreign office, complications
with Vienna, and a possible crisis that might mean

---

[1]French Prime Minister René Viviani (1863–1925).

war. This set us all speculating, though we treated the subject with only passive interest. Troubles with Vienna were chronic, and we had been on the verge of war a dozen times. We even felt humiliation, remembering how some years before we had been obliged to swallow the insult of the Bosnia and Herzegovina annexation by Austria,[2] without a gesture of protest. After dinner my husband, who had been on the point of starting for a business trip to our estates, gave up his plan and his leave of absence and joined our party for the theater. This was the first indication I saw that he had regarded the table talk with any seriousness, though even now he gave only his curiosity as a reason for deferring his trip, by way of explanation to our guests.

As we reached the theater, laughter and pretty clothes were our first impression, and we found the usual gay groups of officers, court functionaries, and women standing about on the wide piazzas. Only tonight, faces were more excited than ordinarily and discussions more animated. All the conversations were on the same new subject that had occupied our thoughts since dinner. Here, too, had come the visitors from town with their gossip.

The bell rang and interrupted comment, and we entered to find our places and to stand near them until the emperor came in, followed by his court and the

[2]Austria had annexed Bosnia and Herzegovina, by decree, on 6 October 1908, thereby creating a crisis in Austrian-Russian relations that lasted until the world war.

Chevalier Guards dressed for an Imperial Ball, 1903

Courtesy Hoover Institution, Stanford University

The Imperial palace, Tsarskoe Selo, outside St. Petersburg

Courtesy Hoover Institution, Stanford University

functionaries of the camp on duty; at their head the Grand Duke Nicholas Nikolaevich, commander of the Imperial Guard and of the camp. Amid a great noise of spurs and sabers, the sovereign having seated himself with the grand duke on his left, the whole house did likewise. The orchestra played its best under the Imperial eye, and the curtain rose at once on one of the favorite fairy tale ballets.

The emperor looked pleased and at rest, and seemed really to enjoy the scene before him. He loved to get away from forms and ceremonies; and this night, in the simple surroundings of our military camp, his shyness found relief from his duties.

Quite evidently, the political news we had heard had not yet reached the sovereign's ear, or else had not impressed him, for his brow showed no trace of preoccupation other than of interest in and appreciation of the pretty "ballerines," who danced and posed for his approval. In the light of later events, I am inclined to think this act of ballet was the last hour of careless enjoyment our emperor ever knew. Afterward I learned that Cantacuzene's trip had been given up at the telephoned word from the grand duke, who all that afternoon had been following the international news with keen realization of its weight.

Toward the end of the first act, a slight movement marked the arrival of M. Sazonov[3], minister of foreign affairs, who quietly joined his colleagues in the front

[3]Sergei Dmitrievich Sazonov (1860–1927), a career diplomat, was minister of foreign affairs from 1910–1916.

of the audience. It was so unusual for a member of the
cabinet to be late when the sovereign was present at a
fête that it at once set us whispering and gave color to
the reports of the early evening, especially as the man
looked weary and was quite evidently consulting with
his neighbors on either side. All three were oblivious
of the scenery and motions of the ballet. The act
ended; everyone rose; and the emperor, recognizing a
face here and there, left the hall, which at once emptied itself onto the piazzas.

More curious than ever was the crowd; and then,
after a few moments' conversation with Sazonov, the
emperor ordered out his motors. The whole cabinet
followed His Majesty to the small palace he occupied
in camp. All the diplomats present felt they wanted to
return to town and send cipher messages to their capitals; and the military element became intensely anxious to leave our frivolous surroundings and to spend
the night at offices and barracks, in case orders must
be received or given suddenly. So we departed from
the building, where, alas, there will never again be
such a meeting.

The news Sazonov gave the emperor was of so serious a nature that a council of ministers was called at
once, the sovereign presiding in person. The council
lasted late into the night and was of immense historical importance. It left a feeling of confidence between
the sovereign and those who formed his government.
I was told, by two of the ministers, how shocked the
emperor was and that he showed deep patriotism in

his remarks. Sazonov took courage from the promise of support, though he was put under orders to avert the catastrophe if possible.

That night, few slept in the cottages, barracks, tents, and officers' messrooms scattered over the hills of Krasnoe camp. Hearts were too heavy and anxiety was too keen, as we sat or lay awake, waiting for the ringing of our telephones. In the small hours of the morning, the summons came—orders to move all our regiments to their winter quarters in the capital or its environs, wherever they belonged, as a mobilization might be called for in a few days. Our own unit, the "Chevalier Guards of Her Majesty the Empress Mother," was to leave first, at nine that same morning, it being the ranking regiment. But it was immediately to be followed by other cavalry, then the infantry and artillery regiments and batteries, until the whole busy camp should be turned into a vacant plain in unbelievably short time. Through the few days and nights I lingered on in our home, I was never free again from the monotonous tramp of hooves and feet past my garden gate. The troops moved in a continuous stream down the high road to St. Petersburg, and this sinister procession was silent and orderly. It contained the flower of our empire, some 50,000 strong, those who would be the first to go out to the sacrifice if war were declared! I carried about with me an insurmountable depression and tore myself with deep regret from the garden and cottage, which had been our summer resort for many years. Not so the men, keen for the fray and hoping this time we should not be led into giving way to German arrogance.

For two or three days there was some uncertainty. The chance of a peaceful solution remained. There was as yet no mobilization. However, on Wednesday, Sazonov seemed despairing of any further possibility of a peaceful issue and ordered mobilization.

I shall never forget the stress and strain of those few days, from the twenty-sixth until the twenty-ninth of July. Disturbances and strikes were feared and predicted in the capital where German agents were arrested, and German money was found and confiscated among our factory workmen! Yet during this time, the German embassy remained with us, talking and negotiating, gaining time for themselves and accusing us of having mobilized. All St. Petersburg lived in a state of indescribable nervous tension, and gossip said the pressure brought on the emperor by certain court influences against war was so heavy that perhaps His Majesty would still be persuaded not to uphold our fine Slav policy of defending Serbia.

To us of the military element the week from the twenty-fifth of July to the first of August was a time full of change and excitement, work and anxiety. My husband, at the first talk of war, had given up his leave on the grand duke's suggestion. Then, within twenty-four hours, he had seen his chief and had a long heart-to-heart talk with him, begging to be set free, entirely and definitely, from his duties as aide-de-camp to his Imperial highness, and asking permission, instead, to go under fire with his old regiment, the Chevalier Guards. The chief listened to my husband with his usual kindly interest. Seven years this aide-de-camp had been constantly near him, abroad and at home. Through the hard period of the revolutionary days, when in 1905 the grand duke took over the command of St. Petersburg, quelled the troubles, and brought order out of a chaos that had menaced the Imperial throne, my husband served him. Also, during the brilliant days that followed, when the emperor had delighted to honor his cousin, and when the grand duke's place in Russia had been unique, he had always shown my husband the most generous understanding and confidence; had given him a filial place in his household, calling him familiarly "Mishka," and using with him always the "thou" of affection. He counted on Cantacuzene for various kinds of work of a delicate nature, charged him often with difficult missions, and accepted as if with grateful recognition the sincere devotion and loyal service my husband offered.

So we felt that perhaps his desire to leave the grand ducal court at this moment might be subject to misinterpretation, but Michael's mind was set at rest immediately. The splendid old chief showed himself greatly touched and pleased with "Mishka's" point of view and replied that not only did he entirely sympathize with my husband and would grant his desire, but if he had been in his shoes, he would have wished to act in the same way; and he envied extremely the possibilities his aide-de-camp would have. He added his wishes for success and said he would watch my husband's career with pleasure and interest, and be ready to help him at any time.

When he returned home, Michael was radiant from the spirit shown him in this interview. It was the only difficulty to overcome, for the old regiment hailed with delight the idea of having an ancient comrade in its midst as a junior colonel. But he was considered somewhat crazy to leave his easy, safe, and brilliant berth at court, to chance rough life at the front.

After this, Michael moved instantly to the regimental quarters in town, and because he feared for us at the deserted camp, I packed and moved with the children to the Orlovs' villa at Strelna, where their kind and hospitable thought had called me in the first moment of excitement. This arrangement had the double advantage of keeping my little people in the country surroundings, good for them, and yet bringing us considerably nearer the capital.

With the home and children no longer on my mind, I gave all my attention to the long shopping expeditions, necessary to turn a "maneuvering kit" into an outfit for serious war. Business consultations and arrangements also filled our time in town.

Brave and brilliant days flew past all too rapidly, though they were hard to live. The city was covered with flags and draperies, and streets and shops were crowded with groups, soon to break up. It was a time of gentle twilight, lingering conversations, and caressing music, played by gypsies; and we all sat late into the night, being Russians.

Saturday morning, the first of August, I woke to read in the paper that the die was cast. War was declared! My husband would be going in a few days, and behind him stretched to the very horizon of my realization the faces of all the friends I had made in twenty years, headed in the same direction.

I was struck anew each time I went out in Russia by the order at large gatherings. There was always plenty of space and time, not to mention proverbial good nature; and these qualities gave a Russian ceremony a note of charm and distinction all its own. The day set for a service of prayer in the Winter Palace was no exception. The ten or fifteen great reception halls were already filled with people holding gentle conversation when I arrived—old men in court uniforms, young ones in fighters' khaki, women in light gowns and pretty summer hats. They all looked tremendously tense and alive, as if gathering up their strength to offer it collectively to their ruler. It must have given the sovereign pleasure to see all that mass of Russians, so seriously coming to him in the hour of need.

The religious ceremony was not long, but its intensity was extreme; and never had the intoning of priest or the singing of choir been more lovely. Certainly, also, the prayer that went up to heaven was profoundly sincere. As it ended, and we rose from our knees, the sovereigns turned and stood a moment facing their subjects, the empress taking her husband's arm. Quite spontaneously, from some 5,000 throats broke forth the national anthem, which was not less beautiful because the voices choked with emotion. Then cheer upon cheer came, until the walls rang with their echo!

It was the first time, I fancy, the emperor had been offered such a tribute. He was paler than usual and seemed somewhat startled but not displeased. He advanced with the empress still upon his arm, and continuing its mighty cheers, the crowd parted in front of them, forming an aisle from the altar to the immense double doors opposite. Old men and young, red in the face and hoarse from the effort, kept up the noise. They, and the women too, bowed low, or threw themselves upon their knees, as their rulers passed; His Majesty, in absolute silence, showed no recognition of any special face. Our beautiful empress looking like a Madonna of Sorrows, with tears on her cheeks, stretched her hand in passing to this or that person, now and then bending gracefully to embrace some woman who was kissing her hand. Her Majesty that day seemed to symbolize all the tragedy and suffering that had come upon us and, feeling it deeply, to give thanks to this group for the devotion their attitude implied. Her expression was of extraordinary sweetness and distress, and possessed beauty of a quality I had never seen before on the proud classic face. In passing me, she stretched out her hand, and as I put my lips to it, she leaned over, kissed me and said, "Your husband, too?" and continued, in reply to my affirmative,

"Then you must help me with all the work there is for us women to do." I cannot forget the beautiful, touching Madonna of that day, stooping to console and encourage her people, drowning her own sorrows in her tears of sympathy for her subjects! Until then through fifteen years, I had seen only a statuesque and austere presence, presiding at feasts and ceremonies, with an almost inhuman severity of expression, and entirely repressing the tenderness this situation had brought out.

The Grand Duke Nicholas Nikolaevich was the observed of all observers. He had been told that morning he was to be entrusted with the supreme command of all the Russian armies! He had neither asked nor hoped for so great an honor, and his gratitude and emotion enhanced his intense personality, until he dominated the surrounding throng completely. He was to everyone the ideal leader in an emergency. We turned to him, with gratitude that the conduct of our armies was to be in his good hands, and as he realized the sentiment expressed, his appreciation showed in his flashing looks and in the sudden beauty of his rare smile.

I was told from a sure source that in accepting his appointment that morning, he had begged two favors from his Imperial cousin: First, to go to the front quietly and without official leave-takings, avoiding the noise that had attended General Kuropatkin's departure for Manchuria ten years before. This request was granted; but not so the second, which was that he might name his own staff. General Yanushkevich was already nominated as his chief of staff, he was informed; and General Danilov was to be the chief of his military bureaus. Both these were supposedly friends to Sukhomlinov,[4] and at headquarters the chief was allowed to choose only his personal staff and not his military one. This measure struck everyone (except the generalissimo himself) as dreadfully unfair, since he must work with these men as instruments and be responsible for their acts. Those devoted to the grand duke felt a first move of his hidden enemies.

At this same hour Wilhelm, in Berlin, was making speeches to the multitude in front of his palace, trying to inflame their patriotism by his eloquence. But Nicholas stood before his subjects without a word or gesture, and they knelt in adoration to the "White Tsar"[5] of history and gave him thus the greatest hour of his life!

---

[4]General Vladimir Aleksandrovich Sukhomlinov (1848–1926) had been appointed minister of war in 1909. Antagonism between Sukhomlinov and the Grand Duke Nicholas Nikolaevich, grounded in differences over issues of military reform, was long-standing.

[5]*Belyi Tsar,* a familiar title for the rulers of Muscovite, pre-Petrine Russia, in which "white" was possibly a geographic designation of Tatar origin, meaning "western."

XII

First Days of War and Then Retreat

Fʀᴏᴍ ᴛʜᴇ ᴍᴏʀɴɪɴɢ of the third of August—Monday—began the distress of parting for us, with the departure of my brother-in-law, Count Theo Niroth, commanding the Dragoons of the Imperial Guard. Knowing poor Theo to be living through his troubles alone, I motored to his barracks at Peterhof that morning early, to say good-bye to him and see if I could be of any use. I found him very occupied and entirely calm, while his regiment seemed well in hand, officers and men going about their unusual business with the utmost order and rapidity. Theo was greatly distressed not to embrace his family before leaving. The war had come so suddenly that though he had wired them, he could scarcely hope to see anyone arrive from the faraway country estates. As I was making my *adieu,* his wife, having made a forced voyage, with great good luck appeared at Peterhof an hour before the Dragoons departed. So at least of her he had a glimpse, and said good-bye.

Our Chevalier Guards were to leave the following morning; and Monday there was a most touching function, when in the courtyard of their old historical barracks, the regiment in battle array was reviewed by its commander (Prince Alexander Dolgoruky) and all its ancient or retired officers then in St. Petersburg. The senior ex-commander of the regiment said a few heartfelt words of good wishes from those too old to go to war; then, squadron by squadron, the men, with their officers, knelt and were blessed by the regimental priest.

As they were to leave at daylight next morning, we had but a few hours for preparations and no time to think. Baskets were prepared with food, literature, and small comforts, which might help out the tedious hours of a long trip on a military train.

Our little girls came up from Strelna to lunch with us that day and to say good-bye to their father. We tried to make the parting as easy as possible for them, so their young minds would not be weighted with the tragedy we elders were living.

Our boy remained the night in town with me and had his first experience of real drama At five a.m. we rose and went to the railway, where we saw the beloved regiment, in the midst of which we had lived so many years, entrain. Perfect order prevailed, but the embarkation took several hours. Each squadron occupied a train: freight cars fitted up for soldiers and horses; platform cars for baggage and provisions; and at the end a car or two, second class and far from clean, for the officers, doctors, papers, etc.

With the actual parting, there was a general breakdown, hurried kisses, choking blessings; then a rush for the platforms. The trains moved off, and lonesome small groups of relatives faced the long days of anxiety

Empress Alexandra and Anna Vyrubova, ca. 1910
Courtesy Hoover Institution, Stanford University

War workers in Petrograd, including the Dowager Empress Marie, mother of the Tsar

My Life Here and There

and emptiness ahead! It seemed dreadful to see our men go! Besides my husband, these trains contained many of our oldest friends, and we knew they would be put immediately under fire. At the last moment I had been charged with packets of valuables and with letters, and had promised to look after and send news to various families unable to be with us on that sunny morning.

There were Red Cross units pushing their preparations to start as soon as it was possible to organize. They greatly needed supplies of all kinds, nothing having been foreseen of the events that were upon us. In the capital itself hundreds of hospitals were opening, governmental as well as private. A great need for pity and charity appealed to the country's womanhood; and one and all responded, giving of their riches in money, time, and personal labor.

There was a movement to rally about the empress for direction in this; and many like myself, who had until then avoided Mme. Vyrubova, called upon her knowing that for all the Imperial war work she was chosen by the empress to represent her personally. Madame Anna Aleksandrovna Vyrubova had been named lady-in-waiting to the empress and taken to live in the palace at the time of her debut. In looks she was very fat, with clumsy walk and figure, a pretty head, soft curly hair, blue eyes that always looked sleepy, and fine complexion and teeth. She had no conversation, except to make compliments in a soft voice; and she posed for being very shy, sentimental, and stupid. By this method she succeeded for years in allaying suspicions of her real ambition and in covering her conduct. On entering upon her career, she at once adopted an attitude of abject flattery, which at first surprised, then pleased and touched the empress. As time passed, Her Majesty admitted the self-styled "slave" more and more to her presence. Court gossip said Mme. Vyrubova sat at her mistress's feet, kissed them, begged for the meanest tasks as an honor, and talked to the empress in picturesque language of the Orient, addressing her as the "Sun and Moon," or her "Life" and claiming she had been saved from dying during typhoid by the adored mistress's presence at her bedside.

About seven or eight years before the great war, Mme. Vyrubova had married, at the wish of Her Majesty, a man the latter chose. Her husband was persuaded to leave his active service in the navy and live at court where he was given the position of aide-de-camp to the emperor. To everyone's amazement, he insisted upon divorcing her after a few months and left the court and his honors to return to sea. He never reappeared and was dubbed mad for the story he told of his married life. After this episode Mme. Vyrubova remained always with the empress, was called simply "my friend" by the sovereign, and became her favorite and confidential attendant. She was given an apartment in the palace and also occupied at times a small house rented outside, where she could entertain with freedom and where her Imperial patroness was often

asked to meet people whom it would have been difficult to introduce at court. Soon the evident dislike
shown by loyal subjects to the Vyrubova ways was explained by the favorite as covert criticism of the empress's friends and tastes and occupations, and a very
delicate situation was created. The sovereign's mind
was poisoned with a morbid belief in the hostile attitude of Russia's aristocratic society toward her, and
thus more and more was she separated from healthy
influences. About two years before the war, Rasputin
was introduced at court by the favorite, and his min-
istrations to the empress were encouraged.

When the war came, a number of women felt with
me that nothing counted but our patriotic duties; and
in a desire to make a demonstration of loyalty, we all
called on Mme. Vyrubova, asking for any work in the
various Red Cross organizations that would be organized by Her Majesty's orders. From then on, it was
impossible not to admit Mme. Vyrubova's influence
on events. We were told by her that "Her Majesty was
suffering from one of her frequent attacks of nervous
pains"; and all those wishing to help were begged to
join in the work at the Winter Palace, where the doors
would be thrown open as they had been at the time of
the Japanese War. In a few days the papers announced
all was ready at the palace, and the afternoon opening
was a spectacle marvelous to see. A vast crowd of
women presented themselves to the presiding committee, the members of which were ladies-in-waiting
from the palace, with Mme. Vyrubova at their head.

Wives of government and court officials, wives of officers, wives of simple soldiers, and work girls from shops and dressmaking establishments were there, rubbing shoulders, all filled with zeal.

Daily we hoped the empress would appear, especially to thank the humbler element for their time and generous effort, which meant loss of money in their bread-winning lives. But as the weeks passed and Her Majesty never came, the rumor spread that she was entirely preoccupied with her own small private hospital, installed in the Tsarskoe Palace, and took no interest in the capital, leaving everything there to Mme. Vyrubova.

I found myself drawn into the stream, making and packing bandages like all my friends, while we talked of the daily news. The latter was most encouraging and gratifying to our national vanity. The campaign in East Prussia progressed rapidly, and we captured town after town until our armies had advanced far on German soil.

In the early days of August, the emperor and empress, with the children and court, had moved from Peterhof Palace to Tsarskoe, as there was fear of the Germans bombarding our coast, where the former residence stands. For the same reason, and because of her many interests in Red Cross work, Princess Orlov moved to town also, bringing my children with her to her home there and vacating Strelna. I was personally glad of this change, being very busy; for besides my afternoons in the palace bandage factory, my mornings were spent in the throes of settling our newly bought house. In the conditions of that time, it was an appalling undertaking to arrange even so small a place. The workmen I counted upon were always being mobilized for war purposes, and my own servants had nearly all been taken. I had to resign myself to a great waste of time and energy; but then various friends came to my aid, and in spite of all complications, I began to hope I might move into our new quarters toward the middle of August.

I loved St. Petersburg in those fine first weeks of war and admired my compatriots as never before. In the streets everyone hurried, everyone was busy, and autos, houses, and women wore the sign of the Red Cross. The humbler elements especially were touching, and each poor shop readily sold things "for the soldiers" at a discount, just as each poor work girl gave of her strength in the good cause. The rich were vastly generous; not only of their money, but their time and thought, palaces and motors, filled out and completed the omissions in the government's care for its sons.

Then one evening the weight of a hammer blow fell on us. The offensive in East Prussia had continued brilliantly, and the thrilling news of daily progress had kept us women in high spirits. A day came when, in the taking of Kauschen on the nineteenth of August, the Chevalier Guards and the Horse Guard Regiment suffered losses, which carried anguish with the tale of triumph to mothers and wives in the capital. So many officers and soldiers were killed. The list of wounded was enormous, too!

My husband had led the three squadrons of his regiment who, dismounted, had attacked in a charge the fortification on one side, and at the beginning of the movement, he had been shot through the liver. He had not wanted to give over the command in so grave a crisis and had continued in action some twenty minutes, until weakness from the terrible loss of blood overcame the artificial strength excitement had loaned him. Then, upheld by a young comrade, Baron Pilar von Pilchau, he went to the regimental first aid station just behind the lines. The doctor and his aide were so rushed with work that the regimental veterinary had been pressed into service. It was the latter who, with Pilchau, dressed Cantacuzene's wound. Then he was put on a horse and, with a soldier to accompany him, rode back eight miles to the hut where the regimental commander was installed. Here, the wounded were stretched out in a small orchard, on straw that had been scattered for their comfort.

All that hot day they lay without any food or care, until in the evening the end of the battle brought back the surgeon and his aides. Then with the voluntary help of one or two officers, the doctors went their rounds in the suffering crowd, doing what little they could to give relief with the slender means at hand. My husband heard about him laments and broken phrases, and recognized some voices; but he could not turn to identify his neighbors in the orchard. He understood that there was as yet no organized service to look after the wounded at the front and that he was thought to be dying. His wound was not re-dressed, but he was lifted by comrades' hands gently and carried into Prince Dolgoruky's room, where the latter ordered a bed of fresh hay arranged for him, and he was given doses of brandy and morphine. That night remains a painful memory, though his commander gave him what care he could. Constantly men came and went with reports and orders. If they knew Cantacuzene, they would approach his corner and offer a few encouraging words. In the morning there was a slight improvement in his condition, and he was so anxious to leave for home with the other wounded, who were to be transported to the railway, that the commander and the doctor consented. More morphine, more brandy, and he was again lifted by comrades and put into a springless peasant cart, where his soldier servant and belongings had already been loaded. Michael's servant, Davidka, who had been attached to him for years and had been mobilized with him, was from our country place, of our own peasants; and his devotion showed in the long trip when he followed the doctor's orders as to how he must handle his master. His excellent care was certainly one of the reasons why my husband lived through the torments of that voyage.

Two days the procession of rough carts traveled backward toward the home country, shaking passengers over rough roads. Their slow pace was torture.

Part of the time in delirium, part of the time vague somnolence from weakness made for forgetfulness; while for the rest it was agony so great that my husband never refers to it in conversation. What I heard of their adventures came to me from a wounded fellow officer, traveling in a cart behind, who moved up from time to time to see how my husband was faring. Davidka, who sat many hours holding his master, told me that a traveling surgeon, in passing, stopped their cart and, taking my husband into an abandoned stable near the roadside, washed his wound, changed the dressings on it, and unpacking Michael's small trunk, changed all his clothes that were saturated from the bleeding.

Finally, they reached the railroad, with our patient still living and conscious, though very weak. Here a train was made up of empty cars, which had brought troops and provisions, and was returning to St. Petersburg for more. The wounded were loaded in, pell mell, foodless, and without attention. The faithful Davidka put his master into a berth and installed himself nearby; and for more than two days they traveled thus, Davidka helping where and how he could.

A telegram was sent me by Prince Dolgoruky, who had for years been the emperor's companion. My husband also sent one on the way; so we were expecting the sad train, and I went to meet Michael, taking our boy, on Sunday afternoon, the fourth day after he had been wounded. Because he was not dead, there was still hope, but that was all. He had had no food on the journey but the stimulants administered at the beginning and now and then a glass of milk given him at the stations along the way by women, who, hearing of these wounded and their wretched plight, played the Good Samaritan and offered what they had—bread, fruit, and milk.

I met my invalid with an ambulance, a stretcher, and Dr. Cresson of the French Hospital, who was kind and talented and full of interest in getting his first war patient. He heard the latter was so gravely wounded as not to be expected to hold out through the trip home. He entered the car to gather up this individual. He found his patient standing in the corridor. To his question of, "Where, can you tell me, is Prince Cantacuzene, shot through the body and dying?" The man addressed answered with a vague smile, "I am that person!" He was helped out of the car at once by the frightened Cresson and the faithful Davidka, and having told me he was "all right and would not go to the hospital in an ambulance," he collapsed on the stretcher we had ready for him and was carried away. His next sentence was that he "would certainly be well in three weeks, and would then return at once to the front." To this, Doctor Cresson and I agreed with enthusiasm, on condition that for those three weeks he would allow himself to be nursed properly and would not fret about the war.

Then he gave himself up to the weakness, which for days he had held at bay by sheer will power. Seven weeks he lay at the hospital, unable to raise an arm. Intense suffering, danger of blood poisoning, pleurisy, high fever, nothing was wanting. All that science would contribute was given him, and the comfort and nursing of the hospital and sisters of St. Joseph were beyond praise. His good constitution did the rest. After about a month, a slight change for the better was noticeable. The doctors promised he would live, though probably as an invalid and with no possibility of ever taking up his career again.

During these weeks everyone was immensely kind. It would be impossible to count those who inquired or came to see me in the first days; and later, as he was able to see them, at the hours allowed, my husband had a congregation of convalescent wounded comrades and other friends about his bed. Men and women had heard of the pain endured, and the feat of Kauschen's capture had made a great stir in our world. The dear maternal Grand Duchess Anastasia brought us letters and telegrams from her husband, in which the old chief[1] in the midst of all his activities found time to congratulate Cantacuzene, ask for his news, and to say that since he had consented to my husband's leaving him and going to the front, he felt personally responsible for his being nearly killed. Now he was hoping to have Michael join the staff, where he could be kept out of further mischief, as soon as the cure was enough advanced to permit his leaving

[1]Grand Duke Nicholas Nikolaevich.

Grand Duchess Marie and Grand Duchess Anastasia visiting wounded soldiers

Red Cross train carrying Russian wounded

Courtesy Hoover Institution Stanford University

home. My husband was delighted with this arrangement. Another great pride and comfort was the Golden Sword of St. George, awarded him unanimously by the committee of that order, with a rare dedication as to his merit and courage in continuing the duty entrusted to him after the enemy had shot him.

He had several unexpected visitors. One day the Empress Mother appeared quietly at the hospital door, having arrived without announcing herself, and asked her way up "to Cantacuzene's room." Her Majesty sat nearly an hour, with her lady-in-waiting, at the bedside, saying that she came as his "commander" (the Empress Mother was honorary commander to the Chevalier Guards) to see how he was and to thank him for his services. She explained that she had chosen Countess Mengden to accompany her that day because she knew the latter to be a childhood friend of her host's.

Two days later my husband awakened from a short sleep, during which I had gone out to drive, and thought himself dreaming. The emperor stood in the door, smiling with his charming, gentle smile, alone! As Michael made a painful movement to rise, His Majesty stepped quickly forward, putting a hand on his shoulder to hold the invalid down; and shaking hands, he found himself a chair and was seated near the bed. For some time the visitor stayed, made the sick man tell him all about his experiences at the front, asking many intelligent questions, and showing the keenest interest in all sorts of details connected with our troops, organization, transportation, and so on. On leaving, he thanked Michael for the services rendered the country and himself, and told him to "get well soon and afterward to take care of himself." With all sorts of good wishes, the emperor departed as quietly as he had come, and the heads of the hospital nearly collapsed over this visit! In compliment to my husband, His Majesty had brought as his attendants on this day two of the ex-Chevalier Guards—General Voeikov,[2] commandant of the palace, and also Count Sheremetev,[3] aide-de-camp. I heard from them that he had let them wait in the corridor during most of his interview with Cantacuzene, calling them in at the end of a long hour for some general talk and the *adieu*.

My husband was deeply touched by the sovereign's attitude and the spontaneous manner in which he had paid him the rare compliment of his visit, for such things were not habitual with Nicholas II. Especially was my husband moved by hearing afterward from several sources that the emperor had said he "never heard from anyone so clear a description of a battle or from any officer such appreciation expressed of the plain soldiers under him and such comprehension of their value and qualities." The sovereign had noticed

[2] Major General Vladimir Nikolaevich Voeikov (1868–1947), commandant of Imperial palaces.
[3] Count Dmitri Sergeevich Sheremetev (b. 1869), a childhood playmate of Nicholas II.

this, as when occasion offered, he himself always tried to show his love for the plain, poorer people.

When after two months my husband could leave the hospital, our new home was ready to receive him, and the children and I had been in it several weeks. It was in fair working order, in spite of the losses to our staff of servants caused by the mobilizations. The interest of seeing the new house had helped Michael through the month when he was still condemned to the life of an invalid at home. Then he went to the grand ducal staff, where the old chief received him with deep affection, established him in a compartment car next to the doctor, and gave minute directions to the latter to have a severe eye on this new patient, taking his orders by letter from Cantacuzene's doctors in St. Petersburg.

Through the winter my husband remained at the staff, gaining strength slowly. He made two delightful trips. One, in the late winter, attached to General Sir Arthur Paget and the British mission, took him to Rumania to meet these guests, then back to the capital, where many official entertainments were given for the envoys; after which he conducted them down the front into Galicia, where the English saw our troops under fire and were forced into great admiration of their bravery and patience, their capacity to stand cold, hunger, and fatigue, and yet fight on. This trait, in both officers and soldiers, seemed to strike every foreigner attached to any part of our front and called forth enthusiastic comment always but especially in the later disasters of the retreat of 1915.[4]

Better still was the second trip, in the spring, when the emperor joined the chief at the staff, and together they made a triumphal tour of inspection through Galicia. Everywhere they were wildly acclaimed.

This journey impressed the sovereign with the importance of the conquests made, and it gained his interest to the cause of winning from Sukhomlinov the delivery of ammunition, needed to go on with our advance. Before the chief undertook his offensive into Galicia, there had been much discussion, as the grand duke, mistrusting Sukhomlinov, had counseled not commencing the campaign until cannon and ammunition should be on hand in great reserves. These were promised by the war minister for the end of the winter, and the emperor had guaranteed his word. The offensive was then made and had proved such a success that not only town after town became Russian, but the enemy's troops were joining our flag in large numbers, sometimes entire units of Czechs or Slavs passing over to our side, with their music, officers, and banners; and our armies looked down already from the summits of the Carpathian Mountains on the Hungarian plains and menaced Budapest. But we could go no farther without the wherewithal to shoot; and while we stood still, the Germans were rushing

[4]The great German offensives of May-September 1915 drove the Russian army out of Poland, Lithuania, and part of the Ukraine.

their picked troops south, to reinforce their fleeing allies. His Majesty was delighted with the new acquisitions offered him. Then he returned to the waiting circle at Tsarskoe and listened to their commendations of Sukhomlinov and to the war minister's own honeyed words of explanation.

All the country and the army joined in feeling this issue to be of paramount importance. Sukhomlinov went to a session of the Duma about the beginning of February and publicly gave his word of honor that by the middle of March the promised supplies would be served out, all along the front—cannon, guns, and ammunition, in fixed quantities, which he named. In the meantime, he and his friends at court (Madame Vyrubova, Voeikov, and their clique) represented that Sukhomlinov had been ill-treated by the liberal elements of the Duma because of his old-fashioned ideas of loyalty; that the grand duke, for personal reasons and from ambition to hold the military power alone, had constantly suspected his intentions and had joined the liberal movement; that the grand duke was trying to get undue popularity with the army. And "who could tell how he might use his power when he arrived at this result?" He had gone with the emperor on a trip into Galicia and had been acclaimed also.

Such a plausible, insidious campaign was inaugurated that the empress's indignation was roused; and she put herself frankly at the head of the Vyrubova-Sukhomlinov party, to save her husband from the results of his too affectionate and trusting nature, and from the liberals, who wanted to undermine his rights; also from the possible rival she saw looming large on the horizon. The emperor demurred, refused to take action, but was duly interested in the case presented to him, and his jealousy of the grand duke was somewhat aroused. Orlov bravely tried to stem the current.

For a time the emperor remained vacillating, but the daily sowing of distrust in his mind was beginning to bear fruit. Sukhomlinov was not pushed; and when, thanks to his failure to make good his promises, the retreat began and the grand duke demanded that the minister of war be dismissed, judged, and shot for his treachery, nothing was done to him, though the whole country was indignant at such weakness. Then the commander-in-chief—who felt that in loyalty to the crown he could not give his resignation now in the face of the disaster that had come to pass—uttered the solemn warning that the protection of such a traitor as Sukhomlinov risked putting the army and the people into a frame of mind that would make for the easy acceptance of any revolutionary propaganda. The soldiers knew they had been ruthlessly sacrificed, and the people felt this also.

This protest of the grand duke's was spread about. It was felt he had been sorely abused, and he was more adored than ever. The Sukhomlinov party, with the empress at its head, came forward for the first time to play a political role; and because of the empress's origin and of the fact that Sukhomlinov was discovered to have protected various spies of Germany, it was called loudly and continuously the "German" or "Occult" Party at court. It comprised Rasputin as its prophet and other picturesque but shady characters.

The grand duke found himself counted the head of an opposing party, quite unconsciously and against his will. In fact, at this time the city of Moscow sent a deputation, asking him to overthrow the emperor and take the throne himself. This I knew of because His Imperial Highness refused even to receive them, and my husband was charged with the delivery of the grand duke's refusal to consider or discuss any such propositions. On the side with the grand duke, for an open pursuit of spies, stood the Duma, and the opinion of honest men of all classes as did also many members of the cabinet.[5] The emperor stood between. He hesitated and was uncertain.

Orlov was the ambassador to and from the staff and handled these delicate missions with consummate tact and discretion. Finally, after several months of retreat, after the loss of nearly all our conquests and the massacre of tens of thousands of Russia's bravest sons and

[5]The author here identifies entirely with the partisans of Grand Duke Nicholas Nikolaevich, who included most of the generals and the Duma's Progressive Bloc, against Sukhomlinov. In the wake of the military reverses of 1915, Sukhomlinov was dismissed, arrested, and accused of corruption and treason. He was eventually convicted by a provisional government court in 1917 and sentenced to life at hard labor, only to be liberated by the Bolsheviks after the October Revolution. The charges appear to have been mainly insubstantial. The rumors and accusations about collusion with Germany in high places, beginning with the empress, have never been substantiated.

with our riches in our harvests, cities, and provinces handed to the enemy or destroyed; with our army fighting with naked fists and sticks, or unloaded cannon and guns that had bayonets only; unbeaten, undaunted, we retreated to Warsaw, losing men and ground as little as was possible; using every natural protection of swamps or woods; tearing down buildings to employ the bricks for ammunition; holding our lines and rallying again. Many were the regiments five times renewed in personnel, patient always, with almost no food or rest for weary bodies; yet never was our line broken through.

And the grand duke in his misery had the one supreme satisfaction of knowing that all the world bowed down to his strength and military ability, and that he had saved his army from a complete rout. Never in all our history was so grand a page as the story of those terrible months of the retreat in 1915; and crowned with the glory of his courage, towering above his men, was the noble figure of the old chief, the leader and inspirer of all, adored by the whole country except those people who owed him most.

A slow and sickening waste of opportunity, and suddenly the emperor made up his mind. Sukhomlinov was summarily dismissed and was replaced by the extremely liberal General Polivanov[6] wounded during the last war and with a record of intelligence,

[6]General Aleksei Andreevich Polivanov (1855–1920). His tenure in the war ministry lasted from 13 June 1915 to 15 March 1916.

honesty, and bravery, something of a politician, and a
friend of the Duma. Not only this; but the Duma,
which had been closed indefinitely in the spring, was
called again for the first of August, and all Russia was
on tiptoes with hope and expectancy.

During the spring's early months, my husband had
been able to ride again, at first slowly on a quiet horse
and with the doctor in attendance; and, as time passed
and he gained daily in strength and energy, it seemed
impossible the dying man of ten months before could
be the normal individual clamoring to depart for the
firing line again. Yet the grand duke kept him at staff
headquarters, to Michael's indignation and dismay.
All of his companions reported when they came to
Petrograd[7] the discussions that Cantacuzene had daily
with his chief on this subject, and the fatherly kindness and severity of the latter. It was characteristic of
the grand duke that he sent me a message at this time.
He said that he was not at all frightened by the invalid's violence and that I was not to be so either. He
had considered that he (the chief) was to blame for the
awful wound at Kauschen, and he was infinitely grateful for Cantacuzene's recovery. He also considered
that my husband had done his entire duty for the
country now and could, without possibility of criticism, remain in the staff where he had his normal work
to do and where he filled his place extremely well. But

[7]St. Petersburg was officially renamed Petrograd at the beginning of the war, the "German" (actually Dutch) original being replaced by its Slavic translation ("grad" = "burg" = "city").

the man wanted to go away so much, and he had such a vocation for soldiering, that undoubtedly he deserved by his record a command of responsibility at the extreme front. Would I tell him what I thought about it; and would I also see the surgeons who had cared for Cantacuzene and ask if, in their opinion, he could begin life under fire again? Malama, his doctor, had written them a diagnosis of the case.

Orlov, who bore the message to me, added, "The chief said he would promise not to speak of all this to your husband, if you would make the same promise about him, as he believes you will both be given a very bad quarter of an hour by Cantacuzene if the tale of our conspiracy comes to light."

I saw the doctors and they seemed to believe from Malama's report that the patient could stand the rough life again. I had had a comparatively tranquil winter, mentally, and that was more than I could have expected. I knew this was due to his kindness; and I could only be grateful now, if he gave my husband the much-desired command on the firing line. So Michael had a leave for two weeks, the first he had taken since his sick leave of hospital days; and I was enchanted to see how he enjoyed it and how his vigor gave him back confidence in the future and renewed his joy in life.

XIII

Life in Petrograd

I CLOSED UP our townhouse with regret, when at the end of May we started for the country. I had promised to spend the summer with our children at my mother-in-law's. I had enjoyed my winter very much in spite of the war that had filled it; or perhaps because of that, for I was very busy. Besides the interest I took in all our personal business, which my husband had turned over to me, I had undertaken work for two hospitals—those founded by the women of the Chevalier Guards Regiment and by the nobility of Petrograd. Also, I had gone into the supplying of our regiment with necessities and comforts at the head of the committee of officers' wives and mothers. These things gave me a great deal of occupation at irregular times. For daily work, I had joined with great enthusiasm the bandage factory arranged by the Empress Mother at the Anichkov Palace.

These gatherings were small, informal, and cozy. The members were comrades and friends, and our Imperial hostess frequently dropped in to see how we were getting on, giving us always an encouraging compliment. Tea, served daily at five, ended our labor, and we were sent home with a delightful feeling of being very useful and greatly appreciated! Our hostess would sometimes put on one of our great, white aprons and would sit an hour, working at the long table, folding or packing. She showed herself very indignant at the changing of the capital's name from "St. Petersburg" to "Petrograd," saying, "As if we had not more important things to do than to be renaming our cities in such times as these!" and remarking that the present government "had better leave Peter the Great's work alone!"

During those months early in the war, the Empress Mother won all hearts and wore her health out, going on long fatiguing rounds of hospitals in Petrograd. She encouraged and helped the wounded, founding charities for families of poor soldiers without resources, and toward spring, working to aid and feed the refugees from Poland, who threatened to swamp the whole country by their sheer numbers. She had both courage and energy, a never-absent gentle smile, and a manner that warmed all hearts to her quiet, dignified person. She understood her role so well that when the revolution came, there was a universal thought for Her Majesty's sorrow; and that she should be among those doomed to trouble in the general upheaval was deeply regretted by high and low alike.

During this first winter of the war, courage was kept up by the news of our fine military record; and though there were no large parties for society, small dinners abounded in hospitable homes.

Toward spring I felt a change in the capital's mentality. Michael's letters from the grand duke's staff, day by day, also reflected the impressions made there by the terrible retreat. In Petrograd the national and individual sorrow was very great, and the cheerfulness that had marked gatherings through the winter departed, once and for all. There was a quantity of gossip about the "Occult" or German forces beginning to influence events, and a general foreboding as to the future created an atmosphere difficult to live in. Parties were forming; and it was a growing complication to steer a straight course among the eddies of suspicion.

June and early July my husband remained at the staff, still fretting to get away to the front, while I remained in the country. About the last of July, he was suddenly named to command the Cuirassiers of His Majesty the Emperor, a magnificent regiment of picked men, admirably well-officered, and already with a remarkably fine record for discipline and bravery during this war. Cantacuzene was enchanted. He left the staff in haste for Petrograd, telegraphing me to join him, as he would be there for the length of time it took his nomination to go through the various departments of the War Ministry. If he went to the front, there were various things to be settled upon.

On 1 August 1915, the Duma met in the great hall of the Tauride Palace.[1] The members were to hear from

[1] The Tauride Palace, a classical structure built in 1783–89, named in honor of Prince Potemkin, conqueror of the Crimea (Tauride), was a central stage of the Russian Revolution: It was the home of the national legislature, the Duma, from 1906 to 1917, and with the February Revolution, housed for a time both the Provisional Committee of the Duma and the Petrograd Soviet. The Sov-

the Imperial ministers the state of affairs in the army and government, and it was hoped they would show a warm feeling of loyalty in upholding the latter. Thus, a renewal of strength might be infused into the cabinet's actions to maintain the army and help it with ammunition and all the other necessities we still lacked so grievously at the front, thanks to Sukhomlinov's reign at the War Ministry.

Always it seems to me an irony of fate that to house the people's first effort at a congress, the building chosen should be the palace of the prince of Tauride (Potemkin), the arrogant and autocratic favorite of our great Catherine! I imagined what he would think were he to see some of the people his walls received!

But this day was not one for contention. On the contrary, Sukhomlinov—accused long since of the responsibility for our disaster—was at last dismissed and replaced by the popular Polivanov, who sat there opposite us. The change had been won from the emperor by the tenacity of the Grand Duke Nicholas and his group, and for the moment the German-Occult party was down.

As the always impressive president of the Duma,

———

viet ("Council") of Workers' and Soldiers' Deputies was constituted in the course of the February 1917 Revolution on the model of a council of representatives from various factories that had met during the Revolution of 1905. The institution was soon replicated all over the country, and an all-Russian congress of soviets was convened in June 1917. The Bolsheviks incorporated this word into the title of their new régime, "The Soviet Union," affirming thereby its democratic, working-class foundations.

Rodzianko[2] went to his place and rapped upon his desk, there was immediate silence. His speech was short and patriotic, much applauded and appreciated. Enthusiasm was the order of the day. Then came the old prime minister. Goremykin was very broken in health, of small stature, bent, and with a poor, low voice, but to this silent crowd his words came clear and full, in promise of better days, of the desire of our sovereign to be strong in defending his land and to stretch out generous hands to all his people, asking for their help, promising them his. When Goremykin finished, what had been only hope before turned to faith in every heart!

Polivanov was pale from the excitement of his maiden effort before such an assembly. Also, he had nothing good to tell us. Warsaw was doomed; nearly all of our conquered provinces were back in the enemy's hands and much of our own territory besides. But, he said, vigorous measures were already taken to obtain the ammunition so dreadfully needed. All must stand together in the country now, behind our heroic army. That day everyone present felt ready to do so.

There had been two vague exclamatory interruptions, from two rather carelessly dressed and rumpled-haired individuals, who lounged in their deputies'

[2]Michael Vladimirovich Rodzianko (1859–1924), the last president (speaker) of the Duma, was a leader of the moderately liberal constitutional-monarchist Octobrist Party; he was a noble land owner from the southern province of Ekaterinoslav.

seats and did not rise while speaking. One, dark, clean-shaven, and of rather a Jewish type was "an eloquent fellow at times, but disorderly and with exaggerated views, named Kerensky,"[3] I was told. The other, "a leader of a party of hot-heads, and always attacking the government was Chkheidze."[4] Both men were to leave their mark on the revolution.

When we left the Duma, it was with a feeling that whatever our troubles and the terrible mistakes that had caused them, they were being corrected now. The crown was well supported by a fine cabinet, and the future could not fail to be good. The days passed, and this impression began to wear away. The retreat all along the line continued. Warsaw surrendered; and many other great cities, rich with our small reserves of ammunition or supplies, were ceded one after another, inevitably, to the enemy. Sometimes the joyful news came into the lines that there "was ammunition behind," but in such small quantities that the soldiers would run several miles back to fetch some part of it before it disappeared among the hungry hands so longingly outstretched to the distributors.

[3]Alexander Fedorovich Kerensky (1881–1970), a lawyer and member of both the Duma and, in 1917, the Petrograd Soviet, was the only socialist (Socialist-Revolutionary) to enter the first provisional government in March 1917, as justice minister. In May he was appointed war minister; in the wake of the July Days crisis, retaining the war portfolio, he became prime minister, which post he held until the Bolshevik revolution in October 1917.
[4]Nicholas Semenovich Chkheidze (1864–1926), a Georgian, was leader of the small Menshevik delegation to the Duma. In 1917, he became the chairman of the Petrograd Soviet.

Prime Minister Alexander Kerensky, with officers

Courtesy Hoover Institution, Stanford University

The Fourth Duma at the Tauride Palace, 1916

Courtesy Hoover Institution, Stanford Universitty

Those who watched us during this period must understand why, as things grew worse, the seeds of revolution, which were being sown by German agents, found fertile ground in the suppressed but general indignation. The fault was not in lack of our patriotism nor lack of funds at this moment. The finances of the country were admitted to have been well managed, and Polivanov was rushing his orders. Everyone said immense energy was being shown; and all realized they were only paying for past faults, which had disorganized the transportation and the administrative departments, making them helpless. The fatal intrigues of the dark powers made them most generally and cordially hated for creating all this. That party still fought the strong, loyal group of ministers who, with liberal views like the commander-in-chief's, demanded and implored that everything should be done to find a satisfactory solution of the terrible problems.

Despair gradually shut down about our hearts. One day at this time, I met with the devoted wife of the commander-in-chief, and I was greatly shocked to notice how worn she looked and hear what she said of the chief and his sufferings over the army's plight. Ammunition ordered by Polivanov could not be brought to the front, he knew, for some weeks yet. He was straining every nerve to obtain better supplies from the helpless powers in Petrograd, and the distress increasing among the troops weighed upon him to the point where the grand duchess feared that her husband would have a complete nervous breakdown.

A few days later I went by appointment to call on Mme. Goremykin. Arriving at her cottage on the islands, I found many ministerial motor cars before her door, and the larger of her two salons was filled with a group of men talking in animated voices, which reached us from time to time through the closed doors. My hostess and I sat in a smaller room. I said laughingly, "You have a large gathering, Madame. It cannot be a cabinet meeting on a Sunday afternoon?"

And she answered: "Dear Princess, it is a sudden meeting my husband called today. He is very anxious over the grave news just received." I inquired if there was something wrong at the front again, but she said, "No, it is much, much worse, and more tragic than that; but I must not divulge it, and perhaps—they hope—it can be yet prevented."

The next morning, news was passed about that the grand duke had been dismissed from his post and banished to the Caucasian front—with the title of viceroy, it is true, but without more than a brief rescript of official thanks. We knew the bearer to him of this news was General Polivanov, who had begged to be spared the painful duty assigned him. We heard also that the whole cabinet had unitedly done all they could to prevent the sending away from the staff headquarters of Russia's great standard-bearer, the lion-hearted commander-in-chief. The Empress Mother had for once thrown aside all her prejudice against mixing in politics and had remonstrated with her son, begging him to spare the grand duke. But all to no avail. The empress's party now appeared openly and aggressively in politics. The grand duke's command was to be taken over by the emperor.

Two days later it was announced that Prince Orlov was dismissed from court and ordered to accompany the Grand Duke Nicholas to the Caucasus. Orlov received no explanation of his sudden disgrace. He had no interview with, and no message from, the sovereign, near whom he had been for so many years. He was quite broken down by the manner of his dismissal.

All sorts of wild stories were current at this time. Of course, everyone said it was Rasputin's influence that had accomplished this disgraceful act, to dislodge two of his enemies; and the most detailed accounts of interviews between the false monk and those he had influenced were whispered about. As a matter of fact, I believe Rasputin took little part in these events, save that dictated to him by Mme. Vyrubova and others, who undoubtedly engineered their business in the name of the man they put nominally at the head of their party. Ever since the grand duke had obtained Sukhomlinov's dismissal, in the conspirators' minds he himself was doomed; and the charges made against him by the empress's protégés were largely because of his extreme popularity everywhere in the country and the adoration of the army for its commander-in-chief. Falsely, it was represented to the emperor that this feeling was being worked up with disloyal intentions by the grand duke himself, and might, by the latter and his followers, be used in a manner to menace the crown.

With reference to this, an official story was told me by one of the ministers, which, knowing the emperor's great sense of duty, seems to me worthy of belief. M. Bark[5] told me, and his loyalty and truthfulness gave it weight. He said that in July 1914, the moment war was declared, the emperor stated to his assembled council of ministers that he had always reproached himself for not going to the front during the Japanese war, sharing the hardships of the troops and the responsibilities of the commanders and that in this war he would not repeat the same mistake. The cabinet united to dissuade him from carrying out his wish, as they feared the danger to his person, also the danger of leaving the government to the regent's care. To them it seemed better to have the responsibility for possible disaster carried by someone who might be replaced on occasion, and thus keep the Imperial credit intact. Their arguments had prevailed with the emperor, and after reflection he had named the grand duke to the supreme command. M. Bark felt that possibly the retreat of the spring and summer of 1915 had brought back this old thought and that it was a desire to make his army feel he stood with them, which in part influenced His Majesty to change the grand duke to the Caucasian front and take command himself at the height of the drama.

[5]Peter Lvorich Bark (1869–1937), minister of finance, 1914–1917.

XIV

The "Occult" Party

AFTER THE EMPEROR took personal command of the army, he made only flying trips to Tsarskoe, and his ministers wasted much time going back and forth to the staff. The emperor often went on tours of inspection to the front and was several times under fire.

The empress went occasionally to the staff, always accompanied by Mme. Vyrubova. The heir to the throne, a fragile boy, lived there with his father. Most people who knew what was happening deeply regretted an arrangement that took the sovereign away from his government. There was continuous trouble politically; the slight improvement in the fortunes of the armies was scarcely a consolation.

The prime minister, though loyal and dignified, was of another generation, and he thought our empire could be strong only on the old lines of a pure autocracy. The mere existence of the Duma disturbed him vastly. There was a prolonged struggle between the two groups in the cabinet, and relations were very strained among its members. Finally, the Duma was closed by Imperial edict. This measure caused violent irritation everywhere and was again attributed to Occult influences. At this time the men who composed the ministry were of unimpeachable honesty of purpose and devotion to the crown, and the basis of their difficulty was only as to which method would obtain the most quickly the results desired—winning of the war and strengthening the emperor's hold upon his people.

Goremykin was for a strong rule, and he felt all concessions to a liberal policy would show weakness; also, that one concession must lead to another. The school of thought preaching that the emperor must join with the parliament, keeping the old promises made ten years before, and that he would only gain force by such actions was represented by a most able group of men: Polivanov, in the war ministry; Sazonov, in foreign affairs; Bark, in finances, while Krivoshein, who was in agriculture, was their head. Optimists regarded him as the prime minister of the future, if his ideas prevailed in the present. But Goremykin had an influence to back him, which was of more weight than all others in swaying the emperor's judgment. The empress was his supporter; and Krivoshein's group, after a short struggle, was entirely defeated. Krivoshein immediately resigned; and, though the emperor asked him to reconsider this step, after ten days' wait he resigned again, and definitely. The others of his persuasion remained in the cabinet, feeling it to be a patriotic duty on account of the war; but they well knew their road from then on would be a difficult one.

This was the second marked triumph of the reactionary party, and the Occult influences were indeed at work. All the liberals prepared for the struggle to come, feeling that they must carry it on with a hidden enemy undermining their reputations and putting their best efforts in a light that would appear disadvantageous. Krivoshein was somewhat criticized for deserting his party in such a moment, while on the contrary, his admirers thought his act the only course open to him. He went at once to the front, as head of one of the army Red Cross organizations, where he did excellent work. In the division of the cabinet that caused his resignation, the government took the last turn in the road that led to disaster.

I spent the early autumn in the country, returning to Petrograd for November and December to see to Christmas things, which must be prepared and forwarded by our women's regimental committee, for the Cuirassiers, who were then on the Polish front. They had had a most active autumn, since the cavalry had been doing heavy work protecting our retreat, which continued, though more slowly and with less difficulty since the army was receiving some provisions. My husband joined me for a few days at the capital where he came on military business, and he asked them for an audience with His Majesty, who chanced to be at Tsarskoe for a time. It was the first time he had seen the sovereign since taking over the command of His Majesty's Own Cuirassiers, and as he had been for so long aide-de-camp to the old chief and was known to be devoted to the latter and to have received his present command from him, Michael felt the interview with the new commander-in-chief might prove a somewhat trying experience.

Far from this being the case, the sovereign received him with quite especial kindness, going back to their talk at the hospital more than a year before and telling my husband how pleased he was to know "his" Cuirassiers were in such excellent hands. Then His Majesty asked various details as to the work the regiment was doing. He granted immediately the requests Cantacuzene made for things required to help the regimental efficiency and gave an order, among others, that two motors be delivered to the regiment as a gift from himself, one for trucking and one for the commander's use. After a lengthy conversation, when my husband saluted, the emperor shook hands with him and, with good wishes for his and the regiment's luck, said good-bye most graciously. As my husband reached the door and opened it, His Majesty suddenly called him back. Cantacuzene went and stood in front of him awaiting orders. "Don't you think you are very young to be in command of such an important unit as my Cuirassiers?" he asked. My husband answered, "I don't know, Your Majesty. It is for you to judge," thinking it possible there was a change coming to him. He was only a colonel, yet he occupied the place of a brigadier-general. "I think you are much too young and of rank too low," continued the emperor. "We must mend matters at once, so I name you major-general and congratulate you upon belonging to my suite!" Cantacuzene was quite stunned by the two honors coming at once, and just when he thought he might be less favored than others because of his past career. But the sovereign perhaps wished, on the contrary, to draw about himself some of the old grand duke's followers; or perhaps he remembered the story of Kauschen's capture, and of Michael's grave wound, and gave him credit for his record there and the hard fighting he had been doing since in the last five months.

When our emperor chose to exert it, he had immense charm of eyes and voice and smile; and early in this time of his command at the staff, the stories of his interest, kindness, and intelligent understanding in the handling of the people who came into contact with him were very sympathetic. They created a certain personal popularity, which lasted until he fell entirely under the influence of the Occult group, after which he became so inert, distracted, and vague, that color seemed to be given, by his behavior and changed looks, to the rumor that he was being drugged by Mme. Vyrubova's agents near him.

Goremykin finally left because it became a necessity to recall the Duma he had dissolved, and he found his cabinet grown entirely unmanageable. In February the Duma was reopened, and the emperor, inspired with a sudden wish to make a demonstration toward his people's representatives, quite unexpectedly appeared at its inauguration. He came from the staff, and for the only time, he showed himself in the house of parliament, where he was vastly acclaimed.

Stürmer, who was an unknown quantity, had just

been named prime minister and was given the portfolio of the interior as well. It was hoped at first this meant a desire on the part of His Majesty to meet the people half-way, and it was said Stürmer was of moderate views. But soon it transpired, he was the nominee of the empress, and he became immediately a weak instrument in the hands of the Occults.

From our quiet hearth on the country estates, where I spent the late months of the winter, I was only in touch with events by newspapers and such correspondents as I had in the capital. Their letters were full of frank anxiety, and I knew they felt things were not going well. In March I returned to town to find the tension vastly augmented.

These were the conditions I found in Petrograd; and when in May, Viviani and Thomas[1] came on a visit of negotiations from our French allies and to gather impressions, they saw how the country and the government were laboring against great odds, to carry on the war. Much entertaining occurred around these two distinguished Frenchmen, and I felt greatly interested to meet them at a few of the political dinners. After their departure Kitchener[2] was to arrive; but to England's loss and ours, that great man was drowned

[1] Albert Thomas (1878–1932), leader of the socialist faction in parliament, was French minister of armaments from December 1915 to September 1917.

[2] Horatio Herbert Kitchener (1850–1916); Lord Kitchener was British war minister from 1914 to his death on 5 June 1916 by drowning when the Cruiser *Hampshire* hit a mine off the Orckney Islands.

on the trip over, together with O'Beirne,[3] the eminent
diplomat, who was Russia's true friend after a residence among us of seventeen years. He spoke our language and knew the country well; and he was deeply
regretted by all our well-intentioned ministers, as well
as by his many personal friends.

Then we, in turn, sent abroad the delegation from
our parliaments. Protopopov[4] was member of this,
and it was the report he made to the emperor, on returning from his voyage, that was the beginning of his
meteor-like career. Pokrovsky[5] also made his trip to
the economic conference in Paris and returned with
his reputation greatly added to, while Bark's able negotiations during his hurried tour of London and
Paris made him stronger than ever on his return.

During the absence from Russia of Pokrovsky and
Bark, Sazonov suddenly one morning read in the
newspaper a "rescript" of thanks and a dismissal,
putting him out of the cabinet! Stürmer replaced him,
to everyone's amazement, as he had no experience for
such a post. When this, then, was followed by the
nomination of Protopopov to the post of ministry of

[3]Hugh James O'Beirne (1866–1916), career diplomat, was
councillor to the British Embassy. As early as 1892, he had been an
attaché in St. Petersburg.

[4]Alexander Dmitrievich Protopopov (1866–1918; executed by
the Bolsheviks), Octobrist deputy and vice chairman of the Duma,
was appointed acting interior minister in September 1916 (minister in December), in defiance of party discipline.

[5]Nicholas Nikolaevich Pokrovsky (1865–1930) was state con-
troller in November 1916, when he was appointed foreign minister (last foreign minister of the tsarist government).

the interior, there was indeed a loud and continuous cry of indignation.

During the summer and early autumn, Raev's[6] nomination to the Holy Synod and Rein's[7] to that of the ministry of public health were declarations by the Rasputinites of their intention to reduce opposition to them to a minimum in the cabinet meetings. The minister of war, Polivanov, was then soon dismissed and Beliaev,[8] who owed his career to Sukhomlinov's protection, was put in his place. These were the men of the cabinet who were to face the Duma at its opening on the first of November.

[6]Nicholas Pavlovich Raev (b. 1856), last "ober-prokuror of the Holy Synod" (government minister in charge of Church affairs), appointed 30 August, supporter of Protopopov.

[7]George Ermolaevich Rein (b. 1854), medical professor and last minister of health under the old régime.

[8]General Michael Alekseevich Beliaev (1863–1918; executed by the Bolsheviks), last Imperial war minister, appointed 16 January 1917.

XV

The Murder of Rasputin

ON 14 NOVEMBER 1916, the Duma opened. Up to the last moment a feeling of uncertainty as to whether it really would open at all reigned in Petrograd. It was said the Stürmer-Protopopov group was frightened at the idea of facing the nation's deputies and that they hoped to prevent parliament's meeting. I heard also that the liberal-minded members of the government—as also society, the provinces, and the army—were all hoping the Duma's criticism would finally open the sovereign's eyes to public opinion and persuade him to overthrow the bad influences at work about him, once and for all.

I was going with, if possible, more interest than to that other Duma-opening, a year and four months before. But of how different a quality it was! My friends in the ministry were looking so preoccupied, and such hideous rumors were afloat, of dishonesty, both political and financial, of treachery and disloyalty, that there seemed little hope left of saving our government as it was. The night before the inauguration, it was suddenly officially announced that the prime minister and cabinet would not make the usual series of speeches, but that after Rodzianko's address they would leave the lower house and go on to the opening

of the Council of the Empire (or upper house). The
two ceremonies, which usually occurred at several
hours' interval, were fixed this time for three o'clock at
the Duma and four o'clock at the Council; and there
is nearly a half hour's drive between the Tauride and
the Marie palaces! To make matters worse, the ambassadors were invited to one and to the other; and by
special message from the prime minister, they were
asked not to miss the later function. Everyone realized
that Stürmer and company knew what they deserved,
and would get, and that they lacked the necessary
courage to face the attacks of the deputies. So they
took refuge in escape from answering for the acts they
had on their consciences. I ended by being so worried
as to what might happen that I decided not to go at all.

The next day it was about six o'clock before anyone
appeared at my tea table. Then came a diplomat or
two, who had hardly realized the importance of what
they had seen and heard at the Duma. Later, one of
our cabinet ministers came in, and though I had never
known him to show nervousness, I saw that for once
his calm smile cost an effort. He was very silent but admitted he thought the afternoon's performance "had
not left a good impression of the government." I was
not surprised to learn later that as Stürmer rose to go,
he had been hissed and had retired from the hall with
cries of "Down!" and "Away!" and "Traitor!" following him. There had been a most violent and open attack on Stürmer as head of the Imperial government
by the most able deputy of the "kadet" party—right—

Miliukov,[1] with humiliating accusations as to correspondence with Germany and workings for a separate peace; and extracts had been cited from a German newspaper of repute, in which an editorial spoke openly of the Russian prime minister as "our man," and of the *"Deutschgemeinte Kaiserin"* (German-intentioned empress), who had put Stürmer in power to help her Fatherland.

That evening each person expressed it differently, but all put into words the one opinion, that after this day's proceedings there were only two courses open to the emperor: Either he must declare the Duma closed, or he must have the accusations investigated and, if found true, shut his wife up in a convent as a criminal or in some villa a safe distance as insane; throw the impostors she protected into prison; clean up the administration with the help of parliament; and reorganize the country to prosecute the war with vigor.

I have never understood how it could be, but really nothing happened at all on the lines of these prophecies. I do not know whether the emperor was ever given a true account. Things were so often kept from his knowledge that he may have heard only what the people surrounding him wished. The Duma remained open, and Stürmer remained a week or so as prime minister, with all the conspirators still in their places.

[1]Paul Nikolaevich Miliukov (1859–1943), historian, founder, and leader of Russia's principal liberal party, the Constitutional Democrats (Kadets), and foreign minister of the first provisional government.

The empress and Mme. Vyrubova directed their creatures more openly than ever, and the emperor remained at the staff, so wavering and inert that the most terrible rumors were put into circulation about his incapacity for action. We heard that the Persian doctor, whom Mme. Vyrubova protected, was drugging His Majesty by degrees into imbecility, with the empress's consent, so finally she would be able to announce his inability to reign, put their son on the throne, and be herself the regent; also that she knew of, and encouraged, the emperor's taste for drink; and that Voeikov had orders to ply him with wine so Her Majesty could manage affairs comfortably, at least until a separate peace could be arranged! A thousand tales such as these floated about, and the reticence of loyal members of the court, and of the few ministers still remaining who were devoted, was considered to be a tacit confirmation.

The Imperial family felt greatly disturbed; and the trips various ministers and grand dukes made to the staff, in hope of awakening the sovereign to a full realization of the situation, were most numerous. Nicholas Mikhailovich,[2] Kyril Vladimirovich,[3] and even the Empress Mother; the ministers Trepov, Bark, and,

[2]Grand Duke Nicholas Mikhailovich (1859–1919), the uncle once removed of Nicholas II (his father was the brother of Alexander II, Nicholas's grandfather). After completion of his military career in 1903, he was active as historian and scholar, president of the Imperial Geographic Society, etc.

[3]The Grand Duke Kyril Vladimirovich (1876–1938) was Nicholas II's first cousin. He supported the establishment of the

very noisily, Ignatiev, went, explained, begged, and prophesied. Each one was kindly received, graciously listened to; and each came home believing he had succeeded and that the tangled political knot would be at once straightened out. And then time passed again, and everything remained the same.

I heard much of these journeyings from relatives of the persons who went in several cases, and at first-hand from the rest. At a luncheon at his mother's, I sat next to the Grand Duke Kyril on 19 November, and he told me he had arrived in the capital from the staff but an hour before. On my saying I feared he had brought sad impressions, he replied in a cheerful tone, "No, thank God! Everything will be mended shortly."

The Grand Duke Nicholas Mikhailovich, who had always been the "revolutionist" of the Imperial family, wrote to the Empress Mother and persuaded her to use her influence to save the crown while there was time. He also saw and discussed the situation with some of the ministers and liberals in the Duma, encouraging them to do what they could. Stürmer was dismissed finally, and we almost counted on some of the promises made coming true; but as the news of this and of Trepov's nomination to replace him reached the capital, the empress ordered out her private train and went to the staff immediately, accompanied, of course, by Mme. Vyrubova.

___

provisional government in March 1917. In 1924, he proclaimed himself emperor of Russia.

We heard the discussions there were long and very dramatic. On her return Her Majesty told the Grand Duchess Victoria that she had been but a half-hour too late to save "poor Stürmer from dismissal, as the emperor had already signed the rescript putting him out and Trepov in his place; but I luckily stopped all the other prepared changes and upset the plans of busy-bodies, who from envy and lack of occupation, want to tear to pieces all the fabric of traditional autocracy in Russia and then throw the power of the throne to a lot of howling disloyal liberals."

The grand duchess protested, saying it was not at present a desire for liberalism but, on the contrary, anxiety for the welfare of Their Majesties and the country which moved people, and that all of society and the nobility felt greatly disturbed. She, Victoria, knew it from many friends, whom she could trust to be truthful. Whereupon Her Majesty displayed anger and said, "If one listened to a lot of silly women who gossip about in society, one necessarily heard nonsense" and that she was better informed by her friends.

Soon all the population of Petrograd grew nervous. Officers told us a tremendous revolutionary propaganda was secretly being made among recruits and reservists who were coming into the barracks, and they, the officers, were not able to discover who the agents were or to prevent their action.

I had asked for an audience with the empress before leaving for the Crimea and was surprised to be "commanded" to go to her at five on a certain day, with my husband. Old Mme. Narishkin had just told me Her Majesty was not receiving except on business, and my request had been made purely from a desire to show loyalty.

I found that we were to go in together—my husband and I—to the Imperial sitting room at Tsarskoe; and there was but one lady-in-waiting, who received us in a short walking costume and conducted us immediately to Her Majesty's door without the usual ceremony. Her Majesty, as we entered, was standing, dressed in her costume of a Sister of Mercy: all black, with white collar, cuffs, and headkerchief. She had grown very thin in the six months since I last saw her; and her loss of flesh, together with the simplicity of her costume, augmented her beauty vastly. She looked worn and sad though, and very severe, except when she smiled; then she was briefly illuminated. She was gracious and cordial, altogether charming, and spoke with energy of the sufferings of all the allied countries—Belgium, France, and Serbia, and our own, especially in its Polish provinces; and she spoke also of the absolute necessity of our going on to the end and winning the war.

She kept us sitting with her for about an hour and embraced me upon my arrival and departure, though she knew me for no friend of Mme. Vyrubova's. I imagined Her Majesty wished us to feel she was not for peace, or for Germany. She spoke with touching care of the poor people all over Russia and of how generously they were giving toward the war charities, and she made no criticism of anyone but was gentle in word and gesture. While with her, I was convinced that none of the accusations of evil intention, or of pro-German work on her part, were in the least truthful. In spite of her fine brain and nature, and strong will, she had, through her illness, fallen completely a prey to the conspirators about her, who by degrees had separated her from all normal and truthful influences. They persuaded her she was the only one who could save Russia and that the way they suggested was the only manner in which this could be done. They also succeeded in explaining away or hiding their own guilt and in blackening to her eyes those who were not of their party. She never saw anyone at all who was not of this group. Her nervous pains and illness; the bad health of the young grand duke, her son; her difficulties early in her married life in understanding Russian society and our point of view; her mysticism and that of the emperor had all been used by Mme. Vyrubova to poison her mind completely against the people who should have been about her. This designing woman had played on Her Majesty's best qualities and on her pride, making her feel abandoned except by the conspirators. They dared now to do any harm, and they ruined their patroness in the avidity for importance and power. Though it is impossible to uphold the policy the empress protected or to express sufficient contempt for the people with whom she surrounded herself, I am sure her intentions and ambitions remained noble. She seemed to me always as tragic and sorrowful a figure as those in the background were criminal.

On the emperor's fête day, 19 December—Saint Nicholas Day—the sovereign came home to Tsarskoe. It was hoped and expected His Majesty would on this occasion keep all his various and positive promises and remodel the government on decent lines.

Otherwise, it was known Trepov would leave the cabinet, with several colleagues; probably all those whose honesty, loyalty, and patriotism were being outraged and who consequently would not consent to stay in bad company any longer. The Grand Duchess Elizabeth, elder sister of the empress and widow of Grand Duke Serge (who had been assassinated while governor general of Moscow in the 1905 revolution), arrived from Moscow on the morning of 18 December, to spend two or three days at Tsarkoe. While her people were unpacking the baggage of the grand duchess that afternoon, they were amazed suddenly to receive orders to cease this and repack with all haste, as their mistress was returning to Moscow that same night. A stormy interview had occurred, during which she (the grand duchess) had thrown herself on her knees to the empress, defending the intentions and devotion of Mme. Vyrubova and Rasputin, also their political program, which now Her Majesty had made her own. Finally, she ordered the grand duchess to leave the palace, not to return under any circumstances, and the latter was going.

The nineteenth then passed. As usual, nothing occurred, and everyone gave up all hope now of improvement. It was seen that no matter what promises the sovereign might make, they could not be carried out. The Duma had been closed, with an announcement—in which no one believed—that it would be opened again in January.

When I arrived in the Crimea, I found at first the quiet country life delightful by comparison with the capital's mental atmosphere. But soon I discovered that all letters from the north were severely censored; and the papers were allowed to contain little concerning politics.

The emperor's uncle, Paul Aleksandrovich, and his brother Michael both went back to Petrograd from the Crimea soon after our arrival there, to be nearer the center of interest; and the poor Grand Duchess Xenia, the emperor's own sister, planned a trip to her city home for the holidays.

I saw much of her these dark weeks, and she roused all my sympathy by the weight of care she bravely carried and by her anxiety for the safety of her brother and family. She fully realized the dangers ahead, yet could do nothing to save those she loved. In fact, it was her son-in-law, young Prince Yusupov, who opened the dramatic action of the revolution by killing Rasputin with his own hand at a supper party given for that purpose in his Petrograd palace.[4] This

[4]See chapter X, note 4. Prince Felix Feliksovich Yusupov, Count Sumarokov-Elston (1887–1967), married to a princess of

hideous business which was planned and carried out in cold blood, made a sensation impossible to describe all over the country. Everyone breathed with relief at Rasputin's disappearance. Some openly hoped it would lead to a series of murders, including Mme. Vyrubova's, Protopopov's, and even their august protectress's, as these crimes would finally rid the nation of tyranny, they said, and save us from a bloody revolution, otherwise inevitable.

Some few optimists hoped that once their "prophet" was gone, the clan of evil-doers might fall to pieces and the empress's eyes be opened at last to their sins. But just the opposite happened. Rasputin had never been the brains of his party, only a mask behind which the real conspirators hid themselves, and his sudden death turned him into a martyr, as well as a saint, in Her Majesty's eyes. The ex-"followers" made much of his remains, which were brought with great honor to lie in the chapel of the Tsarskoe Palace, where night and day the women of his group watched and prayed by them. Then he was buried in the Imperial park, and a daily visit was paid the spot by the empress.

Meanwhile, Protopopov announced (with great presence of mind) that Rasputin's spirit had descended on himself; and he constantly and suddenly

---

the Imperial line, heir to one of the greatest Russian fortunes, recently graduated from Oxford, was studying for an officer's commission in the Russian army when he carried out the plot to murder Rasputin in December 1916.

exclaimed, while talking to Her Majesty, that he saw Rasputin leading her, that he saw the Christ standing behind her, holding out his arms in blessing because she had befriended, protected, and honored the saintly apostle Rasputin had been! These tales were current gossip and seemed to be founded on truth, as I received them from some of the palace ladies, afterward upheld by a quite different source of information—one of Protopopov's colleagues. The Grand Duke Paul's son—the Grand Duke Dmitri—and the Grand Duke Nicholas Mikhailovich were implicated in the Yusupov plot, the latter as an adviser and abettor, the former as having actually lent a hand in the performance of killing Rasputin and of getting rid of his body. Both were banished from the capital immediately, Nicholas to his estates in the provinces, and Dmitri to the Persian front, without any of his own household to accompany him.

Both departed at once, and the Grand Duke Nicholas sent his resignation to the emperor, left His Majesty's suite, and removed his aiguillettes and uniform once and for all. This very able and brilliant man did not reappear in the life of Petrograd until just two months later, when his sentence expired, on the eve of the revolution. During that dangerous period, he held out a helping hand to many a poor Imperialist, saving lives, both in and out of the government, by his influence with the revolutionists.

XVI

The Revolution

I RETURNED to Petrograd soon after the New Year, remaining there four weeks on business. I was perfectly shocked at the changes I found. The cost of living was much higher. No one had any confidence in the future of the government. General depression was extreme and very contagious, since one heard the most sober and reliable people stating facts that did not seem believable but were nevertheless quite true. The silence and the anxious faces of members of our court and government, who were the most loyal, were perhaps those marks of coming downfall that struck me most.

We believed the Grand Duke Nicholas's prophecy was coming true and that our soldiers and people could not longer be forced to defend a government of which so much evil was commonly known. Long lines of poor stood waiting hours to receive insufficient rations of bread and other necessities; the weather was exceptionally cold—twenty or thirty degrees below zero—and fuel was scarce; everyone was suffering, and there were continuous strikes and great discontent.

Society's tongue was let loose, with all barriers broken down. Mme. Vyrubova had completely dropped her mask of humility, except in the presence of the sovereigns; and she gave, I heard, official audience to all sorts of shady people. She spoke openly of how she had done or had decided this and the other measure; and she used the term of speech, "*We* shall act about this as *we* see fit," as if she were at the head of affairs.

The days of the international conference at Petrograd[1] came and passed; the foreign representatives returned to their homes with many delicate questions settled to the satisfaction of all parties. It seems amazing to me that men of such exceptional ability, as were several of those who were members of this mission, should have remained blind to our interior situation, as their reports proved them to have been.

It got about that a palace revolution was being planned, where assassination would clear the way for a new era. Everything else had been tried to no avail, and this was the only remaining remedy.

"They seem there at Tsarskoe to be completely demented," said a most quiet and loyal member of the cabinet one day with a sigh. "And they don't see they are going rapidly to their destruction. On the contrary, they grow dizzy and hurry, pulling, dragging, and pushing one another along."

And really one had the sensation of insanity in looking at the situation. When I was leaving for the

[1] The allied conference to discuss the provision of Russia with war materiel and the future course of the war met in Petrograd from 1 to 20 February 1917. It was attended by delegations from Britain, France, Italy, and Russia.

Crimea again, at the beginning of February, I said to M. Bark, "I leave you still in power. When I return in April, shall I find you so?" He looked at me with an expression of great sadness, grown habitual now to his previously cheerful face, and replied, "I should be glad to leave but cannot do so now. Something ought to be done, either one thing or the other, if the government is to survive, whether in autocratic or in liberal form. But nothing is being done, and everything is being decided backward and forward. I fear you will soon hear bad news of us. I hope and pray not, but I feel it is very probable. You have many friends whom you will not see again when you return; and I am glad you are leaving for a quieter place, and a safer one." His foreboding was so dreary, and he seemed so sincere in the fear and regret he expressed, that it rang in my ears, far on the road to the sunny southern land.

Again I found there the poor Grand Duchess Xenia, more than ever alarmed. I lunched with her immediately upon my arrival, and she made me give her all the details I had gleaned from every source, asking with emotion what I had heard of this one, or how that one felt and stood. A few days later, she, being unable longer to resist her desire, went north, remaining there through the week of the revolution.

My husband joined me for ten days in the Crimea, coming from the front, while his regiment was put by in a small town back of the firing line to rest, recuperate, and feed their horses. He reported conditions in the army were very bad—fodder for the mounts and food for the men growing scarce, clothes difficult to obtain, even for the guard regiments, which were much better served than the poor men of the line. He said also the feeling was anxious there. Wild reports from the capital were coming out, making people nervous—both officers and men. Soon he departed for Petrograd, where he was to meet his mother on some business for the eleventh and twelfth; and then he was to return to his command, in time to go under fire again, on 18 March.

By telegram he arranged to stop at the staff on 14 March for an audience with the emperor.

I had two letters from my husband sent back to me as he went northward to Petrograd and then a dispatch stating his safe arrival. After that no news until Tuesday, 13 March, when a telegram came, saying "all the family are well" and that my mother-in-law had moved to her daughter's, Countess Niroth's, home. This seemed eccentric, as the princess had had an apartment of her own at the Astoria during the whole winter. This was followed by daily wires from my husband, saying "All are well," and adding in one, that my boy "had moved to the Niroths' also," while Michael himself was detained in the capital!

By Saturday morning I was thoroughly disquieted. The northern papers had not arrived for several days past, and no news came save the reassuring telegrams as to the health of all the family and recording the perplexing moving of the princess and my boy from their normal habitations to my sister-in-law's. I became so puzzled that my nerves got the best of me, and I decided to make a day's expedition into Yalta, stopping on the way at the Grand Duke Nicholas's place, Chaire, to see its beautiful gardens and talk with His Imperial Highness's attendant, a gossipy old acquaintance of mine.

We started early, and the drive through the beautiful morning somewhat calmed us. When we reached Chaire, I was in better spirits; but the old attendant met me with an air, as if he were about to weep, and said, "Has Your Highness heard the terrible news?" I felt on the verge of fainting at this, and with visions of crimes and murder, I asked impatiently what had occurred. He said he knew nothing, save that the telephone girl at Yalta told him, "The emperor had abdicated, with the tsarevich. Michael Aleksandrovich was declared emperor."[2]

"And our grand duke?" I asked.

"Alas, I know nothing, Your Highness, but they tell me he is going to the staff again, to command; but our emperor is gone, and I cannot understand! Perhaps it is worse than that! They know so little at Yalta."

My interest in the gardens faded, and we at once regained our carriage and rapidly started for our goal. As

[2]Grand Duke Michael Aleksandrovich (1878–1918) was Nicholas II's younger brother. On 15 March, Nicholas II had indeed abdicated for himself and his son Alexis in favor of Michael, but the next day, when representatives of the nascent provisional government told him they could not guarantee the safety of his person, Michael refused the throne, declaring he would accept it only from the Constituent Assembly.

we drove into the town of Yalta, people were buying sheets of telegraph bulletins and then standing transfixed in the middle of the street reading them, so astounded they seemed of stone, and we nearly ran over several who did not hear our driver's shouts to clear the way. Of course, we stopped our trap; bought telegrams, too; and read the emperor's last sad proclamation, from Pskov, his abdication in favor of his brother—of his own rights to reign and those of his son. It was a beautifully worded document, containing no protest and no complaint, saying the act was for the good of the country, and begging all officials, both civil and military, to remain at their posts and serve their country, defending it from the foe. Deep tragedy in the last words of *adieu* and blessing. I wondered if he felt relief to lay down his burden at last and to rest after so long and dreary a reign. "Where do you suppose the empress was?" said my companion, one of my sisters-in-law, who was excited almost to hysterics.

There followed in the telegrams an order to the Grand Duke Nicholas to go at once to the staff, and a telegram saying he had already left Tiflis; and there was evidence of a "provisional committee" in some orders sent from Petrograd to the local Crimean authorities, but without explanations. The emperor's abdication was dated 15 March, and it being neither from the capital nor from the staff seemed incomprehensible. Why had the sovereign gone to Pskov, unless he had fled for protection to General Ruszky's headquarters? What was occurring in the capital and at

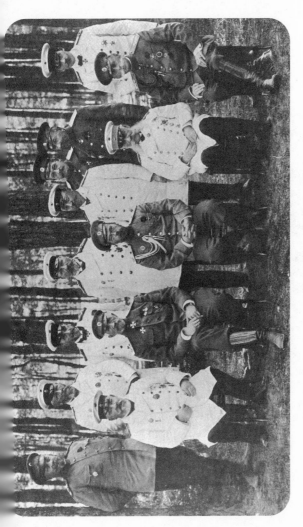

The Russian general staff, 1915; Nicholas II is in the front row (middle) with Grand Duke Nicholas Nikolaevich on his right

Courtesy Hoover Institution, Stanford University

229

The Soviets meeting in the Tauride Palace, after the revolution

Courtesy Hoover Institution, Stanford University

Tsarskoe? Something dramatic, or my husband would not have wired me so regularly they were all well. No one knew anything in Yalta, so perforce we awaited news with what patience we could.

Letters from my husband, my mother-in-law, the Niroths, and my boy, and letters and telegrams from a number of friends who had thought of reassuring me, soon gave me first-hand and rapid information, which was supplemented later by what I was told by word of mouth. The letters were all forwarded me by a messenger, so that after being deprived of knowledge, I was suddenly supplied with a feast of information, and many details from actors or eye-witnesses of the occurrences in the north. In spite of my pity for some and my solicitude for others, I was carried over this terrible period by my intense interest in the immensity of the historical facts. They lifted me quite above the actualities and dangers of the moment, in the wonder of what the future would bring Russia. As for our own personal fortunes, they seemed to be threatened.

The emperor had come from his staff when parliament opened, but then His Majesty did not visit the Tauride Palace. He only was within reach of his ministers, in case of necessity.

All went quietly; in fact, people became nervous over the very calm, after so many threats had been uttered. They felt it was ominous. After some days had passed, during which speeches from the discontented deputies filled the Duma's sessions, the emperor decided on his return to the staff at Mogilev. Then before departing, he called his cabinet together. It met, with His Majesty presiding, on the afternoon of Thursday, 8 March, as it turned out, for the last time in the history of the autocracy.

His ministers in concert decided on a desperate effort. They talked frankly to the sovereign, explaining with a heat of eloquence they had never reached before, the dreadful dangers hanging over Russia. They spared no argument that might strengthen the cause they advocated.

So long they spoke, and so fervently, that before the emperor left the council chamber, he had promised them he would sign two edicts before his departure for the staff: one granting the responsible ministry the Duma had been demanding and the other—to be offered as a free gift from him, if the first seemed not enough to quell the storm—was to be an edict bestowing a constitution upon Russia! This last was an almost unhoped-for concession.

The orders were given for those two edicts to be written out in due form and then brought that same evening to Tsarskoe for signing, and His Majesty bade his ministers good-bye, leaving them with the sensation that at the eleventh hour the ills of our much-abused country were to be healed, that the Duma would soon be carrying with themselves the terrible weight of the responsibility, which up to now had been only upon their shoulders. They could trust to fate that the first act of the new era would be Protopopov's departure from their midst.

When His Majesty returned to the palace, he naturally told of the great decision taken and that he was giving way in this to the ideas of his cabinet and the Duma, upheld by his own convictions. A dramatic discussion ensued and lasted all evening. Protopopov, who had come with the papers to sign, being of their party, reinforced the empress in her violent denunciations of the folly of men who offered such counsel to their master.

If there were a revolutionary movement, it would be local to the capital, and the minister of the interior promised to handle it alone, with his own police, reinforced only by the city's garrison. His Majesty could go to the staff with a quiet mind and fear nothing, leaving the situation here to his devoted servant. At the most, General Ivanov[3] could be sent to the capital with a few picked men to uphold the government's courage at the critical moment.

The empress could give any necessary orders, and all would go well. Then Her Majesty used all her talents to strengthen the policy advocated by her protégé; and before morning, the two promised edicts (prepared that afternoon) had been destroyed and were replaced by a signed blank, put unconditionally into Protopopov's hands. Also, permission was given

[3]General Nicholas Iudovich Ivanov (1851–1919) had been sent from the front to Petrograd on 12 March with a train containing 800 special troops and dictatorial powers to put down the revolution, but the expedition never reached the capital due to dissension in the troops and, in short order, the countermanding of the order from headquarters.

him to tell his colleagues at his own time of their sovereign's change of mind. Then His Majesty departed for the staff, as he had planned, on the following morning, 9 March.

That day, Friday, there were strikes and bread riots in some of the outer suburbs of Petrograd. The former had been occurring for some time; but now, with the dragging of the winter and the increasingly intense cold, the workmen were growing ugly. The crowds of poor who stood for hours in the street, waiting their turns to buy insufficient bread, were ready to show violence at the slightest opportunity.

Saturday there was more trouble, and it grew nearer to the center of the town and included some encounters with the police and shooting. The ministry believed all would soon be well, and its members were secure in the Imperial promise—supposing the edicts that were to mend matters would be published that evening or the next morning.

Sunday, the eleventh, appeared in the papers an Imperial proclamation over the emperor's signature, but not that which was expected. This one *dissolved* the Duma! The latter, in closing its session twenty-four hours before, had announced the following one for Tuesday (the thirteenth) in perfect confidence.

Everyone was thunderstruck! The ministers, all except he of the interior, were completely astounded and, for a moment, without any comprehension or explanation of what had occurred. To plan and prepare

a measure so wise and then follow it by this act was de-
mentia, and without warning them!

That day was one of heavy, angry silence. In the
streets, no tram-cars, almost no sleighs or autos were
in circulation, and few people walked out. In various
directions shooting was heard, and sinister rumors
floated about threatening law and order; yet nothing
could be done. Rodzianko and the members of the
parliament were deeply disturbed.

If they could have managed to bring about a responsible government, in association with a liberal
Duma, all the well-disposed elements (even of the
working and soldier classes) would have certainly upheld it. And now this proclamation, spelling defeat
for all the liberals' hopes, came on them like a thunderbolt! To mend things seemed past praying for, and
the Duma, like the cabinet, felt trapped and sold to
the enemy. If there were any conversations that day
among leaders, they were of a private nature; and as far
as the public knew, Sunday passed in a dull, heavy depression, while the storm clouds rolled up to break
into the worst tempest the nation had ever known on
the morrow.

Monday morning, the twelfth, it had come. The
town was in an uproar. Public buildings were burning.
There were encounters in the streets in almost every
direction between the loyal troops and the revolutionists. Wild shooting on all sides. The cabinet met, and
having news from the staff that General Ivanov was
soon arriving by a special train with some 800 picked

"St. George cavaliers"—soldiers decorated for some unusually brave feat in battle—to take command as dictator, the members limited business to putting out from their midst, by unanimous vote, Protopopov. I think this must be the first time in history a minister had been dismissed by his colleagues. Then they wrote out their resignations, to be sent collectively to His Majesty, and to take effect as soon as possible, which could not be, however, until these were accepted, according to the Russian tradition. During this session at the Marie Palace, there was fighting in several adjacent streets. On St. Isaac's Square in front of the palace, a vast surging mob made a demonstration, demanding that Protopopov, "the traitor," be handed over to it. The latter, who was so bravely going to stem the torrent of any public demonstration, broke down completely at the meeting. Cringing, he begged the protection of those he had injured, as the mob approached, and he tried to hide, running to various parts of the building, weeping, and finally losing his head completely, fleeing in a motor to the house of Mme. Vyrubova's other protégé, the Persian doctor Badmaev.[4] Here he remained until late in the week, when, the revolutionary government being formed,

[4]Dr. Peter Aleksandrovich Badmaev (1851–1919) was in fact neither a Persian nor a Tibetan, as he is often identified in the literature, but a practitioner of Tibetan medicine and entrepreneur of Buryat Mongol origin. Badmaev had many acquaintances in high places and was indeed close to Rasputin and Vyrubova at this time; he had introduced Rasputin to Protopopov.

he threw himself on Kerensky's mercy, coming to the Tauride Palace of his own accord.

The other ministers one and all remained calm at the Marie Palace and went after their morning's work on foot through the streets to their homes and returned for the afternoon session in the same manner, or else remained at the Marie Palace for luncheon.

My husband met Bark near the club at noon and took him in there for a few minutes to avoid the bullets flying about, while the minister told him news of the whole cabinet's resignation. Each of these men afterward said to me how cool the other had seemed; and each admitted that circulating on the streets that day—with troops firing volleys up and down, revolutionists firing wild shots from revolvers and rifles, machine guns mounted on motor trucks, and the secret and ordinary police firing from the housetops and windows—was far from a pleasant pastime.

The Hotel Astoria, opposite the Marie Palace, was shot at and sacked on Monday by the mob. My mother-in-law, who was living there, luckily escaped with her maid and a small dog to the home of my sister-in-law, a few blocks off; but all the windows of her rooms were smashed, and I counted later twenty-seven holes in her walls where bullets were lodged. The ministers at their session of Monday afternoon decided they could do nothing further in the present crisis and that their only duty now was to remain at their ministries until they should be relieved by the sovereign's order or forced away by revolutionists.

They hoped this last might not occur, but within two days nearly all had been arrested. The Duma met early Monday morning, spontaneously, in extra session. The members were drawn there doubtless by a common anxiety and the desire to confer upon what measures, if any, could be taken to restrain or direct the troubles. Many deputies had hoped and wished for a revolution, perhaps even planned it; but all of these had desired a dignified performance, kept well in hand and managed by their own group, with a well-disciplined and grateful nation to uphold them, and with applauding allies looking on. They were not ready yet and were shocked and frightfully upset over the dangerous situation developing. Singing, howling mobs of workmen and regiments of soldiers poured into the Tauride Palace and its garden, purporting to be friends of the Duma; but their wild shouts and violent behavior showed them to be unreliable and highly inflammable, ready for anything.

Rodzianko and other leading men met and discussed the situation. Then they acted with consummate adroitness and presence of mind. They made speeches to the populace, using their eloquence as never before to quiet wild elements who threatened to swamp them and who had now settled in permanent session in the Catherine Hall—the great ballroom of the ex-palace. Kerensky, the socialist, was drawn into Rodzianko's group; and with his then-sincere enthusiasm, he undertook the task of quelling this bedlam. He managed to do so amazingly well; and that the

Duma was not massacred, it owed to his eloquence. Having a name and personality well known to the masses, and a large sense of patriotism also, he had been given over completely the mission of handling the rabble.

Rodzianko, in spite of the injury he and his followers felt had been done them, telegraphed in the most respectful form for the second time to the emperor, giving him the history of events in town, urging the extreme danger, and then asking for instructions. This telegram was sent over the emperor's private wire, was taken down by the operator at the staff, and then delivered instantly to General Voeikov's secretary, Colonel——. The latter then said to my husband that he took it in person to Voeikov, who decided it was not worthwhile delivering it to His Majesty and agitating him! Probably he had been instructed by Protopopov. So life at the staff went on that day in the usual quiet and monotonous routine.

The empress, in the evening, spoke to her husband directly by private wire from Tsarskoe, saying that from the palace she could see a fire or two in Petrograd and that she heard there were some insignificant disorders there, which the police were handling capably. She was pleased to think Ivanov would soon arrive to take command, and then she went on to give her husband news in detail of the children's health and of the palace life. Mme. Vyrubova and her confederates had not seen fit to disturb their mistress with the truth, if they knew it, any more than the emperor at the staff was favored with information of what was happening! That night the two sovereigns were probably the only people in their neighborhoods who slept unconscious of danger.

Rodzianko's telegrams on Tuesday were grown quite terrifying in their note of warning. He said it was now too late to do naught but face events, and that not having received orders, he would be obliged to act on his own responsibility. Voeikov was at last frightened and took three telegrams—after the arrival of the second on Tuesday—to His Majesty. The latter read them, was silent for a moment, staring at them and at Voeikov uncomprehendingly. He said he did not understand how this could be, when Protopopov and all had assured him there was no real danger. Then perhaps it dawned on him that those in opposition to his favorites had had truth on their side. A sharp exclamation of anger escaped him; and peremptory orders followed, in a voice that made Voeikov move rapidly, as if driven by a whip. "If Orlov had been here this would not have occurred," heard the favored Voeikov; and what hurt his pride more was that others heard it too.

With rapid preparations the Imperial train was made up, and the sovereign started for his capital within two hours early Tuesday evening. He expected to arrive there on Wednesday morning, 14 March, and he wanted to go straight to Petrograd and face parliament and the people. But his advisers begged him to return first to Tsarskoe and summon the cabinet there, while just before his starting, an anxious wire from Her Majesty called him also, for her protection, as she said; the population was making demonstrations and the situation in town seemed acute.

The emperor took with him only his immediate household for the trip, with Voeikov in command, of course. Orders were given by wire all along the railroad line to clear it and let the Imperial train through with utmost rapidity. But the night was young yet when Voeikov was awakened by the trainmaster, anxious because he found he could not reach Petrograd by the usual quick route, "the line being blocked ahead." He wanted orders. Voeikov, roused to the danger and the importance of time, had the train switched to another longer road, which it seemed was clear; and he retired to bed again, bitterly thinking this change meant the loss of several hours and that they could not be at Tsarskoe now before late the next afternoon.

Wednesday morning came, and they ran into the station at Pskov and definitely stopped. The officials at this station informed Voeikov they had "orders from the chief of transportation, not to let this party proceed farther." I believe it is not on record how the commandant of the palace translated this curious news to his Imperial master, nor what the latter said of such a situation!

General Ruszky, who was in command at Pskov, presented himself. He was sent to telegraph over his staff wire to Rodzianko, in the emperor's name, asking for news and telling the actual predicament of the Imperial traveler. Ruszky came back to say that the Duma president had formed a "provisional committee" and that he had already sent two deputies to meet His Majesty. They would reach Pskov that evening to confer with him.

Until their arrival, the emperor spent much time in walking on the station platform, from which the public was not cleared away, but where people stood about watching him. He also talked with the empress by private wire from Pskov. Her Majesty gave descriptions of what she saw from her windows. She seemed courageous and cool, and was mainly preoccupied by the condition of her children, who were all down with measles, one of the little grand duchesses and the young tsarevich being seriously ill.

That evening late, the expected deputation arrived from Petrograd. It consisted of Guchkov,[5] afterward minister of war; and Shulgin,[6] editor of a very brilliant paper in Kiev. General Ruszky accompanied

[5] Alexander Ivanovich Guchkov (1862–1936), a founder of the Octobrist Party and sometime chairman of the Duma, became first war minister under the provisional government (March–April, 1917).

[6] Vasily Vitalevich Shulgin (1878–1976) was a Russian nationalist and Kiev newspaper editor (*Kievlianin*). As a deputy to the Fourth (last) Duma, Shulgin was an outspoken critic of the government and, in early 1917, proponent of Nicholas II's abdication. He had an extraordinary post-revolutionary career and died in the Soviet Union at the age of ninety-nine. See V.V. Shulgin, *The Years: Memoirs of a Member of the Russian Duma, 1906–1917* (New York: Hippocrene Books, 1984).

them and remained in the Imperial salon-carriage during all the historical interview. It was the first time in the life of Nicholas II he had received anyone who had not dressed in full uniform (civil or military) before entering his presence. These men came as they had been on their trip, and indeed they had probably not re-dressed since Monday morning when they had gone to the Tauride Palace.

In attendance on His Majesty were old Count Frederiks,[7] minister of the court; General Narishkin,[8] head of the military bureau; one aide-de-camp; and probably General Voeikov. The emperor received the envoys with calm, and when they were seated, asked them to state their business. They did; first reciting the history of events since the Imperial departure on Friday morning and telling how just now they had left the capital in an uproar of battle; the government powerless, since nearly all its members were arrested; the mob in the street ready to burn and sack the city; and the troops, now having all passed over to the revolutionists, leading in the disorders. They said the Duma had met and formed a provisional committee, being

[7]Count Vladimir Borisovich Frederiks (1838–1927) was one of Nicholas II's closest associates, bearing the titles of minister of court, chief of Imperial cabinet, and headquarters commandant. He countersigned Nicholas's abdication manifesto. Under arrest for a short time by the provisional government, he later emigrated to Finland.

[8]General Kirill Anatolevich Narishkin (1868–1924), a childhood friend of the emperor, was head of His Imperial Majesty's Field Chancery.

unable to hear from the emperor, and that this handful of men was now struggling to bring chaos to an end and to find a solution for the many difficulties. Ivanov and his followers had been stopped, and their train not allowed to enter the city; and there was no knowing what might happen to Her Majesty and the Imperial children, or to the country, unless the sovereign made up his mind to the only step left him—that of abdicating the throne, allowing the tsarevich to replace him, with a regency of the nation's choice to conduct affairs.

The emperor listened, showing no temper, regret, or surprise. At the end of their speech, he declared that he refused the succession for his son, not wishing to separate himself and the empress from their boy. He said he would abdicate his rights, along with those of the tsarevich, in favor of his brother Michael.[9] The deputies consented to this and gave him a paper to sign, which had been prepared beforehand on these lines. With no show of emotion, the emperor took the paper and moved into the office next to his salon, leaving all the company behind him. In a few moments he returned, with a typewritten sheet in his hand, presenting it to the deputies to read. He asked if it was what they had wished. Upon hearing their affirmative, the sovereign put his signature immediately to

[9] In fact, Nicholas had first abdicated in favor of his son, with Michael as regent, but a few hours later, realizing this would mean their separation, he withdrew his first statement and signed the manifesto that was made public, abdicating in favor of Michael.

the document. The emperor asked the deputies what he should personally do for the moment. They told him that he was entirely free to return to the staff.

This plan was carried out as soon as his unwelcome guests had departed. Amazing calm had been the emperor's attitude. Helpless in the hands of conspirators until now, the emperor was apparently equally unable to resist these new dominating spirits; and he neither protested nor complained at his fate nor showed the slightest desire to defend his inheritance. On the contrary, he gave in at once, without argument, and did as he was instructed. He seemed to be entirely content to feel he might now lead a quiet life and was to be free from his burden of state affairs. It never occurred to him to order these deputies arrested or to make any other demonstration of self-defense. Though he again conversed with the empress by special wire from Pskov, after the departure of the Duma's deputation and before his own, the emperor did not mention to her the fact of his abdication!

At the staff the emperor had left the supreme command to General Alekseev[10]—his chief-of-staff until now—and he did not take the command again nor return to the palace he had occupied in Mogilev. He remained on his train, which was drawn up near that of

[10]General Michael Vasilevich Alekseev (1857–1918), Nicholas's chief of staff, was instrumental in persuading Nicholas to abdicate. He became supreme commander of Russian forces in September after the "Kornilov affair" and later founded the Volunteer Army to fight against the Bolsheviks.

the Empress Mother, who had joined her son from Kiev on hearing the news, to offer him the comfort of her presence and affection.

Four days they spent in this manner, the emperor enjoying entire personal liberty, driving about the town with Her Majesty and dining or lunching with her, or she with him. Voeikov tried, without success, to abandon the sovereign and get himself transferred to the suite of the Empress Mother, which he considered would be safer. Finally, this unfaithful servant fled and was arrested near Moscow on a train and brought to Petrograd, where he was interned in the Fortress of Peter and Paul by the revolutionaries.

One of the Empress Mother's gentlemen-in-waiting told me in detail of these sad days they had spent at the staff; of the gentle bravery of the great lady, her tender solicitude, and her self-control; also of her son's inertness in the face of changes he could scarcely ignore. At the church he heard the service read with his name and those of his family left out, but he made no sign. At meals also the conversations went on much as usual. The fourth day it was announced to him he must consider himself under arrest and must proceed to Tsarskoe with a deputy of the Duma, who had come to fetch him as his guardian. With the same inconsequence, he heard the sentence, made his *adieu* to his mother and to all his own suite, and then departed for his palace of Tsarskoe without a word of regret or a wave of his hand to the tender, aged figure in black, the Empress Mother, who with a breaking heart stood alone and watched his train disappear in the distance.

On this trip the emperor was accompanied only by Prince Dolgoruky, who of late had been made his marshal of the court, and who had asked permission to share the sovereign's fate. The Duma's representative and a military guard completed the passengers of the special train. The emperor had heard of the arrest of his wife and had since then been unable to communicate with her, but His Majesty seemed to feel no anxiety for her, anymore than for his own fate. Everyone who saw him wondered if he at all realized the danger of their situation.

Arrived at the palace, in spite of the fact that both sovereigns were now prisoners, they were allowed to see one another at first tête-a-tête. It must have been a tragic interview when they faced one another and contemplated the hopelessness of their situation, together with the reasons that had caused this drama!

But one of Rasputin's old predictions was that if anything happened to him, disaster would overcome the Imperial house, so perhaps his patroness still believed in her prophet; and possibly she explained to the emperor that the death of their inspirer had cost them their throne.

At any rate, a day or two later Kerensky, who was minister of justice in the new-born provisional government, came to the Tsarskoe Palace to ask of the emperor some needed information and papers. He was cordially received by the Imperial prisoner, in the latter's library, and they were seated, smoking and discussing some details, when Nicholas II said, "I regret so much that I have never met you until now! It would have helped me greatly if, during my reign, I had known men like you and had been able to introduce such elements into the government!"

Just then the ex-empress walked into the great room silently. Kerensky rose at once, and the ex-emperor presented the socialist to his wife. The minister kissed her hand and drew up an armchair for her near His Majesty's. "You need not offer me a seat in my own palace," she said, and stood in continued silence by her husband's side. Her proud spirit was far from broken; and soon the new government felt obliged to separate the couple, allowing them to meet only at meals and with a revolutionary officer present to watch them and follow the conversation even then.

"She is too strong, and he is too weak," was the explanation given me when I asked why the new government had taken this measure.

XVII

The Provisional Government

I<small>N THE</small> small hours of Thursday morning, the deputation to Pskov returned with our emperor's last proclamation in their hands. Rodzianko published it through the city and placarded it on doors and on walls. It said, freely translated:

> At this decisive moment of the fortunes of Russia, we find it our bounden duty to take such steps as will enable our people to attain the unity of purpose and power, indispensable, for the earliest possible conquest of the enemy; and in accordance with the advice of the Imperial Duma, we abdicate from the throne of Russia and renounce the high powers attached to that office. Not wishing to part with our beloved son, we pass the succession to our brother, His Imperial Highness Michael Aleksandrovich, with our blessing on his accession to the Russian throne. We command our brother to govern the country in strict accordance with the wishes of the ministers who are to be chosen by the people and that he swear this oath for the sake of our dearly beloved country. We also command all true sons of the Fatherland to fulfill their sacred duty of obedience to him as tsar, in this dire moment of the troubles of our nation and to help him and the people's representatives to guide the Russian Empire to victory, happiness, and success. So may God help Russia!

> N<small>ICHOLAI</small>.

Early on Thursday morning a committee waited on the Grand Duke Michael. The grand duke was offered the throne. But it was said he declined the proffered honor, under pressure from the deputation who did not want him to reign. He announced in a proclamation of his own, made public that same day, that he would accept the crown only if he were "elected to it by the people's vote in a constituent assembly."

It was immediately decided to form a provisional government to carry on the war and the administration of the country. That same Thursday a ministry was named. It included all the best liberal thinkers and theorists available. It put Prince Lvov,[1] at the head as prime minister; Miliukov took the portfolio of foreign affairs; Tereshchenko[2] and his millions were set to guard our finances; while Kerensky and his idealism occupied the chair of justice. Nearly all the men in this cabinet were honest and inspired with a fine ambition to set the country on its feet. The American ambassador, Mr. Francis, knowing their value, was anxious to strengthen their position; and he obtained, by Sunday evening, the recognition of the provisional government

---

[1]Prince George Evgenevich Lvov (1861–1925), a prominent figure in local self-government before the revolution, was the first prime minister and interior minister of the provisional government in 1917.

[2]Michael Ivanovich Tereshchenko (1886–1956), industrialist and financier, deputy to the Fourth Duma, member of the progressive bloc there, participant in the plot to remove Nicholas II. First finance minister of the provisional government and Miliukov's successor as foreign minister in May 1917.

by the United States. England and France followed the example of the United States almost at once, and by Monday evening, the new chapter of Russia's history was begun. Quiet reigned again in Petrograd.

The revolution had lasted but a week. When the old ministers had been arrested, none of them had been seriously ill-treated, though a few had suffered from exposure to the cold or from the hardships of poor lodging and inconvenience. The ministerial meeting rooms in the Duma were used to contain all the prisoners, whom the self-appointed revolutionary guards had arrested and brought in. There were an extraordinary number scattered about the rooms, where they were detained a few hours or a few days, after which they were liberated, like M. Bark and Kochubei,[3] or turned into the Fortress of Peter and Paul for a more permanent sojourn.

Senators, members of the council of the empire, members of the ex-court and the government, about 200 of them, lived in these very crowded rooms for five or six long days. Each morning and evening Kerensky made a tour of the rooms, chose out a few men to be liberated and a few more to be sent to the fortress. At one side of the impromptu prison could be heard the discussions and the movements of the Duma's members, while from the other direction came the roar of bedlam let loose, for in the Catherine

[3]Prince Victor Sergeevich Kochubei (1860–1923) was a general and member of the Imperial suite, director-general of Imperial domains from 1899 to 1917; a Cantacuzene in-law.

Hall the deputations of soldiers and workmen held forth—criticizing, threatening, acclaiming; demanding reports of all that was being done and the right to veto or approve every measure presented.[4]

Many times the lives of all occupants of the palace hung by a thread, and always the situation was saved by Kerensky's eloquence and his clever handling of his clients. When he accepted a portfolio in so conservative a cabinet as was the provisional, he almost lost his hold on the ultra-Socialists, who feared he would no longer be their man. The first days after his nomination, as he circulated among the prisoners, he was attended by a "guard of honor," one soldier, one sailor, and one workman as aides-de-camp; but he said afterward, these had really been spies, placed by the Catherine Hall crowd to watch his words and movements. During this time, he was severe and curt in manner with the prisoners, but as soon as he became free from supervision, he was quite unpretentious and human, trying to help and to liberate all those he could.

Hundreds of prisoners were set free immediately after their arrest, while others lingered many days. A number ended up at the fortress, dragging out a miserable existence for months. None was actually ever executed, as one of Kerensky's first measures was the suppression of capital punishment.

[4]The Petrograd Soviet shared the Tauride Palace with the rump Duma Committee that formed the provisional government.

XVIII

The Arrest of the Empress

M{Y HUSBAND}, who had gone to Petrograd on business, had reached the capital on the morning of Sunday, 11 March; and finding all traffic stopped and no means of locomotion, save his own feet, had with his soldier servant, Davidka, carried their light baggage across the silent city to his club. He said everything looked ominous to him, the town dead, and that he found his friends at the club greatly excited and concerned for the safety of the city. It was reported the revolution would be upon them in a few hours. Michael saw his mother and family that day and found the former much worried. He decided that because of the threatening disorders, our boy should not return to school, as was usual on Sunday evening.

On Monday morning, when the revolution broke out in earnest, with shooting growing more violent all over the town as the hours passed, circulation in the street, even on foot, became almost impossible.

For part of the day my husband watched some of the troops who still held with the government fighting masses of workmen, and other troops already passing over to the crowd. But they were all only reserves or new recruits, living in the barracks of the regiments whose names they bore and whom they expected to join shortly at the front. The officers in charge were few and were entirely helpless against the agents scattered among the soldiers. Most of the reservists had been mobilized from the workmen's class with whom they were now fraternizing.

Early in this game, the ministry of the interior ceased to exist. There was no one to give orders to the police, and after two days of bloody defense, these men gave up the struggle. They had at first placed quick-firing guns on all public buildings by Protopopov's orders, and they fired from these points into the streets without other results than to make the mob more furious.

Though many people were circulating on foot, tram-cars and conveyances were all stopped. Banks and shops were closed, and trains only arrived and left the city accidentally, now and then.

On the other hand, the ministers were too brave to fly, save only the trusted Protopopov. They decided each one should return to his offices, attend to what he could of routine work, protect what he could of the Imperial property entrusted to his care, and there await events. This was done. Patiently, quietly, all these strong men sat at their desks waiting through the hours. The arresting of the ministers was done by bands of revolutionary volunteers without authority, and no minister was arrested by official warrant or by the order of the newly created provisional. All the tyrannical or violent acts of the week were carried through by these vague volunteer groups, who visited

public buildings and private houses and, more or less
tipsy, more or less rough, made inspections and req-
uisitions, generally stealing anything lying about and
always carrying off all arms, old or new. Sometimes
the soldiers were well behaved and announced they
were only looking for spies and firearms, and whenever they confiscated property, it was with a pretension of doing it for the public safety.

In all cases, resistance was worse than useless. There
were many victims due to misunderstandings or to hos-
tility shown these soldiers. So it was that General Stackelberg[1] was killed, and some few others wounded.

My husband, who, with his Greek name and South
Russian traditions, also wearing the Imperial aiguillettes and a St. George's sword, was commander of
the Cuirassiers of His Majesty and might have seemed
a safe person. Yet erupting half-tipsy into the club
apartments, ten or a dozen soldier hooligans, after examining these gentlemen's baggage, confiscating their
arms, boots, money, and other property, next examined their victims' papers and, declaring these "not
in order," arrested them as German spies and said
they must go to the Duma at once.

Naturally the officers felt indignant, but they, *nolens-
volens,* had to accept the situation. Although Prince
Engalichev wished to resist, he was persuaded to be
calm and cause no unnecessary irritation as the little

[1]Baron George Karlovich Stackelberg (1850–1917), a cavalry
general who had played a prominent role in the Manchurian campaigns of 1904–1905.

procession started on its long and dangerous walk
through the agitated city. The four men had been previously disarmed by their captors and were obligated
to remove their Imperial aiguillettes. The long two-
hours' walk by the Grand Morskaia, up the Nevskii,
and across town to the Tauride Palace, with their lives
hanging by a thread, was a fatiguing, harassing, and a
humiliating experience. And yet, even these soldiers
treated their prisoners illogically well, and when
Prince Karageorgevich broke down because of an injured foot (which he had come from the front to treat)
he was hoisted on a passing motor-truck and sent on
in that way to the Duma. After the first fifteen minutes my husband took the whole party in charge and
gave his captors orders to conduct them directly to
Guchkov's office at the Duma, which was done immediately on their arrival. This member of the provisional committee was amazed to see my husband and
his party appear. He at once liberated them, returning
their papers and giving them certificates to show they
had already been through the ordeal and were to be allowed now to circulate about the city or elsewhere.
Then Guchkov drove Michael back to the club in his
own motor, and the latter was none the worse for his
trial, except in the loss of his sword and revolver,
which had been stolen. These he had greatly valued,
the sword having been worn through the Turkish war
by an uncle of his and the revolver carried by my own
father through his campaigns. But the loss of these
arms was nothing compared to the dangers escaped!

As to the aiguillettes and the Imperial initials on my husband's epaulets, he never replaced them, since on the following morning the emperor's abdication was announced.

To obey the Imperial will, as expressed by the proclamation, meant to serve the new government faithfully and to aid in driving the enemy from our frontier. So Cantacuzene, with all other officers, remained in their positions. He continued to command the Imperial Cuirassiers, whose designation had been changed to "Podolosky Cuirassiers," in memory of the town from which their original quota had been drawn, back in Russian history.

There was no move at first in the revolution against officers or aristocrats, except in individual cases. The whole drama was made on a seemingly patriotic basis—"For the war and for national liberty," as against the tyranny of the German or Occult party at court. It was an attack on the form of government: autocratic and bureaucratic.

Thursday morning, after the abdicating proclamation was placarded everywhere, suddenly order seemed to emerge from the chaos. People went freely about the city; shooting ceased. It was almost uncanny to see, for underneath the surface nothing was yet established on a secure basis. There was no organization or real power, and no disciplined force could be counted on. Yet all the streets and churches were crowded with smiling people, most of whom were beribboned or cockaded with scarlet; and the town was decorated with red flags. The Imperial arms were removed from shops and palaces, and this without much show of violence or hatred. There had been comparatively little destruction of property and little drunkenness or loss of life. Suddenly, now, there was food and fuel; and the thoughtless public never realized they were living on precious reserves but went about their business, trusting all was well with Russia, since they had what sufficed for immediate needs.

On Saturday my husband was able to leave for the front, having at last transacted the business for which he had gone north. He left the capital quiet and apparently safe, and our boy had returned to school.

Over the whole country the news of the revolution was received with a thankfulness almost religious; and order reigned everywhere, though the police were at once gathered in by mobilizations and sent to the front to fight, leaving our prison doors open, and streets and highways unguarded. Unfortunately, even the frontiers were free to all for six days, so anyone might pass in without question or papers. By the time the provisional government sent soldiers to replace the ordinary frontier guardians, thousands of German spies and agents had passed our gates unmolested and had settled down to their deadly work of organizing and forming the Bolshevik party, which in the beginning had been but a rabble. The dramatic side of this neglect was soon realized by the provisionals, but its results could never be corrected.

In the first wild days a promise was also made that

the troops then in Petrograd should never be sent to the front or disbanded but should remain where they were, to protect the capital—"an honor won them, by their part in the revolutionary movement." This measure came, ready-made, from the Catherine Hall deputies and was signed by the first government. It was afterward much discussed whether the ministry knew what difficulties they were putting in their own path for the near future by placing these (already undisciplined and disloyal) troops in such an unassailable position. This act had far-reaching results. The decree, which was called the "Order Number One to the Army," suppressed all law and discipline and created "committees of soldiers" in each unit to discuss obedience to their officers, and legally put complete freedom into the hands of the lowest placed. These were the weights of stone that later dragged the ideals and the possibilities of the revolution to the depths of the swamp in which they ended. The "Order Number One to the Army" was printed immediately, and thousands of copies were sent by special agents directly to the soldiers all along the battle fronts. It was thus spread among them first, without reaching their officers. This I have been told by many who were on the firing line.[2] Commanders were dumbfounded that a decision of such severe and

[2]"Order Number One" of the Petrograd Soviet had been directed to the capital garrisons but, as the author writes, the order was immediately circulated at the front, with disastrous results for military discipline.

grave importance should have been taken so quickly and sent in this way, instead of through the usual channel of the staff, to be passed on down to army corps, divisions, brigades, and regiments.

I have been told, also, by several reliable officers who were during these days attached to the provisional government in the Tauride Palace, that they had made personal investigations at the time and had found the presses used to print these orders were handled by Germans. Also, that the messengers who had carried off the bundles of proclamations to the front were Germans or in German pay. They had protested at once and had asked the provisional committee to order a small posse of soldiers to arrest these enemies but had not succeeded in obtaining permission, or the men, for such service.

From the first moment of the revolution, the best of the officers were very pessimistic as to the future and saw our only salvation in military help at once from the Allies. But one and all our officers acted with loyalty to the new government, since it was provisional and their emperor had commanded all true sons to remain at their posts and fight the enemy. Thanks to the super-human work of this fine element, the army was held together for months by the old traditions and personal influence, and by the good relations between officers and men. The former ended in accepting martyrdom, rather than be guilty of giving up the cause of our war.

In some strange way, no news of the abdication

reached Her Majesty until a deputation was announced to her during the day of Thursday. She immediately replied she would receive its members in audience in one of the palace halls. As she entered the room, she found that she was facing a group of unpretentious-looking men whose spokesman, a young colonel, announced to her that he had the painful duty of "arresting Her Majesty." She indignantly asked how and why, and was given a short history of events in the capital, of which she had been totally ignorant. "But His Majesty?" she inquired with impatience. And she then only was told that her husband had abdicated the night before, for himself and his heir. At this the empress's knees gave way, and she stumbled forward, catching and bracing herself on a table. "It is not true! It is a lie! I spoke with His Majesty by private wire as he was leaving Pskov, and he said nothing of it."

The Imperial proclamation was handed to her to read. In spite of all the bitterness and despair she must have felt, she drew herself up proudly and faced the deputies, "I have nothing more to say."

They told her she might remain in her palace and would be well cared for and her comfort seen to. "And what about the children? They are ill and cannot be disturbed." They should remain also. Then she asked two favors. That the old sailor who had been near her son as an attendant since the boy's birth should be left to him and that the doctor might come from outside as usual. These were granted. Only she herself must not go out. It would not be safe and was against the orders of those who must guard her. And the ex-empress, now a prisoner in her own palace, passed from the great hall without another word.

She waited in patience, outwardly proud and calm, and told her children nothing. She saw the mob about her gates. Listening to their threatening racket, she saw the Imperial Escort of Cossacks, her guard, pass over to the revolutionary party. Even the corps of palace servants asked to leave her, all save a few who were in her personal service. Only one or two palace ladies remained with Her Majesty, and she had no news of her husband nor of events outside her walls.

Soon Rodzianko sent her word that if she wished to send her jewels to him for safe-keeping, he would give a receipt and would answer for them. She refused the offer and kept her jewels and her children near her. Sympathy was expressed on all sides in Petrograd, as in Yalta, by the humbler classes for her children, who were down with measles; for the Empress Mother; and for the various grand dukes and grand duchesses. But in the whole great empire, where they had reigned for more than twenty years, there seemed no word of praise or pity for the miserable pair who had been all-powerful sovereigns only a few days previously, and not one person raised a hand to defend their banner. This seemed to me one of the most eloquent details of the whole revolution.

Since his arrest and liberation on Wednesday, my husband had gone about the streets in complete freedom. He wore no side-arms, as none of the officers were doing so in town. But he put these on again on Saturday to start for the front, where he found his regiment in a state of amazement and fermentation. The great news was just then reaching the army from the capital, and the Order Number One had been already spread among the soldiers. Cantacuzene was in time to confirm true stories and interpret the extraordinary document in such fashion that his men and officers were welded together in a common desire to prove their patriotism and the value of their discipline. They decided, once and for all, to live up to their past traditions; and they did it through eight months of constant temptation. So remarkably did this unit stand the strain of revolutionary experiences, that they were counted unique on the whole front and made for themselves a reputation that was a great credit to their own and their commander's steadfastness.

Shortly after the revolution my husband was promoted to a brigade command, consisting of his own Cuirassiers and of their sister-regiment, which in old-régime days had been the "Cuirassiers of the Empress Mother." In leaving the head of his regiment, commanded for so many months under fire, Cantacuzene had been very sad to break up the associations. His consolation came only from the fact that, besides including it as one of the units of his brigade, the Cuirassiers' new commander—Prince Cherkassky— and all the officers still clung to him, making a personal group of adherents, almost as if they were his staff. While the soldiers, in spite of the introduction of revolutionary ideals, kept their old attitude, always called Michael "our prince," and came to him with their personal and committee troubles, quite in the ancient, patriarchal manner. They even consulted him as to how they must take the new democratic theories and how to apply them. In late July at a meeting of the regimental "soviet," these men voted unanimously to give Cantacuzene the right to use their uniform for life, doing him an honor that was a custom of the old régime and had been abolished by the revolutionary government.

My husband's new command was ordered at once to Kiev, there to maintain quiet in the city, where upheavals were much feared. Kiev remained the quietest, safest, and best-behaved city in the empire. This was so until the moment when, early in November, everything was taken over by the Bolsheviki and Ukrainian powers, and the provisional government finally fell once and for all. When he was ordered to Kiev, my husband wrote to me of his deep-rooted dislike for the kind of work ahead of him. But since it was in a large and comfortable city, he said he would like me to join him, if all went well, and that he would take a house and settle down to a more stable life than he had enjoyed for two-and-a-half years past. I was only too delighted to go; but I decided to visit the capital for some business first and to see our boy there, as rumors were afloat about the closing of his school.

XIX

Aftermath of the Revolution

THE FIRST WEEK following the revolution, traveling had been almost impossible, and one could not reserve berths, or even seats, in any cars. All the population of Russia seemed suddenly to move about the country. Baggage was constantly being lost, and one was knocked about beyond belief.

Two days before I started for Petrograd, I read in the local Crimean paper that my husband's old chief, the Grand Duke Nicholas Nikolaevich, had arrived at his villa, Chaire, near us, accompanied by his wife, his brother, and his sister-in-law. In attendance were only Prince and Princess Orlov, who had followed the chief through devotion and without salary nor with official position.

Immediately after this arrival came another, sadder traveler to the Crimea. The Empress Mother, with quiet dignity, settled with the Grand Duchess Xenia and the latter's husband, the Grand Duke Alexander Mikhailovich, at Ei-ta-dor, their home. They also had been given a choice of residence.

After so many years of kindness at these people's hands, I felt I must make some demonstration of sympathetic loyalty; so I put myself at their disposal to carry any letters or packages to the capital. Knowing this would be their only opportunity of escaping censors, who I heard now stopped all Imperial correspondence, I found the refugees were glad to avail themselves of the occasion my departure offered. I carried away a large bagful of letters, of every shape and size, in the lining of my dressing case. I was somewhat frightened when I thought of what might happen if I chanced to be searched! Luckily I completely escaped the interest of those in power. The new régime knew nothing, and cared nothing, about my responsibilities; and I was able to deliver documents from Her Majesty to her business man and to the grand master of her former court, and to put one from her to the Dowager Queen Alexandra of England into the hands of a sure messenger in Petrograd, who carried it over the frontier. From the old chief also, to the then-prime minister Lvov and to the minister of war Guchkov, I carried letters, as well as a number of business letters from him concerning the direction of his private affairs. I was enchanted for once to repay a small part of what favors had been shown to me through the seventeen years I had spent in Russia. Certainly I had never supposed I should be granted by fate any such chance, and it was with real joy I undertook the delicate tasks.

I had been to Chaire and had heard from the grand duchess of the revolutionary experiences she had gone through in Tiflis. I had seen the Grand Duke Alexander and heard the details of the four days which the Empress Mother and he had spent at the staff with the ex-emperor, and of the latter's arrest; also of the old empress's return to Kiev, the respectful sympathy shown her there and during her trip. All these members of the Imperial family were hopeful for the future of Russia, and they thought the provisional government would be able to push the war. They believed they would be allowed to live in peace in the Crimea or on their country estates. But they were most anxious as to their financial situation. None had large personal fortunes, and they had depended on the pensions they drew from the emperor's civil lists or from the Imperial family's estates. No single one of them, however, complained of these losses. This group had foreseen the troubles and seemed to me less agitated now than they had been before the cataclysm. Once the sovereign had lost the game, there was nothing more to do but to accept the situation with what philosophy one could.

No member of the Imperial family in the Crimea mentioned to me personally either the ex-emperor or his consort. Daily the newspapers published articles giving what purported to be true details of the "inner" palace and political life of Tsarskoe during the last months of the empire. These appeared vastly degrading and humiliating.

We all agreed the provisional cabinet was well chosen and promised, on the whole, to be conservative and intelligent. We looked forward to the probability of the "constituent assembly" being in favor of a constitutional monarchy. Some member of the Imperial family would then naturally be chosen as emperor; possibly the ever-popular and always strong old chief or the Grand Duke Michael, whose wife came from the merchant class of Moscow; or perhaps Kyril, who was next in succession and who had an Imperial wife.

There was also a chance, it seemed, of the Grand Duke Nicholas Mikhailovich being the people's choice. He was supremely intelligent and had made a study of politics for years. Also he had been a revolutionist in his ideas, while his democratic mode of life had given him occasion to make many friends in every group and class in the empire. He had written several historical books, universally approved; he knew the "intelligentsia" class of Russia; and the artistic classes knew him and his collections and were his admirers. In the Duma and the *zemstvos*,[1] he had many warm friends. He had been banished in disgrace by the ex-empress and had only returned to Petrograd just in time to play an evident role in the debates of the Duma during the troubled revolutionary days, and he was a great favorite of the Empress Mother.

It was with intense curiosity, some anxiety, and much hope that I went to Petrograd at the very end of March. My trip was comfortable and quite ordinarily calm and monotonous.

I arrived in Petrograd on 13 April, Good Friday, when the revolution was exactly a month old. My boy

---

[1] The *zemstvos* were elective organs of limited self administration at the provincial and sub-provincial (*uezd*) levels, introduced in the reforms of the 1860s.

was at the station to meet me with his grandmother's carriage. As the train came in, the platform was packed with a vast crowd of people, mostly soldiers in unbuttoned and untidy uniforms. But all of them were grinning and good-natured. My baggage was seized by ready hands and carried from the train to our vehicle. On my inquiring why soldiers did this work, my boy said the troops now ruled the town. No one dared gainsay them, so they promenaded about, slovenly, careless, smoking, requisitioning what they liked to eat, and even refusing to drill or obey orders. Among other things, they had taken possession of the stations, finding the work of baggage-carriers easy, amusing, and profitable.

My next impression was of the princess's coachman, with a large red bow pinned to the breast of his livery. My boy added to my amazement by telling me that "Grandmama was the most revolutionary of the revolutionists and was full of enthusiasm for the destruction of all the old traditions. She rejoiced in the red flag on the Winter Palace and especially in the closing of his school, which she considered privileged!" This, it seems, was really temporarily the case, and the princess told me at our first meeting how her "French republican heart beat in unison with all the new ideals." The rest of our family did not agree with my mother-in-law in this and seemed very pessimistic. Both attitudes surprised me. I could not but mourn the downfall of what I had seen so brilliant and so highly placed and of all the old poetic traditions. It seemed to me, nevertheless, that Russia's future was full of promise, if only because all the strongest and best elements in the country were ready with heart and soul to give their services. On the other hand, I didn't like to see the beautiful statue of the Empress Catherine in front of the Imperial theater with a red flag pushed into her hand. The revolutionary red, which had floated over the Imperial palaces and the Fortress of Peter the Great in place of the emperor's "standard," seemed to me out of place and very tragic. Besides, I missed the great golden eagles that had been torn down and that had represented, to my mind, more than 300 years of the country's picturesque history!

At the Hotel d'Europe, my usual apartment seemed cozy and homelike, and the servants, all old acquaintances of mine, had much to tell me of their personal experiences in the great days just passed.

My poor boy was bravely facing a very difficult situation. He had not been ill-treated during the days of change, and after the emperor's abdication he had moved freely about the streets. But his heart was bleeding for the destruction of the school he loved with all its beautiful, distinguished traditions of more than a century's growth. I did my best to comfort and console my young student, whose view of the revolution was colored by the unjust treatment from which the Lyceum suffered. It was the first serious calamity in young Mike's sixteen years of life and was an immense blow to all the loyal young fellows in quaint green uniforms who made up the corps, some 300 strong.

This year, studies were to be finished on 14 May, and the school was to be closed permanently. Our son decided to transfer to Petrograd University. This settled, I still had nearly a fortnight to spend with him in the capital. I looked forward with much interest to what I should see and hear.

At first the Easter celebrations had seemed quite strange without the features of the great ceremonies at the palaces and without the dashing court-carriages and sleighs in the streets. But the churches were packed with devout crowds, and there was a new spirit abroad of released hope and a touching show of brotherhood. There was also marvelous order, though not a policeman was to be seen in the streets. The atmosphere of the capital was really very wonderful. The public acted as if there were a solemn function going on, and on each holiday I had the impression of a cathedral atmosphere when I went out. There was food and fuel enough now, and the lower classes were smiling, content, and trustful of the morrow. They showed perfect respect to those whom they had always regarded as superiors. The shops were full of supplies, and everyone was buying, since prices had been lowered by orders of the provisional government.

The optimism of the street was not reflected, however, in the salons where I went, save apparently in the minds of the allied ambassadors, who were convinced the war would be pushed rapidly now that the

Occult forces were overthrown. It did not occur to them that with the old régime all the machinery of administration had disappeared.

Among my own group of friends, I found an entirely different viewpoint. Nearly everyone admired and liked individually the members of the provisional cabinet. They wanted to help and uphold them in every possible manner and to see them last through until the constituent assembly. But the Russians of the upper class, when they spoke of the situation, expressed great fear of certain dangers, which loomed large to their eyes on our political horizon. First, there was an evident and grave probability of the army's complete disintegration. It was fully confessed already that the "Order Number One" had been a terrible mistake. Also, the cry of "Land and Freedom," which the soviets were starting under German suggestion, raised the question of the land's immediate distribution. This made workmen and soldiers desert in vast numbers, vaguely believing what German agents told them, that they must hurry back to their homes to receive their portion of the spoils. What could the government do to obtain this land, which was to be given away to the populace? So to our minds, the army and the land questions were both serious stumbling blocks to law and tranquillity.

Then, also, provision reserves carefully made by the old government were being rapidly squandered now, while nothing was being done to gather new stores, and our transportation was as disorganized as

ever. The police had been destroyed, and the vague
civilian militia that replaced them could be of no service in case of real necessity.

The factories were not working. The workmen all
were members of committees, and they were busy
"governing" or were merely doing nothing and finding life too agreeable to return to their duties. The
"soviets of workmen and soldiers," still in residence at
the Tauride Palace, composed the real government
and were becoming a force with which the ministry
was obliged to reckon. They even made some proclamations independently and insisted that the cabinet
must have their consent to all its measures, otherwise
they "would not be representing popular opinion."
Kerensky still held his party's confidence, and he handled them with genius. But it was difficult for him to
accord the ideas of the workmen and soldiers with
those of his ministerial colleagues, and his health was
breaking rapidly under the strain of his speeches and
travels.

I saw my friends informally, and constantly, as
usual, keeping a salon full daily about my tea table. If
anything, they were better humored than in the winter, and much less preoccupied, having no responsibilities now. I went frequently to all the houses where
I had been a habituée, even to see the families of some
of the men now in the fortress, whom I felt disinclined
to neglect in the moment of their disgrace, and I even
visited them quite openly. The first of May—Labor
Day—passed with great processions and meetings in

the street. Disorders were expected, but everything went off quietly; from this fact, people drew confidence. All the forenoon processions of government employees, soldiers, sailors, poor factory workers of both sexes, and school children wandered about the main streets with red banners on which were written various mottoes, such as "Land and Freedom," "Liberty." They chanted religious songs, or their bands played the "Marseillaise," which had replaced our own national anthem; though I had been warned of possible dangers, twice I walked out to see the sights. The religious progresses were immense, and those who took part wore exalted, soft faces, while their voices were sweet and low, as those of our people always are. There was not a policeman in town, yet no single disorderly incident marred the celebrations anywhere. To see the people in this phase was to love them; and I was infinitely touched by the beauty of the Russian's nature, and its simple nobility!

Albert Thomas, the great French socialist, was visiting Petrograd, and being an old acquaintance of mine, he came to me several times for a cup of tea and a chat. I was greatly interested in hearing him talk of our present situation, which he admitted caused him many surprises. First of all, he said he had been told that he was to come out to converse with men of his party—that is, Socialists. "But your definitions are different from ours in France; and when I found myself facing the representatives of my supposed opinions here, I discovered that these were not Socialists at all, but what we call in France Anarchists and Communards." He was cheerful and optimistic, however, and he insisted the future of our country would be better than the present. He counted upon our being able to reorganize rapidly for a supreme war effort during the summer. He told me one day that there was a very strained situation between Kerensky and Miliukov in the cabinet—"with which I have nothing to do, except that it makes my work more difficult, since as I am sent by the French government to yours, I am directed to act with and through Miliukov, your minister of foreign affairs; and on the other hand, I am charged with a mission from my party in France to their comrades in opinion here (Kerensky at their head); therefore, with a misunderstanding between Miliukov and Kerensky, I am obliged to wait with crossed arms until questions are settled between them, before I can accomplish anything." He said he had come to replace Paléologue temporarily, as the latter had been too closely identified with tsardom to be of much use.

I was very pleased with Albert Thomas. All his theories and hopes for Russia interested me deeply, but I did not see him again after the spring. He remained in our country until late summer and traveled and studied us in our various phases. Before he departed for France, I heard his opinions were greatly changed and that he had declared before he had always thought ill of our emperor for abusing and suppressing the Russians; but now he admired him for having managed to reign peaceably during twenty-odd years.

As a contrast to Thomas, I saw several times the Grand Duchess Victoria, wife of Kyril Vladimirovich, who next after the emperor's brother, was in line of succession to the throne. I was very sorry for her, as I had known her ever since her arrival in Russia and had had many occasions to admire her fine qualities, besides finding her a most sympathetic person. People were saying the Grand Duke Kyril, in joining the revolutionary movement at the very beginning, hoped the Imperial crown would fall upon his head, he and his wife having always been very simple and democratic in their lives and always in opposition to the Occult forces of the old régime.

It was with good reason they had held their positions so well in Petrograd circles, for they were a charming and distinguished pair. Victoria was born a princess of the English royal house, her father being the second son of Queen Victoria (styled Duke of Edinburgh and Coburg). He had married the Grand Duchess Marie Alexandrovna of Russia, sister of Alexander III and Vladimir, Kyril's own father. Victoria had first married in her teens the grand duke of Hesse, brother of our empress, and this husband was her own first cousin on her father's side, since the mother of Hesse and of our empress was Princess Alice of England. For seven years the Grand Duchess Victoria had been a miserable wife but had finally obtained a divorce from her German husband to marry Kyril. Her difficulties during her first marriage had embittered our empress against her, and her being openly in love with Kyril was well known to all the court in Europe and had caused much talk. When a divorce was finally granted her, the emperor of Russia sent for Kyril, his cousin, and forbade him to marry Victoria, who was now free. Kyril replied that he had come to this audience with the express intention of announcing his engagement and of asking for the sovereign's permission, as head of the house, for his marriage; whereupon the emperor refused it. Then Kyril, defying his master, joined the Grand Duchess Victoria abroad and married her anyhow.

Nicholas II, acting at the request of the empress, issued an edict immediately, saying Kyril was deprived of his court rank and his service, and was banished from the empire, since Her Majesty did not wish to receive the divorced wife of her brother. All this noise seemed not in the least to affect the happiness of the new ménage. Each rich in their own right, they did not miss their allowances suppressed from the Imperial civil lists; and they spent three or four years on the Riviera, in Paris, or in the country in Bavaria, where one or the other of them owned homes. In all these surroundings, they made a most charming circle about them, held a gay court, and were greatly admired for their beauty, wit, and charm, and their unfeigned happiness. The young grand duchess was grieved, however, that her marriage to Kyril had caused his exile and his giving up his service in the Imperial navy; and through her mother and his, she brought pressure to bear on our emperor, that finally one summer Kyril was allowed to bring his wife to Tsarkoe on a visit; and after six months or a year more they were officially forgiven and were permitted to return and live in Russia where Kyril again took up his service, received back his rank and aiguillettes, while Victoria became at once one of the powers at court and the leader of the younger group in society.

My husband had been the intimate boyhood friend of the Grand Duke Kyril, and they had first played, then studied, and later traveled together before our marriage. Since I had married, Kyril had been a constant frequenter of our house, and naturally we were enthusiastic over his return to favor; and we found his wife delightful.

When the war came, all the war work organized by the Grand Duchess Victoria was immensely successful, and I had admired her as much in times of trouble as in the gay circle of the old days. Now I wanted especially to show I was most sincerely one of her followers; I did not know whether Kyril had been forced by his marines of the Imperial Guards to accompany them to the Duma on that first day of the revolution, or if he had gone there of his own free will, but I did know of the effort he had made during the previous autumn, in risking his trip to the staff, to plead with the sovereign against the Rasputin-Vyrubova crowd, when so many unkept promises of liberal reform were made to him. For that act I held him in high esteem.

I called up the grand duchess on the telephone,

and she answered in person and invited me as of old
to come with her. I found her in informal dress and
with her tea-table spread, in her small sitting room;
there was the usual beauty and comfort in all the
arrangements of her palace, which kept more an air of
home than any other in the city. With its books and
knitting, soft chairs and lights, and all its treasures in
marbles and collections so disposed as to be merely
harmonious parts of the general scheme of decoration, it was wonderfully attractive. She herself looked
older, seemed grown taller, and was all in black. As
we smoked and drank tea and talked, I heard with joy
her calm, fair judgment of people and things, and I
was won by the uncomplaining way she had of accepting a situation that upset her life so thoroughly.
She asked news of those of the Imperial family whom
I had recently seen in the Crimea, and she spoke of
our experiences; then she told me some of her own.
She said she had heard from every side of the apparent incapacity of the emperor to react against these
circumstances, previous to the revolution. She told
me even the Empress Mother had said after her last
days with her son at the staff, "It is as if someone had
exchanged my son for another man, quite unlike him;
so indifferent he was, and so silent, through all the
great events. He did not at all realize what had happened to him."

I inferred the grand duchess was thinking of the
current report that the Occult clan at court had
drugged the emperor into complete inertia; though

she did not actually say this. Of herself and her husband and their plans for the future, she told me the provisional government had begged them to keep as quiet as possible. They were consequently going to Finland for the summer, where they would not be too far away from the capital, yet where they could get country life and quiet for themselves and their children. She was very simple and uncritical of the old régime, as well as of the new; but she seemed on the whole full of hope for the future of the country. She had long known Rodzianko and others of his group, and believed in them and their intentions but thought they would be treading on difficult ground before very long.

On the third of May, I lunched with Prince and Princess Kochubei (my husband's aunt and uncle), and from their small party, all of whom were the cream of the old régime, I heard also only broad-minded political opinions expressed. The party seemed unusually optimistic, and they prophesied that Russia soon would be a flourishing republic.

The Grand Duke Nicholas Mikhailovich was there, and he drove me home to my hotel, leaving me with a promise to return again for tea later that afternoon when he had been to his club for war news. We had spoken together in crossing the city of the perfect order in the streets and of the fine behavior of the public, even though there was no sign of authorities about to keep order.

The grand duke had been most enthusiastic over

Nevsky Prospect, St. Petersburg, ca. 1900

Princess Julia Cantacuzene

Courtesy Library of Congress

the masses who were showing such a capacity for re-
straining themselves, even after years of repression,
from which a reaction was to be expected.

"I should be neither surprised nor afraid to see
them form a republic soon," said his Imperial Highness.

"And would you consent to be their president,
Monseigneur?" I asked.

"Well, not the first one."

"Their second president, perhaps?"

"It would be easier." And the grand duke laughed.

Later, when he returned to tea, he told me he had
come down the Nevskii ahead of a great demonstration—a procession of soldiers and plenty of rabble
about them, with black banners of anarchists, and
shots and shouting against the government, while on
one banner in large letters was written, "Down with
capitalists and conservatives!" As one never knew
what might happen, he advised me to remain at home
for the rest of the evening.

For two days the town was up in the air with sharp
fighting and shooting going on in most of the main
streets, especially the Nevskii. The shops were partly
barricaded, yet between the fights, people went about
and attended to business. It was my "baptism of fire,"
as I had not been through the demonstrations in
March. My boy had now finished with his school. As
his year's marks were good enough for him to receive
his diploma without examinations, we had taken our
accommodations to leave the capital for Kiev in the

evening of 5 May. Our train was scheduled for six-thirty. The streets were still turbulent, and the confusion at the railroad station very great. My boy took the maid, trunks, and tickets to the depot about three o'clock that afternoon to insure our baggage being put on the train in time. Toward four o'clock, a number of people dropped in for good-byes and to bring me sweets and flowers, in kindly Russian manner. I ordered tea, of course, and while we sat chatting, suddenly our attention was attracted by the sound of quick-firing guns and salvos of infantry quite near. One of the hotel servants rushed in, pale with excitement, to say I was to close my windows at once, as there was a battle going on in front of the hotel. Although my rooms were more protected than most, by their outlook on the quiet square and the Imperial museum opposite, the hotel director begged me to avoid showing myself at the windows. The windows were already closed, so we went on with our tea and began to discuss how I should manage to reach the station. Everyone was entirely philosophical, as we gradually were being trained to these small inconveniences. Then, after half an hour, as the acute firing subsided, General Knorring[2] volunteered to go down and see what was occurring in front of the hotel. He returned, saying the crowd was enormous on the Nevskii. In his opinion, I had better leave now and profit by the moment's calm to cross the Nevskii, in-

[2]Most likely Baron General Vladimir Romanovich Knorring.

stead of waiting until later when I did not know what might happen. I hurriedly put on hat and coat, and with M. Bark and General Knorring, I descended and went out into the street. There was no shooting, so we decided to cross the wide street at once, and on foot. We were quite ten minutes doing it, not wishing to seem in haste with a crowd so large, almost stationary, and containing elements of variable and possible hostile temper. M. Bark's horses had taken fright from the noise, it turned out, and his coachman had driven them home, leaving a message for his master. But we didn't regret this, as liveries would have attracted attention and perhaps created a disagreeable incident. My two cavaliers conducted me safely over the battlefield of a few moments before; the general left me under the Bazaar Arcades along with my un-uniformed companion to protect me, and he wandered off to search for a cab. This was found shortly and General Knorring returned in triumph with his cabby, who proposed he should be paid ten rubles to the station, instead of the usual two. "As one is apt to run into any kind of danger on the way, Excellencies!"

Naturally we were very glad to accept these terms and his services. I arrived safely at the train depot, an hour and a half ahead of my train time, to find my boy standing on the pavement in front of its entrance with a pale, anxious face, which lighted up at the sight of us. We heard the firing of the infantry's salvos back of us, as I made my *adieu* to my kind bodyguard, and with gratitude we left the stormy capital.

Our train went unmolested to Kiev, and we had no disagreeable experience on the way, though the corridor of our car was crowded with soldiers, who talked politics violently through the thirty-six hours the trip lasted and who expounded to us the most muddled and impossible theories of government, which they were going to introduce into practice. I felt, after the helplessness the government had shown in the uprising of the past three days, that we should be living on a volcano for many months to come. It would be well to place our children somewhere in safety before I undertook to settle down with my husband in Kiev. So I decided to propose to the latter sending the three little people for whose welfare we were responsible to my mother. This arrangement would give me time and independence to settle in Kiev and follow the developments of the revolution. We could attend to any duties that imposed themselves on us, with reference to Michael's service or the estates, with a knowledge that our children's lives were entirely sheltered from storms. If anything happened to us, which seemed quite possible considering Cantacuzene's marked situation in Kiev, the children would be with their natural guardians in America.

I found my husband had made the same reflections as I had, and he at once fell into my plan with enthusiasm. We secured the first accommodations possible out of Russia by the trans-Siberian road. But these were only to be had for the early part of July. So I planned to visit now for a month in Kiev, then go to the Crimean coast for another month with the children, and from there take the little group to Petrograd and start them on their long trip.

These arrangements once made, I felt a weight already off my mind. I enjoyed the time in Kiev and was keenly interested in all I was told and shown there. On the day after I reached Kiev, the papers announced that all difficulties between parties had been settled satisfactorily in the capital by the complete triumph of Kerensky and his followers. The government had seen the necessity of giving way to the socialistic tendencies, and Miliukov had thereupon first protested and then resigned. He was replaced at the Foreign Office by Tereshchenko, and Shingarev[3] had gone into the latter's ministry (of finance).

Our group regretted the departure of Miliukov, as it meant one strong honest patriot the less in the cabinet; but since it was all a temporary affair, people were encouraged to think it did not matter much. The important thing seemed to be to preserve law and order, and to continue the war, until the great elections came off, toward autumn. The more the Socialists were brought forward now, the more they would be obliged either to make good, which of course would be better for Russia, or to damn

[3] Andrei Ivanovich Shingarev (1869–1918), medical doctor and prominent *zemstvo* man and Constitutional-Democrat, Duma deputy, first minister of agriculture in the provisional government, succeeded Tereshchenko in the ministry of finance in May 1917. On 20 January 1918, Shingarev was brutally murdered in his hospital bed by a band of pro-Bolshevik sailors and Red Guards.

themselves in public opinion, and so lose their chance of finally holding power.

Almost everyone concurred in this opinion, and Kerensky personally still kept the general admiration. He, an ardent revolutionist as always, had shown tremendous patriotism, moderation, and lack of personal vanity in the crisis. He had, since his placing in the ministry of justice, handled questions connected with the detention of the ex-sovereigns and members of the old-régime party with more generosity and dignity than anyone could have hoped. He also showed himself a consummate leader of his own party and managed its unruly elements with a skill altogether remarkable. His eloquence continued to excite the multitude's admiration, and even the most retrograde gave him their respect. I found in Kiev, as in Petrograd, that everyone considered Kerensky was going to be the greatest man of the time, and all groups joined in wishing him success.

XX

Kiev

MY HUSBAND was established in Kiev with his Cuirassiers about him. They were the great attraction in the public squares and parks, and were shining lights in a town that was apparently full of holiday makers. It was overrun also with deserters and careless soldiers, who could dress now as they pleased and salute their officers or not on the streets. Against this background, the spick-and-span, well-groomed, picked men of our Cuirassiers contrasted strongly. Their pride was in their looks and discipline, and they thoroughly enjoyed their successes. My husband was delighted with the way his officers and men had taken the revolution; and he almost hoped he might be able to hold his command together, and really keep the city in order, until the occurrence of the constituent assembly. This was to be arranged for in September, the government's proclamation promised.

Kiev's attitude was much more optimistic than had been Petrograd's. The hotels and restaurants were crowded. There were musicals, plays, and festivities, with enormous numbers of arrivals and new settlers. All the Polish aristocrats, who were refugees from the war-devastated provinces, had settled here in 1915. Among them were many pretty women in attractive homes, wanting to forget the sufferings they had been through.

On our estates in Poltava, the prices of labor had been pushed up somewhat, but otherwise things were going smoothly. Our "peasant committee" had acclaimed my brother-in-law when he had recently been to Bouromka. Our intendent, who was of the peasantry, was on excellent terms with the villagers. But it was decided that my mother-in-law should not go to the country for this summer, as she was in a bad condition of nerves. Though the place remained vacant, many others round about us were occupied by their owners, who were satisfied all was going well locally and would go even better later, since confidence existed between proprietors and peasants.

Shortly, there began to be talk of a Ukrainian movement, "intended to bind together the groups of Little Russia, as against the disorderly ultra-socialistic waves that may come into our provinces from the north!" We knew there were German agents working among us for the Bolsheviki, and both the upper and lower classes of people wished to keep these out of Kiev and the surrounding country. My husband became interested in finding out the origin and aims of this mysterious propaganda. In two or three weeks, after a casual first mention, the word "Ukrainian" was in everyone's mouth. To his great annoyance, he discovered a nest of Austrian agents at the bottom of a clever plot to unite the ancient provinces that had first formed the Ukraine, thus creating a "nationalist" movement to

Riverfront in Kiev

Courtesy Hoover Institution, Stanford University

Street scene, Kiev

separate them from the Russian central government. Their scheme was later to bring this whole section of the Russian Empire under Austrian influence and, if all went well, to annex it to Austria. It was a deep-laid and intelligent plot of the enemies, whose agents in Kiev were either Austrian spies, or Poles and Russians, their dupes and paid agents. Reports were at once sent to the central government in Petrograd, accompanied by proofs. Orders came back to my husband and others that the Ukrainian propaganda was to be fought to a finish. Consequently, some of the leading men of that party were pursued and run out of the town, and a counter-propaganda was inaugurated. The nationalist movement was being given a black eye, though there was a group still among Little Russian peasants, Poles, and the deserting soldiers who liked the new ideals—or the enemies' money—and who said they wished to see an autonomy under Russian sovereignty, but with Ukrainian newspapers, banks, money, and army. A committee was formed to represent the interests of this party. They gave the authorities some difficulty and anxiety since a "committee" could not be suppressed, with the then-ideas of freedom. Neither could spies be executed, as capital punishment was no longer permissible.

Early in July the Ukrainians sent deputies to Kerensky begging him to do justice to their party, saying their desire was to keep law and order, and to remain under the wing of Russia. They wished for an autonomous government, to use their own language, to form their own regiments, but the latter would be glad also to fight side by side with their Russian comrades. Tereshchenko, the minister of foreign affairs, was sent by Kerensky for the delicate mission of conferring with the leaders of both sides, because he was a native of Kiev, had large interests in the industrial life of the city, and would probably, therefore, be a just and capable arbiter. Among the Ukrainians there was great rejoicing over this choice. He was persuaded that he personally, in his sugar-factory interests, and all other industrial and property owners in and around Kiev, stood to gain by a Ukrainian régime, since the latter would be conservative and a bulwark against the Bolsheviki, also that the lower classes (peasants and soldiers) would have their patriotism awakened by a nationalist propaganda and would behave better.

Before Tereshchenko left Kiev, he saw everything through spectacles put upon his nose by the plotters. He had admitted their perfect right to form a government with a senate (which they called "rada"), also a ministry with different departments to handle local questions. They were to make up a given number of volunteer military units, these regiments to be formed by soldiers drawn away from the Russian formations, through open and permitted propaganda. Such troops were to be officered by Ukrainian nationalists, though they would obey orders from the Russian War Ministry sent by way of their own minister for war.

Tereshchenko was seemingly quite sincere in his belief that such decisions were for the best from every point of view. Apparently, he never realized that his act was giving the lie to his own central government's former policy and that he was putting a military force in the field that might some day fight the provisional government and overthrow it. My husband and others saw this reverse side of the shield. They pointed it out, first to the minister himself, afterward to the central government. But they received reply that their business must be to watch the development of all the different branches of the movement, see that it did not get beyond bounds, and that the Ukrainians really carried out their promise of sending troops to the front.

Kerensky had tried his eloquence to make the national army take the offensive in July on the Galician front, and the disaster of Tarnopol had been the result.[1] He seemed still to hope from the northern front some sort of recompense for the drama at Tarnopol. The ambassadors of the allies actually were told that the great number of deserters were not deserters at all but represented a spontaneous permitted demobilization of certain classes of older men who were being allowed to return home to cultivate the land. Afterward, remaining army units would be strengthened

---

[1]On 1 July, the Russian army had begun an offensive on the Galician (southwestern) front in the hope of repeating the successes of the previous summer against the Austrians in that sector. What began as an advance turned into a rout when the Germans and Austrians counterattacked and, in the Battle of East Galicia, retook Galich, Tarnopol (24–26 July), and Chernovtsy (3 August). This was the end of the Russian army as an effective fighting force in the world war.

by new recruits and would at the end of the summer be ready to take the offensive all along the line with vigor! The American ambassador told me this, and said when I protested that "it must be true, as the minister of war had told him of it, and he was of course a reliable authority!"

Since the officers felt sure of defeat, they begged that no offensive be tried, that the Russian army be left, a mere curtain, to hold certain of the enemy's troops in front of them. It was the extreme limit of good to be expected under actual conditions, and the officers claimed it would serve the allied cause better than would another tragic failure and defeat. Meantime, some shock battalions of picked men—mainly officers or young boy cadets from the military schools, all volunteers—were being formed. One of them, under Mme. Bochkareva, was called the "Battalion of Death" and showed up magnificently through all the troubles that were to come.

From late July on, whenever he went into the street, my husband was followed by various strange-looking individuals, sometimes in hooligan's shabby dress, sometimes in uniform. I was on the qui vive, and these apparitions dogging Michael made me somewhat anxious. He personally treated the whole matter as a joke and amused himself frequently, leading the mysterious spies on wild-goose chases about the city or stopping unexpectedly with a loud remark about them and their interest in his affairs. In the streets Cantacuzene was now a well-known figure. He was constantly being

Women's Battalion of Death, Petrograd
Courtesy Hoover Institution, Stanford University

*May Day 1917, Winter Palace Square, Petrograd; left banner —
Long Live the Socialist Republic; right banner — Long Live Socialism*

saluted, pointed out, or spoken to in a friendly, grateful spirit.

At the Crimean seaside I spent a delightful month, waiting quietly with the children for the date of their departure to America. I had many friends about me and greatly enjoyed my "cure," in spite of anxieties which the long trip before my little people caused me.

It was during my stay in the Crimea that Admiral Kolchak,[2] who until now had kept the most perfect order and discipline at Sebastopol, was obliged to resign by an uprising of the sailors of the Black Sea fleet that he commanded. He was replaced by an officer of the sailors' election, and from that moment, excesses were feared all along the coast, especially where the members of the Imperial family and their suites were scattered. The Imperial exiles were under arrest now, and we heard of motor-loads of half-drunken Bolshevik sailors scouring the country, robbing and assassinating the well-to-do people who had taken refuge anywhere on the peninsula. We were glad to turn our faces northward, since a strike on all the railroads was threatened, and this announcement made me impatient to see my young travelers beyond our borders.

[2] Admiral Alexander Vasilevich Kolchak (1874–1920; executed by the Bolsheviks) was appointed commander of Russia's Black Sea fleet in April 1916. Having initially greeted the revolution as a prerequisite to revitalization of the war effort, he resigned his post on 20 June in protest against the collapse of discipline in the fleet. Later, from late 1918 to January 1920, as "Supreme Ruler of Russia" in the civil war, he directed the civil-war struggle against the Bolsheviks in Siberia.

Letters from Petrograd seemed to reflect very uncertain conditions. Senator Root's mission had come and gone, and he had written to me twice, giving me news of my family, from whom he had brought me many messages. Besides this personal information, his letters reflected what seemed a rather *determined* optimism as to the Russian situation, and a desire to believe the best of our capacity to live through the revolutionary period. Knowing the reliability of his judgment, I was very keen to have him receive a variety of accounts and impressions, and not alone the official history of events, which I felt must be that necessarily presented by men he would meet in the capital. His limited stay and the surrounding influences would keep him away altogether from certain questions, while the government would naturally try to inspire him with confidence in its ability to take an active part in the war. Unless someone of the military or of the old régime group was near to predict the sadder possibilities in our revolutionary movement, I feared a false version of our recent experiences would alone be told. I heard afterward that the senator had seen Sazonov and that one or two others also had presented our view; but he left just before the Tarnopol offensive, and I fear with greater hopes for Russia than the country was able to justify.

XXI

Kerensky and Bolsheviki

IREACHED Petrograd on 14 July, a Saturday, and settled down at once in my old apartments at the Hotel
d'Europe to the complicated measures necessary for
supplying my company of travelers with passports,
money, and so on, for beyond the frontier. We had
been forewarned by everyone of the great difficulties
we should encounter on the trip from the Crimea to
the capital. But we had suffered no inconvenience at
all, save from heat and from the crowds everywhere,
which made it impossible to move about at any of the
stations. We had supplied ourselves with provisions
and were therefore able to eat and live in our reserved
compartments. There we were quite unmolested by
what seemed to be the millions of deserters, swarming
like flies on the roofs, in the corridors, on the platforms—everywhere. They were noisy but perfectly
good-natured and entirely willing to fetch and carry
for us and make themselves useful. With these three
days successfully behind us, and with the supreme triumph of finding all our baggage still on our train and
intact, my optimism grew as to the children's long trip
through Siberia. I was glad enough, however, to see
their time for starting nearly at hand, for I had noticed
both on the railroad and in the capital a queer general

effervescence, which was vastly increased in the past six weeks. It could scarcely be expected an improvement would occur with time.

On Monday I must present myself with petitions for each passport, photographs of each member of the party, also with all the travelers in person and with two sponsors for my veracity, who must viva-voce assert the destination and all possible details as to the proposed trip. Our large party, which consisted of three children, nurse, governess, a business man, and myself, together with General Zolotnitsky[1] and M. Tatishchev,[2] attracted immediate and amiable attention from the old régime officials, who were still in charge and who had been prepared to receive us. The business was put through with much effort on all sides in record time, about an hour and a half. In spite of the prepared written petitions, many questions still had to be answered, explanations made, and everyone had to sign six times or more. Then we were told the passports would go that same evening to the general staff, for the military visa, and that I might call for them in two or three days—on Thursday afternoon, perhaps.

After starting the children back to the hotel, Tatishchev kept me a moment to say, "When are you really in need of the passports?" I told him the children's tickets were for the trans-Siberian train of 24

[1]Peter Nikolaevich Zolotnitsky (b. 1874), a war ministry official.

[2]Boris Alekseevich Tatishchev (b. 1876), career foreign service officer; at this time head of the Foreign Office chancery.

July, a week and one day off. "Then if you want to get your documents, spare no urging, for the offices are slow and disorganized now, at best, and there is a crisis pending, which may cause all work to be stopped within a few days. This afternoon there is a cabinet meeting being held to treat of the gravest questions. It is again as in May—the conservative element locking horns with the ultra-democratic crowd. I fear it means disorders in the streets and resignations from the cabinet unless a compromise can be found today. I do not say this to alarm you, but so you will follow up your papers and push them through by every means in your power."

This coming from Tatishchev, who was unemotional, reliable, and never pessimistic. Thanks to his warning, I at once went on to the bank and begged the manager, an old friend, to take personally in hand the question of the children's letter-of-credit and to push it through with all his powers. The American ambassador, Mr. Francis, had promised to help me with his authority at the finance ministry, so I hoped for the best.

That evening a group sat about my tea-table after dinner—friends who had dropped in for a chat. Someone was reading an article on the revolution that had appeared in an English magazine whose editor was filled with admiration for our great qualities. It was warm, and the windows opening on my balcony, looking over the quiet park, were opened wide. The noise along the Nevskii came to us vaguely from round the corner. The little girls with governesses and nurses had retired, while my boy sat with us. Suddenly we heard the tac-tac-tac of machine-gun firing piercing the air, far off at first, then approaching rapidly. An uprising beginning! The Bolsheviki! Evidently, the conservative cabinet ministers were holding out. In a moment a hotel servant appeared, followed by my frightened maid. "Will Your Highness permit me to close the windows? The hotel director begs the windows and curtains be closed immediately and lights put out so outside attention will not be attracted."

My guests helped the man and maid do this, while I went into the two large nurseries adjoining my salon and gave orders for closing their windows too, not waking the girls but saying that the attendants should remain dressed for the present.

When I returned to my guests, they were sitting in the light of one small table-lamp with a dark shade. We held a hurried consultation. The hotel director sent me a second messenger to say the Bolsheviki wished to visit the premises, searching for firearms, and so on. He had held them off momentarily and had telephoned asking for a force of Cossacks to guard the hotel, but until these arrived, he could not stand long against the Bolsheviki's arguments, if they insisted on making a tour of inspection. He therefore warned me so I might be ready for their visit to my rooms, in case it occurred.

I decided my guests should leave at once. As soon as their good-byes were said, the maids, the governess, my boy, and I hid such valuables as I had with me in various out-of-the-way places. Then I rapidly changed from my house gown to a rough traveling costume, and we waited with locked doors. We had every intention of showing ourselves hospitable (if the need presented itself) to nocturnal visitors.

From time to time, some one of my acquaintances in Petrograd telephoned to know how we were faring. I had only good reports to give, though the battle seemed to rage all about us through the night, if one was to judge by the continuous firing. Machine guns and musketry, revolver shots and mad shouts, made a bedlam of the streets. At intervals the deep buzz and whir of the revolutionary motor-trucks passing under our windows, carrying soldiers or prisoners, added to the din. Nurse and governess, the maid, my boy, and I remained dressed and on guard for several hours. The two younger children, who had been wakened at first by the shooting, were reassured by being told it was "just the revolution"; they turned over and went blissfully to sleep again.

I was really anxious as to what was happening about us. To think that I had brought my little people into this turmoil of my own accord. I feared it might in some way prevent their departure. Then I tried to believe that within a week all would be tranquilized and to hope that I should be able to push their papers and get everything prepared as I wished within the seven long days ahead. At last, about one o'clock in the morning, nothing dramatic having occurred to us in spite of the continuous firing, I realized we must get what sleep we could and leave the future to take care of its own problems. All our rooms communicated by inside-doors and were at the end of a long corridor, so no one of us could be disturbed without the others of our party being warned. Without undressing, we lay down upon our beds, and my boy and I both slept immediately and remained unconscious of our dangers until nine o'clock the following morning! In fact, the maid had to come and wake me, bringing me a breakfast-tray and the news-sheets. She announced that now we were quite safe, since at four in the morning, the Cossacks had come and were established in the hotel office, while the director had organized a patrol among the servants.

I was told also the restaurant would be open only from twelve to three o'clock, to give us one hot meal during the day, after which we might have cold food and tea, with the children's milk, in our rooms. I found no one would be allowed to come into the hotel (as the doors were barred to the crowded streets), and the proprietor asked that we should not try to go out either. There were disorders everywhere, and shops, banks, and offices were closed. I found out by telephone the government offices were also closed. So nothing could be done to push my papers. We remained where we were that day and the next—Tuesday and Wednesday—as if besieged, in our big rooms with windows closed and curtains drawn to prevent any stray shots from coming in.

The shooting increased and decreased periodically, for no apparent reason. My maid went up on the roof, and from its parapet she saw the street fighting and the pillaging of some shops on the Nevskii. My boy also made trips to the roof and to the hotel office where the Cossack guards were in possession. The male guests of the hotel met to discuss our situation. A number of American tourists (businessmen) were of this group and were greatly interested as to the changes this demonstration would bring. The American ambassador rang me up. I found him greatly interested in the complications, but he hoped the next few days would see a satisfactory solution. From Tatishchev, who telephoned me also, I learned that the question in the cabinet was a difficult one to settle. It would probably and disastrously bring about the resignation of the last conservative elements still in power, thus giving the Socialists another forward push.

Tuesday evening the shooting lessened, and by Wednesday evening the city was entirely quieted.

Thursday the whole town resumed its normal aspect. The trains were running, and we went about our business as if nothing had occurred to disturb life. The anarchists had gained a step in their advance toward power. Prince Lvov had resigned, and Kerensky was made prime minister, with various other socialistic elements put into the cabinet. All patriots, not only those of conservative ideas, were growing anxious at the lost ground each day showed and the increasing power of the mob and their German leaders. It was decidedly marked that Lenin's[3] propaganda was growing more aggressive; and Trotsky, the anarchist (whose real name was Leo Bronstein), had arrived, or was arriving, to inflame the already unbalanced brains and help Lenin to do his utmost.

I was glad the children were leaving, more and more so with every hour. The young travelers were greatly wrought up at going, and though I knew it was the only way to have them reach safety in time, I felt extremely anxious at launching them into the possibilities of the long trans-Siberian voyage. They looked very young and helpless as they started off, in spite of my boy's manliness and his little sisters' confidence in his capacity to take care of them. I was grateful to all the group of friends and officials who had facilitated their preparations and without whom the uprising of the Bolsheviki would have prevented my getting my young people off. As it was, the little party, well supplied with tickets, passes, and funds, started for the ends of the earth in a safe and well-appointed train. Though they had adventures and experiences, even discomfort, they ran into no real dangers and finally reached their destination safely, landing after six weeks in San Francisco, where my mother had then met them.

[3]Vladimir Ilich Lenin (real name: Ulianov) (1870–1924), founder and leading figure, until his death, of the Bolshevik faction of the Russian Social Democratic Labor Party, precursor of the Soviet Communist Party. Lenin had returned to Russia in April 1917 after many years of European exile.

I remained on alone in Petrograd for two days after I had seen the children depart, attending to some business. Before leaving for Kiev, I saw the capture by storm of the Lenin headquarters. These were in the ex-palace of the Ksheshinskaia,[4] first "ballerine" of the Imperial theaters. It was a large, detached palace or villa, opposite the Fortress of Peter and Paul, and near the Trinity Bridge. One side of the building faced on the street, and one on its own entrance-courtyard, while the other sides looked into its charming garden, which made the corner of two streets. A high wall edged these, and where the streets met at the wall's angle stood a small round summer-house, which had been the pulpit used by Lenin and his followers to preach their poisonous doctrines to the Russian world. Lenin had been an exiled nihilist under the old régime and had lived in Switzerland. One of the first measures of the revolution had naturally been the pardoning and repatriation of all political prisoners and exiles. This was without distinction as to what opinions they held or what their individual reputations were. To everyone's surprise, Lenin returned home directly through Germany. Though he explained he was not allowed to stop or get out at any station, we heard he had been the recipient of every possible attention during his travels in the enemy's country. On

---

[4]Matilda Ksheshinskaia (1872–1971), ballerina and former mistress of Nicholas II and of several grand dukes. Her villa, on the "Petrograd Side" across the river from the Winter Palace, was used by the Petrograd Bolsheviks just as the author describes.

his arrival he at once took possession of Ksheshin-skaia's palace, which she had abandoned in terror at the first sign of the revolutionary movement. The ballerine protested at her property being requisitioned by the Leninists, but she was intimidated into silence. Daily, Lenin or one of his lieutenants preached their fiery sermons from the little corner summer-house and distributed pamphlets to the listeners below on the sidewalks. After a time, the new government having proclaimed complete toleration of all political theories, the orators began to make new converts who, as they demanded the maximum of socialism, took the name of "Maximalists"—in Russian, "Bolsheviki"—and became a declared party, though they made no noisy demonstration before the end of April. It was found that certain of their group had German gold coins about them. The government through its weakness in troops could not act, though; and Lenin stayed on at the capital, playing his waiting game, talking, working always, especially among the poor.

Polovtsev[5] now, in the second uprising, decided the nest of this propaganda must be cleaned out. Suddenly one evening, he bombarded it with machine guns, took the fortress by storm, and captured about thirty of the plotters, though not Lenin himself, who had fled into Finland as soon as he had discovered the failure of the uprising. Then documents were even found in the house that showed the Leninists in relationship

[5]General Peter Aleksandrovich Polovtsev (b. 1874), commander of the Petrograd Military District.

to the enemy, and German gold was captured there.[6]

I had been dining that evening at the American Embassy. As the town was only superficially quiet, Mr. Francis proposed when we left, about ten o'clock, to drive another guest and myself home, affording us the protection of his carriage with its American flag. It was still twilight, with a splendid afterglow fading on the horizon and the charm of the soft July sky. This caused the ambassador to say, as we settled into our seats: "It is early yet, and we have all been shut up for so long. I haven't left my desk today. Shall we go round by the Quai and admire the river on the way to your hotel, Princess? It is but ten minutes more drive by that way."

I naturally gave an affirmative reply, and we all drew a deep breath of pleasure as we turned out on to the Quai, the most beautiful street I know, with its great palaces on one side and the swift, vast expanse of river on the other. Soon we were passing the Summer Garden, and the British Embassy stood up in front of us, while the long elegant curves of Trinity Bridge, clear against the sky, spanned the river and joined the Field of Mars[7] to the Fortress of St. Peter and St. Paul.

---

[6]Although the Bolsheviks indisputably received help from the Germans, who supported all anti-war factions in Russia, the so-called "German gold documents" published by the provisional government's minister of justice in July with the intent of compromising the Bolsheviks were only business telegrams.

[7]A vast square on the Neva Embankment just upstream from the row of Imperial palaces, which had been used as a military parade ground since the early nineteenth century.

"It doesn't seem possible we have been so agitated these last days," I said.

"No," said Mr. Francis; "certainly this time the provisional government has held its own."

"See, there are the fortresses of the government and of Lenin, standing opposite one-another, and at peace," I said; and then we both noticed a light playing on them.

"What do you suppose that light means? A signal?" said our host.

"Or, perhaps just one of the naval searchlights being tried," I answered.

Suddenly the silence across the river was broken, and a shot was fired, and then an avalanche of them rang out, and the whole space between Peter and Paul and the Ksheshinṣkaia Palace was alive with soldiers and with guns, flashing and banging—bedlam let loose again!

"Hello, that looks serious," said Mr. Francis.

The coachman, without asking for orders, whirled his plunging horses completely round and started back in the direction whence we had come. I instructed him to turn into the first side street and, avoiding thoroughfares, to take the short cut to my hotel. He was entirely self-possessed and obedient.

When we arrived at the hotel, we found the director who knew of the intended action on the Lenin headquarters and could reassure us as to the general security of the city. Polovtsev had taken the citadel of disorderly propaganda, proved its connection with

Germany, and arrested twenty or more of the leaders of the party. He had obtained the obedience of the men under his orders and had quieted the city within forty-eight hours. Now he even dared publish an "order-of-the-day" to his soldiers, saying he wished to see them appear in the streets with their uniforms properly buttoned, their arms cleaned and in order, and with their general aspect such that he could tell, when he looked, the members of the garrison from deserters or tramps.

Within a short time, in spite of this record, Polovtsev was summarily dismissed, and the reasons for it given out officially were his over-severity with the soldiers as embodied in his order to appear properly dressed, his intolerance toward one political party in these days of freedom, and his having sent to prison members of a legitimate group in the new Russian organization!

The arrested Bolsheviki, though liberated after a few weeks in prison, showed themselves greatly embittered. With the full knowledge and consent of the ministry, they at once took up their old habits and headquarters, continued their propaganda, and finally even published several newspapers. The government apparently was too weak to assume anything but a propitiating attitude toward these avowed anarchists, or else there was no feeling in administrative circles of danger to the nation from the Lenin and Trotsky theories. It all seemed fatal in its menace for the future of the country to those of our class, who had no desires politically and who thought only of winning the war and of preserving Russia. But our military and conservative groups had lost the power even to speak.

XXII

The Rise of the Bolsheviki

F ROM JULY ON, Kerensky seemed to lose his grip on
things somehow and to change both his personality and his policy. Whether this came from ill-health
and his breaking down under the strain of his varied
occupations and responsibilities, or whether he realized some of the dramatic failures of the revolution
and this affected his capacity, or whether it was simply
that he was not the type of man to stand his personal
success, it is difficult to say. In the early days he had
been of the people and disdained luxury. Now he
moved into the Winter Palace, occupied the emperor's suite there, sleeping in the emperor's bed,
using his desk and his motors, giving audience with
much form and ceremony, and surrounding himself
with luxury and sentinels.

The capital gossiped much. The conservative
group, who until now had been full of admiration for
Kerensky's honesty and patriotism, and had trusted
him, became disillusioned. The Socialists felt their
golden statue was uncovering feet of clay, and his own
cabinet was helpless. As the weeks passed, there were
murmurs against him, only vague at first. But his policy was to keep his personal popularity at any cost,
and the price of it became a flow of concessions to

the nation's baser instincts. This lasted through July and August.

My trip back to Kiev was without adventure. I lay awake reading and thinking until late into the night as the train moved southward. In the corridor of the car, a dozen or more soldiers were sleeping heavily. I heard them breathe and turn. One was half sitting, half leaning against my door, which occasionally creaked behind his weight. During the afternoon they had been talking politics loudly, and such nonsense as to what the revolution would do had been passed round that I grew desperate in the thought of their lack of understanding. One old fellow sat silent during all these discussions, and while our berths were being prepared for the night, these rough men made me standing room among them, and I found myself next to the quiet fellow. I was chilled and tired, and I shivered, saying to him,

"It is cold tonight, Little Father."

"Yes," he replied. "And there is no wood to heat the car with."

"True; that is because there is so much disorder everywhere, not because wood is lacking in Russia."

"No, Lady. There is much of all here, but we cannot get it."

And then I ventured, wondering what he would answer: "I am surprised, because I thought the revolution would remedy the ailments of the old régime, and it seems even worse now; or perhaps it is only to my eyes?"

"Oh, no," said my soldier with dreary resignation. "It is much worse. In the old days at least there was order and some wood, also provisions; and then when it was cold weather, there was vodka to be had, to warm oneself with, and that helped much."

Now in the silence of the night his speech came back to me, and I wondered what would become of all these lowly people, some of whom were so ignorant as to be demanding "a republic with a tsar"; and I wondered who would be the more helpless, they or ourselves.

As this thought crossed my mind, the soldier against my door woke up, moved and cleared his throat. Then gently, so low as to wake none of his comrades, he began a crooning, chanting, harmonious song, in a soft minor key, unutterably sad and sweet, full of the pent-up suffering and longing of his whole, primitive race. Though it was uncultured, his voice like many of our peasants' voices was beautiful beyond words. And I regretted my incapacity to gather up this passing thread of sound and weave from it, for a violin to sing in other times its lament for the past and the hope for the future it seemed to contain. A whole hour and more the lovely strain went on. Finally it died away, as the singer fell asleep again.

Now influenced by the poisonous German propaganda, which was being daily injected, these same creatures of the plains and woods were working themselves into a passionate folly and were suffering from hideous moral indigestion, following too much liberty, which might well bring about their own ruin, together with that of the whole country. And seemingly, no one could help us now, while it was still time! Everyone, at home and abroad, was either too busy, or was blind. Some said we had primitive strength enough as a nation to live through our trials, and after knowing these people for so many years, I was of those who kept faith in their final resurrection. I only wept for the sufferings and destruction that the immediate future must bring, and for the reaction of our troubles on the war. It took all my courage to face the months ahead, and I wondered whether I should leave Kiev alive and with my husband or whether we should find our end there.

Kiev seemed enchanting after the capital, with its gay streets and gardens, its charming luxurious homes, and the great, splendid, picturesque piles of ancient monasteries and churches, crowned by their numerous golden domes. All this was reassuring to my sad spirits. It looked and felt like old times here, and I began to believe again in the ideals of the revolution and in its success. I was delighted to pile myself and my small baggage into Cantacuzene's big motor (leaving Élène and Davidka to struggle for the trunks) and to be whirled off by our smart soldier-chauffeur to the pretty house into which my husband had already moved.

Mme. Ivanov, an old acquaintance of ours, had been ordered by the municipal government to lodge some of the military who overflowed the town; and in looking about for people least apt to disturb her ease and her old servants, she begged us to come and settle with her for the time of my husband's detail in Kiev.

We were very pleased to accept. For weeks during the hot summer weather we sat, took our meals, and received our friends. I at once loved the place and grew very fond of the little quaint old lady, its owner. The months we spent with her, and the dramatic experiences we lived through together, only drew us closer to one another.

Kiev was full of acquaintances, and there were even several old friends settled there or passing through. I found my husband was the center of an agreeable group whose motto was openly to "Eat, drink, and be merry, in the insecurity of the morrow." Life was expensive, but people had plenty of ready money and were trying to spend it on their immediate enjoyment, since rumors floated southward that there might be later a general confiscation of ready funds for government needs. Everyone kept open house in the cosmopolitan society, composed of rich Polish refugee nobles, of the members of the French aviation unit stationed at Kiev, of those men who, like Cantacuzene, were stationary in the city, and of the floating elements of officers on leave. Parties on the river, auto-picnics to the chateaux in the neighborhood, dinners and suppers with gypsy-bands and chorus, bridge and even tangos, poker and romances were the order of the day. It seemed even gayer than in the spring, perhaps a little feverishly so. What was happening in the upper strata was also going on among the people in the streets, parks, and cheap restaurants. One had the impression of a wild festival in every class.

We drifted through July and August. There was talk always of the constituent assembly, but no step had as yet been taken for arranging the elections.

The Ukrainians were augmenting their propaganda, with evidences of success. They were now established in a great and beautiful building that had been presented as a museum to the city by one of its rich citizens and which they had "requisitioned," throwing its valuable collections into the street. The donor had vainly tried to save them, and after ineffective appeals to the municipal authorities, he had a heart-stroke and died. In these halls was established the Rada, or senate, of the Ukraine, while their government offices were near-by, in a hotel of ill repute, which had been confiscated also.

Since they now figured in the province's administration, my husband and others had to treat with them on every question pertaining to our estates. All who had visited the Rada and the Ukrainian ministries returned disgusted, saying they had had to do with a lot of second-rate bounders and had found wild confusion, while unlimited pretensions were the marked trait of the new party, whose only effective work was in spreading propaganda of disorder and disloyalty, dictated by their Austrian masters.

Committees became an epidemic everywhere. Committees of workmen at Count Bobrinsky's sugar factories decided when they would work, also at what prices, and when to enjoy a holiday; and they over-ran the Bobrinsky home, camping in the rooms and using furniture and valuables. It was the same at other factories, and production was practically at a standstill. Likewise, committees of peasants on all estates fixed their own wages and labors, and said what should be done with the master's harvests after the year's grain was brought in. The village cows were grazing on proprietors' lawns, the village people walked in gardens and parks, ate fruits and vegetables found there, requisitioned machinery and stock, and though the chateaux were still respected, there was already talk of taking them for places of amusement or for school-buildings.

All this created an atmosphere and situation quite indescribable. Shops were closed, with signs up saying it was because the shop girls had taken a holiday. People were constantly forced to do their own house work while the servants went to committee meetings. Masters were obliged to pay their servants eighty to one hundred and fifty rubles wages, where before ten or twenty had sufficed. All this came by degrees, and with each week there was a new surprise, until at the end of the summer, the upper classes were greatly depressed and lived in dread of further developments whether on their estates, in factories, shops, hotels, or homes. The masses, on the contrary, had reached the zenith of self-confidence and were in a semi-hysterical triumphant condition. We had luck personally, for our old servants were daily proving their devotion, and we suffered no inconvenience from any caprices on their part.

There was, however, a strike declared by the "dvorniki." These men, who cleaned our sidewalks and courtyards and ran errands, were also night-watchmen and looked after passports for the inhabitants of each house (by police regulation). Many large apartment houses kept three or more of them. Suddenly, these now-formed committees, deciding they would do none of their special work, called a strike. Our own Grigory went out with seeming unwillingness, being a good man and with little to do, since our household was small. He had always been content with his place and wages, and had lived with Mme. Ivanov for fifteen years or more. But he was told he must also profit by the new liberties, and "protect the revolution." Otherwise he would be punished by his fellows who were less contented than he. So, dressed in his best clothes, he went out to meetings during all the day, returning home only to eat and sleep, and doing no work, of course. During the week of their strike, a deputation of dvorniki came to call on Mme. Ivanov. The deputation was announced, and it waited in the hall, and seeing our little hostess really frightened, my husband offered to receive them for her. She accepted, and Cantacuzene—followed by Prince Kurakin, who was visiting us; by the ever-faithful Davidka; and by a small boy, our "Buttons" who ran errands for the household—threw both panels of the door open suddenly with a loud noise. The deputation hesitated. These bullies had expected to face one small, old, feeble woman, and not three solid men.

"What do you want here?" Cantacuzene shouted, with his most ferocious scowl. The leader of the band stepped forward. "Comrade," he began in the revolutionary phrase; but he never got any further. Now my husband's vocabulary, already rich for such occasions, had coined new treasures of speech in these revolutionary days, and one after another, rolled forth sonorous arguments and appellations, red-hot! What he thought of these times, with their disorder, of the strikes in general, and what of the dvorniki and of this deputation in particular, he said, thoroughly enjoying having an occasion of letting himself go. We couldn't in detail follow his speech from where we sat in the salon. Our impression was merely of a single terrific explosion. But when he had concluded, the men before him thoroughly understood that Cantacuzene did not consider himself their "comrade." He ordered them out. They, without a word, turned and all together rushed frantically to the front door, pushing and stumbling in their haste, as they fumbled with its fastenings. At last it opened. They tumbled over one another, down the three steps into the street and fled, running at full speed to the corner, where they disappeared. They never returned, and we heard nothing further of the strikers' pretensions. A committee formed for self-defense in such cases categorically refused to grant any of the demands made of them, whereupon the dvorniki gave up their strike and took up their work again quietly, exactly on the old terms! Our own dear Grigory returned to us, removed his best clothes, and with a contented smile went on with his sweeping as of old.

As yet, our country place, Bouromka, was quiet, which was a great blessing. We gratefully attributed this to our intendant's personal talents. He was of peasant birth and of our province, and he showed himself most adroit in handling men. Also, he got on with the village committee, where we knew he was expending money as well as eloquence. But since he succeeded in getting the year's crop sown, grown, and harvested, and kept the gardens, park, stables, and chateau unmolested, we were content. Bouromka was furnishing us with provisions and supplying my mother-in-law with them in her Crimean villa. When the harvest was disposed of, we found there had been a slight deficit, instead of the usual fine revenue; but we were so pleased to have the estate still untouched that we carried this burden easily enough. In September there came to Bouromka village, however, a committee from outside. Ukrainians and Bolsheviki, the intendant reported they were, and these preached the most inflammatory doctrines.

The peasants were still resisting, explaining they were content with us and that their work had always been well paid for and themselves well treated. The agitators then said the land was by right the peasants', and they declared the house, buildings, and stock should be appropriated by them now, as everything, according to the law of our new republic, belonged to the people. Still the peasantry was quiet, but we

Empress Alexandra and Emperor Nicholas II
Courtesy Hoover Institution, Stanford University

EUROPE, 1888-1917

National capital city
City or town
Historical point of interest
Railways the Cantacuzenes used
Other railways
Kiev Locations associated with the Cantacuzenes
Riga Other locations

0   250   500
Miles

White Sea

Lake Onega

Lake Ladoga

St. Petersburg (Petrograd)

Tsarskoe
oe

E U R O P E A N

Dvina River

Kama River

Volga River

Moscow

Ola River

R U S S I A

Tula

TRANS-SIBERIAN   RAILWAY

Samara

U   S   S

Don River

Ural River

Kharkov

Bouromka   •**Poltava**

Dnieper River

AINE

Odessa

CRIMEA

Sebastopol   •**Simferopol**
Balaklava   •**Yalta**
Simeiz,
Livadia–Oreanda Palaces

C A U C A S U S

Caspian Sea

Tiflis

lack   Sea

60° N
70° E
60° E
60° E
50° N
40° N
30° E
40° E
50° E

PETROGRAD
ARSENAL
COMPLEX

Kshesinkaia
Palace

Finland
Railroad
Station

ARSENAL QUAI

PETER

TRINITY

Kronverk Canal

Fortress of
Peter and
Paul

STOCK
EXCHANGE
BRIDGE

Lesser
Neva

River

Neva

ALEXANDER BRIDGE

NABEREZHNAIA

Chevalier
Guard
Regiment

Tauride
Gardens

Tauride
Palace
(The Duma)

Smolnyi
Convent

Smolnyi
Institute

Petrograd
University

Winter
Palace

DVORTSOVAIA QUAI

Summer
Gardens

Field
of
Mars

Laitnyi
Gardens

Great
Neva

Imperial
Admiralty

THE ENGLISH QUAI

ADMIRALTY ST.

Alexandrovich II
Palace

Imperial
Lyceum

Mikhailovska
Gardens

Imperial
Michael
Square

Imperial
Museum

Post
Office

Alexander
Garden

Great
Palace
Square

Imperial
General Staff

NEVSKII

AVE.

ITALY ST.

Hotel
d'Europe

War Office Annex

GRAND MORSKAIA

Ministry
of War

Isaac's
Square

GOROCHOVAIA

Catherine Canal

City Hall

Mikbhov
Palace

NEVSKII AVE.

Marie
Palace

Imperial
Bank

VOSNCZENSKI AVE.

Sinaya
Square

ST.

LIGOVSKY AVE.

Nikoliev
Moscow
Railroad
Station

Neva
River

Griboiedov

Canal

Zarskoselskii
Railroad Station

Obvodny   Canal

Obvodny   Canal

Fontanka

Baltic
Railroad
Station

Warsaw
Railroad
Station

N

0   0.25

Miles

ST. PETERSBURG, 1899-1917

С. Петербургъ.
Невскій проспектъ

St. Pétersbourg.
La perspective du Newsky.

Postcard, Nevsky Prospect, St. Petersburg, ca. 1900
Courtesy Hoover Institution, Stanford University

329

Bertha Honoré Palmer
Oil on canvas, Anders Leonard Zorn, 1893

Ida Honoré Grant
Oil on canvas, George P.A. Healy
Courtesy Chicago Historical Society

*Propaganda poster: October 1905 Manifesto, "The Most High Manifesto,
to which His Highness Major General Trepov put his hand"*

Propaganda poster: Opposing the suppression
of the Moscow uprising, December 1905

Idealized depiction of Emperor Nicholas II leading troops;
shield carries his motto — God Is With Us

Grand Duke Nicholas Nikolaevich and Russian generals

335

"Freedom Loan," lithograph, 1917

Courtesy Hoover Institution, Stanford University

"Nicholas Nikolaevich, Supreme Commander of the Army," lithograph, 1915

Courtesy Hoover Institution, Stanford University

Battle of Lemberg, near L'vov, 1914

"Tsar Announces Declaration of War," Winter Palace, Petrograd, 1914

Courtesy Hoover Institution, Stanford University

Princess Julia Cantacuzene, 1928
Courtesy Chicago Historical Society

knew our hour would soon come, and this anxiety for the old family home was added to other troubles.

My husband was eaten up with the weight of his responsibility and the strain of pouring oil on the troubled political seas of Kiev. Life became so exhausting that we quite gave up all effort to go into society; and we never moved from home, where my salon remained generally filled by various people who came to talk of their troubles and vexations and to tempt us into replying with tales of our own.

Though it was already September, Kerensky's government had kept none of its promises. We were no nearer to the constituent assembly than we had been in March. The army was rapidly disintegrating and was not being supplied with either food or clothing in any sufficient quantity. Deserters roamed the country, selling their uniforms and every other sort of stolen goods, and intimidating inhabitants back of the lines everywhere with their depredations. All Russia was infested with bands of criminals who had been let loose from the prisons, who were plundering, murdering, and burning.

These were dressed invariably in uniforms and announced themselves as "Bolshevik soldiers." There were in Kiev, Moscow, and Petrograd, associations of deserters, as open in their propaganda as were the political parties. Everywhere provisions and manufactured goods were growing scarce, and even the prices of necessities were now soaring tremendously beyond anyone's expectations.

On the other hand, money was almost worthless. In two-and-a-half years of the war previous to the revolution, I was told only three billions of rubles had been issued in paper by the old régime, which had been greatly reproached for its extravagance. While since the revolution, nine billions had been issued in six months; and the government presses were breaking down from the strain of printing so much. The design of the bills was simplified and their size cut down, to save time and paper. The people were suspicious of the new productions; said they represented no value and were not real money. Disrespectfully, the public gave these creations the name of "kerenki," and it was the first open sign of their demi-god's waning favor. Government officials and the army had been paid in "kerenki," while the bills of the old régime were collected in private, some being bought at a premium. It was whispered about that these ancient moneys were passed on to agents who were gathering them up for use by the Germans when the latter should occupy Russia.

Such was the state of the country when, at the great conference in Moscow,[1] representatives of all parties appeared and were invited to express their opinions and advice. All save the Bolsheviki had been called. It

[1]The Moscow State Conference, called by Prime Minister Kerensky to consolidate public support for the provisional government, met on 27 August 1917. It was attended by some 2,000 current and former politicians and officials, representatives of unions, soviets, and so on.

was remarked that General Kornilov,[2] ex-commander of the Petrograd garrison and now commander-in-chief of the army, was given a tremendous ovation by the public when he spoke, detailing all the miserable facts connected with our situation. He implored the government to act and, with a firm hand, to uphold the ideals that had been in everyone's mind at the beginning of the revolution. He especially begged laws might be enacted to suppress lack of discipline in the army and to abolish the ridiculous measures that had made our magnificent fighting machine the tragic farce it had become.

Kornilov spoke splendidly and commanded admiration not only from all his hearers but also from the various press organs, which all over Russia printed his speech next day. He offered to risk acting himself in the matter of the army, begging only that the administration uphold him by its authoritative consent and saying that he would take and face the responsibility and unpopularity any repressive measures would cause to their inauguration.

Kerensky's appearance at the conference had created comment against him, as he had quite evidently lost much of his prestige. He was trying to regain it by expressing a desire for concessions to the very lowest

[2]General Lavr Georgievich Kornilov (1870–1918), who as commander of the Petrograd Military District had arrested the Imperial family in March, had been appointed supreme commander of the Russian army on 2 August. Dismissed after the "Kornilov Affair" (see later), he died doing battle against the Bolsheviks in 1918.

elements. He seemed artificial and had lost his fire. His catchwords, grown old, seemed meaningless and were without effect. Essaying explanations of the dramatic mistakes of the past months, he was unconvincing.

This Moscow conference, from which much had been hoped, broke up without coming to any conclusions. At its end, there was a Bolshevik demonstration in Moscow, with shouted accusations that the government had invited only "conservatives and counter-revolutionists" to take part. As usual, there was no armed forces to protect the cabinet or conservatives, so the conference broke up, and the ministers left Moscow as rapidly as possible. Then the rabble quieted. Kornilov returned to staff headquarters at Mogilev, and the government to Petrograd, while Rodzianko, General Brusilov,[3] and all others who were long since revolutionists, but now were called counter-revolutionists, were forced out of public life and disappeared from view permanently.

[3]General Alexei Alekseevich Brusilov (1853–1926), former commander of the southwestern front and hero of the 1916 offensive in that sector, was Kornilov's immediate predecessor as supreme commander (replaced in the wake of the "Tarnopol disaster" mentioned by the author). He later cooperated with the Bolsheviks in the war with Poland (1920–21).

XXIII

Kornilov and Kerensky

T HE TAKING of Riga by the enemy, with the complete rout of our army on the northern front, a threatened invasion of Petrograd, the tragedies of officers and shock-battalions annihilated, the masses of our soldiers who would not fight—all this followed immediately upon the Moscow conference, proving General Kornilov to have been right in his predictions. It was all too hideous! The massacres and the burning of chateaux and villages by our own fleeing soldiers gone wild, were none-the-less dreadful because we knew how wonderfully courageous, patient, and strong they had been but a short year before.

Immediately after these terrible events, came the tremendous sensation of the "Kornilov affair." News of this reached us as a thunderbolt one morning when our Kiev papers announced that Kornilov, commander-in-chief of the army, was arrested at his staff by government order; that Kornilov was at the head of troops going to attack the capital; then that General Krymov[1] was marching to attack the capital;

---

[1]General Alexander Mikhailovich Krymov (1871–1917), a principal in the "conspiracy of the generals" that led to Nicholas II's abdication in March. Krymov headed the troops that Kornilov ordered to occupy Petrograd on 10 September 1917. After the

and that Kerensky was marching at the head of the city troops to defend himself! Then, for several days, all communications between Kiev and Petrograd were entirely cut off, and for a time we heard nothing further of the drama, either by wire, by post, or through the press. But we had our own excitement, which seemed amply sufficient.

The first morning when Cantacuzene read the news, he foresaw the possible complication that presented itself for our Kiev garrison. Kornilov and a group of his followers were evidently trying to demolish the authority of Kerensky and the provisional government, which they had sworn to serve. Our soldiers' committees would meet to discuss the problem of whether they should follow their military leaders' movement or stand by the government. Probably it would mean bloodshed, a division of opinion, and the town upside down within a few hours.

My husband decided to take the bull by the horns and to meet this crisis as he had that of the revolution in March. Calling together his regimental and squadron commanders, he ordered them to see that the soldiers' committees in each of his units met at once and that all the published and contradictory telegrams should be read before them. The officers were to tell their men that they themselves had but just learned

---

failure of Kornilov's attempt to restore order for the sake of the war effort, Krymov was dismissed by Kerensky and shortly afterwards committed suicide.

this news and they knew nothing beyond what the printed sheets contained; that if anything further reached staff headquarters, it would at once be given out; and, meantime, in the crisis the commander wished everything to be done to keep order in Kiev. Also, that in his estimation, everyone's first duty was to stand by his sworn allegiance to the provisional government. This move would make the officers and soldiers feel at one in their sentiments and would keep the commander informed as to the committees' intentions and would prevent unnecessary difficulty, until more could be learned from the north!

The officers present wanted my husband to accompany them and speak to the men himself, but Cantacuzene refused, saying their strength would be augmented if each officer acted on his own initiative and, as it were, spontaneously. His own influence could be called in as a reserve authority, in case things went less well than expected. Nearly everyone present at the meeting of officers personally admired Kornilov and sympathized with his desire to better matters. But all agreed that the move, by its vague and even disconnected character, could create ill-feeling everywhere between classes—making indignation rife among the lower members of society, who would be for Kerensky and who would accuse Kornilov and the upper strata of desiring to replace the present independence by ancient severities.

Within an hour, all of my husband's subordinates had rejoined their units in Kiev and its environs, and his orders had been carried out with tact and intelligence. After some discussion the decision was taken everywhere by the troopers to await further news quietly. All that afternoon members of soldiers' committees crowded our anteroom and Cantacuzene's private office, questioning personally their old commander. My salon received a continuous stream of officers who spent the hours in conjecture as to what was happening in the north and what the result of Kornilov's move would be to Russia. No one talked of anything else. It seemed evident to us that after his speech in Moscow, the commander-in-chief, who was a self-made man of the people and a true patriot, had lost all hope of the administration ever being able to improve matters. He consequently had decided to take things into his own hands and strike a blow to save the army and our national honor. In case of failure, he would make matters much worse, and it was almost certain such a plot must fail.

In truth, this, the worst, was exactly what happened. The soldiers sent to fight against those of the capital's garrison immediately deserted to the side of the latter. After the troops had fired a few vague shots, they fraternized; they decided then that this was a counter-revolution, planned, of course, by officers and retrogrades. They proceeded to persecute the former element all along the front, in every garrison, and on all our warships for their supposed knowledge of and sympathy with the movement. In some cases the troubles amounted to little more than a disrespectful expression of suspicions. In other places it took the form of arrest and dismissal of officers by the committees of soldiers, accompanied by threats. But in a great number of cases, groups of officers were tried hurriedly and executed or were even killed without trial, in the most appalling circumstances, after the infliction of tortures going back to the Middle Ages for their inspiration.

Certainly Kornilov had been animated by the best sentiments, but it was equally certain that he completely missed his lofty aim and that his conduct had aggravated a thousand times our already terrible plight. One of the officers said with great bitterness, "We had lived through six months and, in many cases, had won over our men to believe in us, and often we had even managed to work in with the committees, getting the best from them and suppressing the worst. And now all that valuable ground is lost, and we stand on a volcano with our lives in our soldiers' hands, minus their confidence, dependent on their caprice."

Two or three days after the bomb of the Kornilov affair had exploded, a soldiers' committee meeting was held at the Cuirassier camp, when a vote of confidence in all their officers was passed unanimously and a young officer, Prince Cherkassy, was elected as president of the soldiers' committee. After this, Michael walked on air as far as the behavior of his own troops in an emergency went. But, alas, these were only a very small part of our army, and the rest were scarcely better than a vague horde of wild men.

All the people I had ever met in Kiev came to have tea with me, in the few days following this act of the Cuirassiers: principally to find out if the fairy tale of their behavior was true and to congratulate my husband upon his triumph and his influence with the men of his command. Soon communications were established with Petrograd again, and we read more of the fiasco and of the large group of generals who were supposedly mixed in the plot and were arrested and confined with Kornilov and with his staff. Curiously enough, in spite of his proclamations, Kerensky never pursued the accused by court martial; while Kornilov invited a trial and announced in the newspapers through the whole country that he had positive proofs to show the plot had been of Kerensky's invention and that he had only followed orders, which he had received from the prime minister himself.

Round this there was much talk, of course, but nothing was proved; and we heard of the farcical battles about the capital, which had lasted but a day. We knew little of the disturbances in the city or of General Krymov's suicide, or murder, after a prolonged interview with Kerensky. The latter, now "dictator" by self-nomination, made a proclamation to all Russia accusing these generals, "upheld by certain other retrograde elements," of making a disloyal attempt to upset "the people's government." He now came before the public in his final role of demagogue, and his hysterical utterances from that moment on confirmed the theory of his rapid degeneration in health and brain. He could no longer be relied upon, and to us it seemed quite evident that the Russian government as at present constituted was doomed to fall soon from sheer incapacity and that the power would go then surely to the Bolsheviki, who, being in German hands, would make peace or even an alliance with Germany.[2]

My husband felt sure he must still stay at his post and do what he could to hold Kiev, until the death of the provisional government. He decided to give up his service, however, when the Bolsheviki took over the power, using at last the right given him by his severe wound (through which he had obtained a complete discharge from the service in 1914). He was deeply distressed over the situation. Some of the nobility with whom I talked felt our worst enemy was the revolutionary disorder in all its forms and our only hope was in getting discipline re-established at any cost—even through conquest by the Germans. Cantacuzene felt, on the other hand, that the poison which had sapped our vitality had come to us through German channels, and not those of the revolution, that we could have weathered all the storms if the enemy's spies and propaganda had been eliminated. He, therefore, following his theory to its logical conclusion, said that the worst thing that could happen to our country

[2]The Bolsheviks did, indeed, make peace with the Germans after they came to power, but the widespread belief, reflected in this memoir, that they were German agents pure and simple, was, of course, erroneous. They had their own revolutionary agenda.

was its mastery by Germany. This would inevitably come with the Bolsheviki's triumph, and he refused to remain in his place to see it.

It appeared to be but a question of three or four weeks, with the German armies overflowing the Riga front, until Petrograd might be invaded. We had left in the capital a number of valuables at the bank, both papers and jewels, and all our furniture was there, as well as some trunks containing clothes and personal effects, which had remained at the lodging of our intendant. We were anxious to get at these and either store them permanently or destroy them in the face of the coming storm. As Michael could not leave his post at Kiev, I volunteered to go to the capital for a few days and attend to these details. With some hesitation my husband consented to my plan, and after much red tape as to passports and the permissions from the soviet of soldiers and workmen of Kiev "to travel northward on business," I departed with the ever-faithful Élène.

It seemed to me heart-breaking to see our proud capital brought so low as I found it now. The pavement blocks in the principal streets were pried up in many places, and these holes remained unfilled. On the great Palace Square grass grew between the cobblestones, and market-women were established along the edges of the Nevskii's sidewalks, calling their wares to the passer-by. All the main thoroughfares were packed with vast crowds, standing, walking, pushing, shoving, and all shouting. I had an intense impression of dirt and din and chaotic movement. The streets off the large arteries were, on the other hand, uncanny and silent. Here and there a frightened-looking pedestrian hurried or a hooligan-soldier slunk along. Everyone who was well dressed looked anxious.

Acquaintances seemed amazed to see me and warned me of danger. But I was fortunately able to attend to all my business most satisfactorily. I found many willing hands to help me in it, not only those of my own class, but also humbler friends, shopkeepers or workmen, whom it seemed I had helped in various insignificant ways in the past and who now showed themselves only too ready to serve me.

It was said to be impossible to engage places on trains leaving the capital, everything being taken for weeks ahead, so numerous were the people leaving to take refuge in the south. The general strike of railroads was expected any day. But I was lucky as usual, as a friend of mine, the hotel clerk, obtained two places for the day on which I had planned my departure. When I told of this last triumph, my words were received with laughter, and it was said, "No doubt the strike will be held over until you reach Kiev in safety! You are certainly the spoiled child of the revolution and lead a charmed existence."

I began to grow really superstitious and to attribute my success among so many dangers to a present given me some years before by an old comrade of my husband's. It was a delightful tiny owl, carved by the famous Fabergé from a precious Siberian stone. I was just starting on a journey once, and this friend had come to see me off and had given me the trifle saying, "Keep it near you. It will inspire you with wisdom in emergencies, and also it will bring you luck, by finding a solution for all difficulties." Since then the lovely little creature had always accompanied me in my dressing case, and during my revolutionary experiences, it had remained ever in my pocket until I really began to believe in its virtues.

In Petrograd, though everything seemed to me so dreadfully sad, I was, nevertheless, deeply interested in the recent development of the historical drama. In spite of the harm it brought us personally, I kept my faith somehow in the country's great strength to live through its sufferings and to recover from the reign of terror, which I knew would surely come.

I found time to see a number of friends during my stay in the capital. Their aspect had greatly changed, for no one wore elegant clothes; and even if one dined or lunched out, it was in a business suit or tailored gown, as if we were all on the point of traveling.

They had no confidence in the present government, and many were the anecdotes told of the life, the waste of time, and the dire disorder of the clan now living in the Winter Palace. Kerensky had lost his hold. He lived from day to day, doing an hour's work, giving a few audiences and then collapsing. His colleagues complained of his inattention and his vacillations. The people complained of his "bourgeois luxury." All those approaching him complained of his despotic ways. In the palace itself, dirt and danger reigned, and Kerensky feared all those surrounding him, even to the enormous bodyguard of troops, whom he had stationed in the palace himself and who were always plotting his destruction.

From two friends of Tereshchenko who had no knowledge of one another, I received the following story of the Kornilov affair, as having been given to each of them by the foreign minister himself.

After the Moscow conference he, Tereshchenko (himself in despair at Russia's situation), had gone to Kerensky, asking the latter to act in conjunction with General Kornilov to bring the country's dramatic drifting to an end. When others of the cabinet had upheld the minister of foreign affairs in this and Kerensky had agreed to the idea, a consultation was held with the commander-in-chief, Kornilov, and plans were made for picked troops to be ordered from the northern front, under General Krymov—who was one of our strongest commanders—and sent to the capital to arrest the heads of the anarchist party, put the present garrison of the capital in its place, and finally start the government on a new chapter of achievement, with at least some chance of success.

It would then be possible, they hoped, to act in like manner in the provinces and, with the army bringing the country to its senses, to continue the war. This was, of course, a last hope and a desperate one; but it had chances of success with Kerensky, hero of the masses and adored by his own soldiers, as one of the leaders. Conservative elements were so sick of the results of our revolution they would be glad to back any group they supposed would be able to inaugurate law and order.

This plan obtained the consent of the two men chiefly concerned, and also of the cabinet of the one and the staff of the other. The day was set for the execution of the scheme, and Krymov was ordered to start from the northern front, where he was then, with his corps. Tereshchenko was sent by Kerensky to the staff, for some last settlement of detail; but he had no sooner started than Kerensky's courage gave out, and he changed his mind completely, seeing only a plot against himself now in the whole affair. He wired counter-orders to the staff. Kornilov wired him back it was too late, that he could no longer reach Krymov (already on the road) to recall him. Kerensky then published a proclamation dubbing Kornilov a traitor and the movements a "counter-revolution"; and he declared the capital to be in a state of siege and sent the garrison troops out to meet Krymov as an enemy. The latter, greatly surprised, finding himself faced by an official army, which he heard was sent against him by the man whom he had supposed to be his ally, rushed into the city to demand explanations of Kerensky, while his army, already converted by the city troops, remained fraternizing with the latter at the gates of Petrograd.

After a discussion with Kerensky, Krymov had died

in the Winter Palace of a revolver wound; and it was said he had committed suicide through humiliation and disgust. Tereshchenko added to this tale that he himself had rushed back from the staff, only to find the capital topsy-turvy, the garrison and Krymov's regiments the best of friends, all the cabinet dreadfully frightened, and Kerensky hysterical. Driving straight to the Winter Palace from his train, and bringing into play all his temperamental powers, Tereshchenko treated the dictator to a scene of such violence that the attendants were vastly impressed. Finally, the minister of foreign affairs, having relieved his mind, handed in his resignation and departed, slamming the door.

I heard Kerensky wept; and having quieted his nerves, sent for Tereshchenko, begging him to reconsider his measure, as he was the last conservative in the provisional government and, if he retired, Kerensky would be obliged by the "ultra-left" to replace him with Chernov, uneducated and an extreme Socialist—and then "where would Russia then be, all through Tereshchenko's lack of patriotism? And how could they negotiate with their Allies; how would the foreign ambassadors confer with such a person as Chernov?" Tereshchenko accepted again the burden of his portfolio after Kerensky had gone on his knees to him.

I don't know what truth was in this story, which came to me twice over, at second hand. It was much talked of, and Tereshchenko had grown immensely in public esteem, especially with the upper classes. It was being said that if the present dictator and ministry fell, perhaps the minister of foreign affairs would make a good head for a new provisional cabinet in spite of his youth. People were so tired, worn, depressed, and puzzled, they seemed quite tragic and unable to react any more against the slowly advancing destruction; and they were very anxious to discover someone on whom to lean.

Pessimism in all shades was reflected in Russian society. There were those who still believed we might weather the revolution and that there would be a final mutual understanding of the nobility and peasantry, which could re-establish something of the ancient national life. Some awaited a military dictator who would rise as Napoleon did in France. There were those who thought—as I did—that a reign of terror must come, and then Russia would emerge strong and powerful, but with entirely new ideals and desires—perhaps as good as the old nation's or even better, if one could be broad enough to accept them and fit one's life into the new frame.

Everyone was frightened, and with good reason. But there were some splendid examples of courage and dignity in the face of danger. Such a one was old Princess Paskevich.[3] I heard by chance she was in

---

[3]Princess Irene Ivanovna was the widow of Count Fedor Ivanovich Paskevich-Erivansky, Prince Varshavsky (d. 1903), the son of Ivan Fedorovich, a leading military figure of the first half of the nineteenth century.

town and went to see her, having formed long ago warm relations, which on my side were based on grateful admiration grown up through many years of intercourse. She was called the "Little Aunt of all Society," so many were related to her. She was greatly surrounded always, though she was a childless widow, almost blind, and eighty-five years old. Her great palace was on the Quai, and I found the pavement dragged up in spots and the building itself barricaded, as if against besiegers. As I rang, the bolts were drawn at once, and I was immediately admitted by the door porter, an old acquaintance, who greeted me with surprised enthusiasm. "What is Your Highness doing in Petrograd? It is good to see Your Highness; but not for long, I hope." Then, to my question he answered, "Oh, yes; our Princess will be glad to see Your Highness. It is many days since we have had a visitor, and it will do her good."

I was taken to the princess up the grand staircase as usual and through the state apartments to her own blue salon at their end. I found my hostess, as she had been for the last fifty years or more at that hour of the afternoon, seated in her black silk gown and dainty lace cap. The beautiful quiet face was unchanged in expression, as with welcoming smile she stretched out a hand, which in olden days had inspired sonnets and was still admirable. *"Ma chère enfant,* how kind of you to think of an old blind woman in all this mess! Do sit down and tell me of yourself and your plans, and what you are doing here."

We had a long talk, and though she spoke of the situation in deep sorrow, she had faith, as had I, in the future of Russia. "Only it will not be for me to see. I am too old and must go the way of my régime, but I am glad if you younger people keep your courage and patriotism. And I agree that you should all follow the movement and the new ideas. The old ones were bad in many ways, but I was used to them."

I told her I was in town to settle some business and to carry off some valuables, fearing the occupation of the capital by the enemy.

When I asked her her plans for the near future, she said, "I have none. All my family and friends want me to move, go south, and rent a villa somewhere, but I have decided not to do so. My estates at Homel are all confiscated; the chateau is destroyed; so this house is now my only home, and I am blind and eighty-five. In the best of conditions, I cannot hope to live long. There is no one to whom I owe any duty, as I have no near relation; so instead of fleeing elsewhere, looking for a very doubtful safety in some place where I should be threatened with discomfort as well as danger, and traveling over railroads, which are a scandal of mal-administration, I am going to sit still here, until I am killed by Bolsheviki or Germans, or spared and left to die tranquilly in my own bed. Here, at least, I have quiet, and all my furniture and souvenirs about me, and I have space enough to take my exercise in these rooms. Also, I can permit myself a certain degree of comfort until the end."

I was impressed, and delighted, by the princess's attitude, with its simple dignity and courage. When I left her, later in that afternoon, she came with me through the great rooms, where so many treasures of art hung upon the walls or stood about in their old places.

"I've put away nothing, you see," said the princess. "No place is safe, really, and I want at least to enjoy it all, what time I can."

And then she kissed me and she said affectionately, *"Adieu,* my niece, and thanks for coming. It touched me greatly that you thought of me. God bless and keep you and yours!"

Her tiny figure stood more erect than usual at the top of her immense white marble stairs, and I thought of the fine blood she carried in her veins. As I looked up at her, it seemed to me her ancestors would be proud of her courage against the enemy and rabble alike.

In the past, she and her husband had always shown the same spirit, and they had even dared to close their doors to all of the Imperial family because Prince Paskevich had disapproved of something the Emperor Alexander II had done. They had made an exception only in favor of the wife of Alexander III, the present Empress Mother, who was an intimate friend of Princess Paskevich, and who had remained so.

But it was true that no other Imperial guest had ever crossed this great lady's threshold, though she had never in fact spoken even a word of criticism; and I had heard these facts not from her, but from the Grand Duchess Maria Pavlovna.[4]

---

[4]The Grand Duchess Maria Pavlovna (b. 1854), the widow of Tsar Alexander III's younger brother, Vladimir Aleksandrovich (1847–1909), was a former duchess of Mecklenburg (northern Germany).

XXIV

The Bolshevik Uprising

HAVING ACCOMPLISHED all I had gone to do, I left Petrograd as planned and arrived safely in Kiev with a large and varied assortment of baggage.

My husband had been very worried during my trip, feeling that the threatened railroad strike might easily catch me and keep me *en panne;*[1] or that the Germans' arrival in Petrograd might cause a stampede from there and make traveling altogether impossible.

As it was, the Germans decided to advance no farther than Pskov, and they left the capital to their spies and their subordinate agents (the Bolsheviki) for a time. The provisionals still kept a semblance of power and by remarkable feats of adroit politics and concessions, they held on another month. Everyone was nervous, and the crowds in the streets became greater than ever. One had a feeling that the slightest spark would set fire to the whole situation. Michael no longer let me go out alone on foot. After dark it was admittedly dangerous to be on the streets. The French units were leaving, or trying to do so, as rapidly as possible. Many of our class were going to the Caucasus or the Crimea, saying the Germans would soon be

---

[1]"Broken down" (French); that is, unable to go on.

in Kiev; and the peasant committees, having taken over their estates anyhow (under Ukrainian encouragement), they had nothing to gain by remaining and themselves falling into enemy hands.

We had horrid news now from Bouromka, and none at all from the other estates, and we were seriously concerned. We ordered the intendants and certain faithful house servants to bring to Kiev what smaller objects they could from the more valuable collections at Bouromka—ancient silver, the old snuffboxes, the jewelry worn by various ancestresses, as well as a very rare and a beautiful collection of old cameos and the jewels of my mother-in-law and sister-in-law, which had been left in their safes at Bouromka. Finally, we required papers of identification, in case the estates should be confiscated and the chateau destroyed.

The bronzes, pictures, furniture, and collections of china could not be handled or transported without attracting attention and, above all, it seemed important to avoid arousing suspicion among the village committeemen. So these and some 20,000 volumes in the library, some of them of infinite value (intrinsic and sentimental), all the family archives, and a cellar of rare vintages—many of which were more than a century old—remained to their fate.

The worst of these forebodings were soon realized. First, our cattle and horses were confiscated. A few days later the distillery was broken into and burned, and the drunken crowd invaded our farm buildings, taking possession of the chateau stables. Then our house cellar was rifled, and the faithful servants were driven out back to the village, while the crowd captured the parks and gardens, the orchards and espaliers, and rifled the mill and storehouses, destroying machinery, workshops, and so on. The chateau itself was spared, though the strangers advised its burning. But the canny elders among our peasants said it would be a pity to do away with so good a palace. Better let it stand and use it sometime. And so it stood for three or four months more, when it was given in prey to a frantic mob of what had once been our quiet peasantry!

The price of every necessity and luxury soared in a most preposterous manner. Toilet soap, which had been twenty kopecks a cake, reached three rubles and fifty kopecks, and there was no laundry soap at all. Butter had gone from sixty kopecks to ten rubles a pound. Rice was seven rubles a pound, when obtainable. A blue serge, ordinarily about five rubles a yard, was anywhere from seventy to one hundred rubles now; and for a yard of white crepe-de-chine, whose old price was four-fifty rubles, I had recently paid forty-eight! A ready-made dress worth about sixty rubles cost one thousand now!

We had reduced our meals to coffee and black bread with a little butter in the mornings; at lunch, two dishes, generally a stew of some kind, and the second course of potatoes, cabbage, or tomatoes; while our supper consisted of one dish only, which was generally cold and was prepared from the remains of lunch, with coffee, bread, and a little honey as dessert. We had a large supply of honey brought in from Bouromka in the summer. We had collected provisions during a year, and I counted that there was coffee, sugar, and such things as oil—enough to last us a year. Also we had potatoes, cabbages, and various dried vegetables to last, with care, through the winter. Most precious of all was a bag of white flour, which we reserved for us, in case of illness, and had divided up into small packages, which were hidden in the walls and woodwork and in various pieces of furniture.

Everything was sold by card system, but almost never could the quantity allowed really be obtained. Sometimes, even after the servants had spent hours waiting in line before the shops, there was nothing to be had. For our household, consisting of seventeen people, we could get only ten pounds or less of black bread each day, and frequently two or three days passed when none could be had. Everything was divided up by our servitors in excellent good-humor. The cook showed himself truly a cordon-bleu, since he managed to make all our meals tempting, in spite of their sameness; and he prepared excellent thick peasant soups of milk, dried vegetables, and pieces of cheap meat! Luckily, dairy products, fruits, green vegetables, and the native coarse cereals were still plentiful, but the outlook for winter was unpromising. We foresaw food riots, with the famine which must soon come upon this city through the disorder in transportation.

There was lack of fuel, too. We had put in our supply of wood in the summer, and we hoarded it with care, heating baths and stoves with utmost economy. We all took our tubs as nearly successively as possible, and the kitchen fire was reduced to what was necessary for one hot meal each day.

I was more afraid of our provisions being requisitioned than of any other danger. But our luck held, and when we left Kiev, we passed on fuel and dried vegetables to our successors in the house, while we took my mother-in-law a royal present of our coffee, sugar, and so on. For this the family was immensely grateful, as they had not believed in the dramatic conditions until quite recently, and they had consequently had very few stores to fall back upon.

And thus we reached 25 October, Russian style— 7 November—when we received the first news of the great Bolshevik uprising in the capital, the attack on the Winter Palace, Kerensky's flight, and the complete eclipse or arrest of the remainder of the provisional government! Chaos evidently in Petrograd; and then complete silence, with the telegraphic, postal, and press communications all cut off!

In Kiev there was naturally an instantaneous reflection of the drama in the north. At the first signs of uprising, Michael put the Cuirassiers in charge of the arsenal and the railroad station, while young cadets from the two military schools for future officers were used to garrison the staff building, telephone, water, and electric stations; and when the Bolsheviki began disorders in the neighborhood of their own quarters (at the Imperial palace), these were attacked by the cadets and some Cossacks. In three days, two battles were fought about the palace and in its gardens, while it passed from hand to hand.

Thursday and Friday there were no riots, only processions, meetings, and a general feverishness, and factory strikes out of town. Then the trams stopped. On Friday night, mob-crowds formed, making threats of attack on the staff buildings, which necessitated a strong defensive force quartered there. I watched the arrival of this, which consisted of the young cadets. It was dark, and their heavy tramp attracted me to the window toward one in the morning. A first group entered and disappeared in the buildings, occupying the courts back of the offices. Then another large unit arrived, and the boys spread themselves out all over our sidewalk and street, lighting their campfires, stacking muskets, and settling for the night. They looked immensely spick-and-span and were evidently delighted with their sudden call to duty. Young laughter and talk floated in to us through our open windows. To my expressions of regret, my husband answered that such boys must do this kind of work now, as he hadn't enough Cuirassiers to go round. He had put the latter in the hardest places. These little chaps liked the excitement much better than studying their lessons. Their ages ran from seventeen to twenty, but they felt they were doing men's heavy work. And indeed, they might even have it to do.

Then I could see Cantacuzene didn't like using them.

Small cannon and quick-firing guns were established where they could sweep the street entrances. Our block was all there was of the "Bankovaia," which ran into other streets at right angles on each of its ends, where a building blocked the vista. Our defensive cannon, if fired, would therefore send shell through the rabble and squarely into the houses beyond.

My husband spoke little, but he looked white and anxious. He spent most of his days and nights at the staff, where Kirienko[2] was holding a perpetual session of the impromptu commission formed to decide questions with reference to local defense and the city government's action. Kirienko was remarkable. He was cool, optimistic, encouraging, making quick and responsible decisions, receiving and haranguing people and deputations who appeared, playing poker with Fate truly, and with extraordinary bluffs, winning many points and holding on desperately in the hope that each hour might bring news from Petrograd.

As time passed and still nothing came from the capital, Michael saw his troops wearing out. There were not enough to change them off, with his men so scattered about. More being needed, two regiments of

[2]Prince Cantacuzene had been posted with his brigade to Kiev shortly after the March revolution to maintain order in the Ukrainian capital. Kirienko was the Socialist Revolutionary "commissar" sent by the provisional government to take charge of the civil administration of Kiev and its province. The two apparently got along well.

Czecho-Slovaks were brought from points where they were in reserve back of the firing lines. These arrived on Sunday afternoon and were a great relief to the commander, who hoped he was getting reliable help as he reviewed them in front of the staff headquarters with Kirienko.

Of course, the whole town was vastly excited over this. Cantacuzene's strain reacted on me somewhat, and I never supposed days could be so long and so wearing as these were.

Kirienko, in the absence of orders from the capital, had decided to act at once on his own initiative. On Monday morning he had called together a commission of government men and had then formally invited the Ukrainian Rada and the soviets of workmen and soldiers to send deputies. These should discuss the situation with him and help take measures to insure the tranquillity of our city and the safety of its inhabitants. The soviets made no reply at all to Kirienko's invitation, and the Rada sent representatives. After long wrangling, these Ukrainians came to an understanding with the central government party. They would take over certain administrative departments, principally in connection with the relations between peasants and proprietors, and also certain lines of government control in town. For this gain in power, they in exchange would police the whole province, keeping law and order in the rural districts; also they would help to police Kiev now and prevent a Bolshevik uprising.

When it came to settling where the different military units should be stationed, the Ukrainians claimed "as a compliment" that their national soldiers should receive certain honorary posts in the city; among others, they wished to guard the arsenal. Cantacuzene protested violently at so much being put into the hands of uncertain friends; but the Rada made it the price of its cooperation, and Kirienko thought our party could not risk losing the Ukrainian help. The concession was made them, and my husband was in despair over it. Before the deputation left the staff office that evening, their leader had signed a formal treaty with Kirienko, accepting in the Rada's name an alliance, offensive and defensive, with the provisional central government. From now on these two parties were to act together, and their united efforts, it was hoped, would quiet and intimidate the Bolsheviki.

That night, Monday, we went to bed. Early next morning we were awakened by firing all about us. Poor Michael could not dress fast enough to reach the staff, where he remained some time, while we waited anxiously for news. He had found everything there in mad confusion. Kirienko sent at once for the Rada leader, who came in haste. In answer to his accusations, the Rada leader explained that yesterday he had signed with the provisional government what *he considered a temporary agreement,* while last night the soviets had sent to the Rada meeting a deputation asking for his cooperation. They offered Ukrainians such advantages, in case of acceptance, that at the general desire of all their people, the Rada and ministry (himself at its head) felt obliged to tie themselves definitely to the Bolsheviki. If the people's party came into power now, the Ukrainians would be given the entire administration of the provinces round about Kiev. Consequently, in nationalist interests, he had become the ally of this people's party, of the Bolsheviki. Kirienko then protested, threatened, bluffed; but he could do nothing. The shooting all over town was growing violent.

As the Rada's representative departed, reports began to come in, giving dramatic impressions of our group's desperate condition. At the aviation camp in one suburb, the soldiers had mutinied, had killed or wounded several of their officers, while the remainder of the latter had fled after removing the magnetos from their airplanes so these could not be used by the soldiers for bombing the city. The men of the artillery batteries had behaved in the same way, only the officers there were not able to put the heavy guns beyond possibility of use. Every now and then, a shot fell into the center of the city, causing great excitement and havoc. We still had water, electricity, and telephone service; but we didn't know how long this would last.

Wednesday morning Kirienko was still at the staff; Cantacuzene also. But there was nothing anyone could do now, and the city was in an uproar. Officers were being shot on sight anywhere, bombs were exploding, bullets whizzed through the air and broke windows or embedded themselves in walls. We felt vastly alarmed, especially as in our neighborhood several houses were sacked, hundreds of people arrested, and from time to time, it was reported that the mob of Bolsheviki were marching in our direction.

By the afternoon the Ukrainians demanded that for the general "safety and protection of the revolution," troops of the provisional government must retire from Kiev and be disbanded and that the cadets return immediately to their schools, where they were to be considered prisoners of war. Kirienko was obliged to hear the orders given to that effect. It was quite evident that in Kiev the reign of the provisionals was over and that the power was in the hands of the mob. My husband, indignant, with his soldiers dispersed and banished from the city, could do nothing now but hand in his resignation. This he did. He was consequently without any command. That afternoon we talked of what we should plan further in case we got out alive from this hornet's nest. We decided to go first to the Crimea for a rest.

I knew Michael would be doomed as soon as the Ukrainians took over the power, since all through the summer he had bent his best energies to fighting their propaganda, and revenge would seem very sweet to them. We were both very tired, and he especially was terribly worn by his work.

Suddenly, Colonel Sakhnovsky, then commander of the Cuirassiers, was announced, and saying he must speak with Cantacuzene on urgent matters, he was received in the latter's workroom. When my husband returned, he said to me without preamble, "Can you leave the house in ten minutes?" I answered I could; whereupon he added, "Sakhnovsky has just come from the staff. He says the crowd in power have already shot the commander of the garrison's infantry and are going to arrest any Cuirassier officers left in the town, and that I am being looked for, to be judged and executed. Kirienko is also condemned and has disappeared, having fled. Sakhnovsky wants me either to go out and stay in the Cuirassiers' temporary camp outside town or to hide in town. I've decided to do the latter, as at least I won't be exposing the regiment to trouble or attack. We can spend the night at the hotel, if you like. There is a room already engaged there."

Taking a small bag, into which I put a few valuable papers, with some of my jewels and money that were in the house, I threw on a cloak and my furs and hat.

Our chief difficulty, we knew, would be getting out of the house, through the lines of troops encamped on our doorstep and the sidewalk and also along the streets between us and the hotel. Now, all these troops were Ukrainians who might know my husband's face dangerously well. Luckily it was cold and almost dark, and he was in civilian clothes, which he had never before worn in Kiev. He put on a heavy traveling ulster and a soft felt hat, and threw his traveling scarf about his neck, covering chin and beard. Under his cloak he took the precaution of carrying his revolver and sword. I felt satisfied that in this disguise Michael was quite unrecognizable. Pulling my own furs up high and taking the small bag of valuables in one hand, I covered it with my big muff. The extravagance of my muffs had often been laughed at, but that night I was grateful for this one's size and protection. I also had my revolver loaded and off the safety, in my hand, inside the muff.

We made our *adieux* to our visitors and servants in the hall, then had all the lights put out so the front door's opening would attract less attention from outside. Kurakin unbarricaded the door and held it open enough for Cantacuzene to slip out. I followed him, and it closed behind me again, very quietly. I admit my heart beat hard, and I was wet with perspiration, in spite of the cold air, as we threaded our way sauntering across the street and along the sidewalk of the other side toward the corner. Here stood a sentinel, with a cocked gun. Fortunately for us, he was of the new régime variety. Instead of attending to his business and challenging us, he chattered on, smoking with some comrades, who were having dinner. We slunk by slowly behind him, until we reached the remnants of a barricade, which stretched in disorderly heaps across the street. Once past this, I breathed more freely, and my husband spoke, "Now hurry! Shall I take the bag? Here it seems general traffic is allowed, and I imagine we are all right!" I insisted on keeping the bag so he could the better hold and hide his side-arms. Our walk became as rapid as possible. With the occasional bullets about, this seemed reason enough. We passed a general with his head down going at a quick pace. It was my brother-in-law, Niroth. "Theo," I said, low. He raised his eyes. "Why, what on earth? Misha, too, in this lovely costume! Where are you two going? To a masquerade?"

Cantacuzene said, "Hush," and then, "Come with us"; and Theo turned and kept us company, while we told him in a few words of our experiences since luncheon time, which seemed ages ago. As we reached the next street, we met a cab and with a good-bye to Theo, who promised to report at home our favorable progress through the danger zone and to send us some dinner soon, we jumped into the vehicle and drove on to the hotel. There the porter, whom we knew by having often dined at his restaurant in gayer days, nearly fell over when he saw us and recognized Cantacuzene. He took us to a room on the top floor, which my husband had kept for months in his name, using it for any officer or business man whom he wished to detain in town. It was a piece of luck to have it now, as the house was crowded. Fortunately, as we reached our floor, we heard that the soldiers of the Ukrainian government had just finished inspecting there and had gone down below, looking for arms, examining people's passports, and confiscating valuables. I felt safe as I hid our revolvers.

The room was desperately dirty and upside-down, with beds unmade, soiled water standing in washstand bowls, and all the furniture pushed about, as if by an earthquake. Our windows looked out on a courtyard, so we were safe from stray shots or attack. I had no particular desire to live through more excitement than I was forced to. But my husband, who so far had spent all these busy days in his office, was keen to be free and to see things from the spectator's point of view. He believed his disguise sufficient to protect him; and it seemed easier for him to move about than to sit still, so I didn't even protest at his going down again into the big main street. I began to feel very impatient for the promised supper, when about nine o'clock, Davidka and Élène appeared with cold ham and hard-boiled eggs and various other picnic dishes Mme. Ivanov had sent. Best of all seemed a bottle of hot coffee and a tiny flask of old brandy for Cantacuzene. Also the servants brought necessary linen and clothes for the morrow and our dressing cases. They had braved the street-shooting to bring us all this, and they reported it was quiet at home when they had left. Though some soldiers had called asking for Cantacuzene, after a conversation with Prince Kurakin and Count Niroth, these had departed, not even inspecting the house.

My husband returned, and we dined. I was very pleased because he said my nerves were as good as his own in an emergency, or better. We laughed over my Fabergé bird, which had again brought us luck. We spent a short, quiet evening in our high-perched room and slept, exhausted and relieved, until the morning. Davidka and Élène arrived with coffee and hot toast from home. They said the late evening had been very exciting on the Bankovaia. There had been a lot of violent firing, and our house-party, with the servants, had taken refuge and spent most of their time in a back-corridor, where, as there were no windows, they felt protected from bullets.

Cantacuzene started out to get his discharge papers, promised him by division headquarters at noon, and I went to do some shopping. I found shops and banks open, and as in July in Petrograd, I had the impression of Russia's wonderful intelligence in letting bygones be bygones. If it hadn't been for broken windows and injured buildings and for my husband's civilian clothes, I should have been tempted to think I had dreamed all the events of the last thirty-six hours. In the afternoon Cantacuzene, no longer belonging to the Russian army and with his papers in order, took me back to our house, and we surprised our guests by appearing in time to dine with them. Kurakin and Theo were very jealous, they said, of our new, complete liberty. No one was allowed to resign now, and it was only Cantacuzene's blessing in disguise (his wound) that brought him this luck. We then decided to go south immediately, on the following Saturday if we could get off, and to take Mme. Ivanov with us. Then, if it was possible, to go beyond the frontier soon. We knew the time had come at last to join our children, and I thanked heaven they were safe and away from all we had gone through, or might still have ahead.

XXV

Our Escape from Kiev

TRAINS were running again, and there was news of Petrograd at last. It was announced that the Bolsheviki had been entirely successful there and had taken over the government, while the provisional ministers were shut up in the fortress—all but Kerensky, who had fled in the very beginning of the trouble. The Winter Palace had been stormed and taken after a brave defense by the women's Battalion of Death, which had lost half its effectives. All the other troops, of course, turned Bolsheviki, and everywhere in the capital, there had been a high carnival of bloodshed and riots, assassinations and arrests—a page of the March performance, greatly exaggerated. As far as we were concerned, this meant definitely an end of my husband's work. We must be only too thankful to be among the few who might perhaps escape further danger and misery. All congratulated us and expressed relief that my husband was now leaving the place he had so valiantly defended from the Ukrainian propaganda. He was told he ought to go as quickly as possible, for surely when the new administrators were once in the saddle, they would think of him among their first political victims.

Packing began. I fancied I had brought nothing to

Kiev, but as the servants piled things up, this seemed far from the case. Finally, I saw ten large trunks prepared, impossible to drag with us under present conditions and which we decided to leave to the care of some sure friends, those who were sub-letting our house for the rest of the contract. Six smaller trunks, of valuables and real necessities, we meant to carry on our trip. Besides these, we seemed to have much hand baggage, as well as a huge basket of provisions for the journey. Each one of our acquaintances who came to see us before the day of separation brought some little gift from slender stores—a glass of preserves, a few biscuits, or some sliced ham.

Davidka and Élène, indignant with the fate that had overtaken us but glad now on their own account to abandon Kiev, arranged everything with evident desire to please. We had removed Davidka's Cuirassier epaulets when the regiment had been sent away so he would not be ill-treated on the street by his Ukrainian "comrades."

Saturday, suspecting the difficulties ahead, we went to the station at four p.m. to get places in our train, which was to leave at eight-thirty. The station-master, Biron, was an adherent of my husband's, having had much to do with him because of the guard Cuirassiers, who had worked all summer on the station premises. He, therefore, invited Mme. Ivanov and me into his private office and kept us there, out of the crowd and in comparative comfort and cleanliness for our four hours' wait.

We saw trains come in and their contents of weary, worn humanity empty themselves out of the cars, through windows as well as doors, while waiting mobs surged about in huge waves. No sooner was one set of occupants out of them than the cars were assaulted and taken by storm, with shouts, screams, lamentations, oaths, and blows, crashing of glass, and creaking and breaking of wood. The compartments and corridors were at once re-filled to overflowing. On the roofs, platforms, and steps, khaki-clad soldiers clung like flies. After a time Michael decided it would be impossible for us to fight for places against such odds, and he asked Biron to allow us to go down into the car-yards and get our car there, where we would wait until the train started. Biron consented, and a messenger was sent to find out about places, for there were no possibilities of engaging any now, and it must be always first come, first served. When the man returned, his report was that the cars down there were already packed by hundreds of other people who had had our idea and used it without asking Biron's permission. There were not only no places left, but not even a pin could find space. So we gave up the start for that day, and our party returned to spend the night at home, greatly surprising the servants, who had remained in the house. Next day we would try our luck again. Mme. Ivanov was terribly depressed and most agitated over the dangers of a trip of three days under such conditions. Cantacuzene was greatly annoyed and worried, and I was more than ever determined that, at whatever cost, we must go on the morrow and not defer our trip again, even by one day.

After a bath and breakfast the next morning, we were all less blue, except Cantacuzene, who had not yet traveled since revolutionary times and who had been horrified by his observations of the day before. I was resigned, as I had made one or two trips in almost the same conditions. On our way to the depot, we were obliged to cross the main street of Kiev, and there we found just passing, a public funeral of some of the victims—Ukrainian and Bolsheviki—of the past week's disorders. Masses of excited people packed the sidewalks and the side streets for a considerable distance back, looking on. We were in my husband's auto for the last time, but he himself in civilian clothes and the chauffeur and Davidka minus their epaulets were not compromising. As the hearses finished passing, and only political deputations made up the procession, we noticed our smart machine was attracting attention and hostile glances from the onlookers. Luckily, just then our chauffeur saw in the crowd two mounted gendarmes and saying to my husband, "Those may be some of ours, Highness, and perhaps they would help us through," he begged to send Davidka to investigate. Cantacuzene consented, and within a moment, both gendarmes turned, looked, and gave us a broad grin, but no salutes, not wishing to give us away. They appreciated our delicate position and knew that if the crowd recognized their ex-commander, our car would be smashed to bits and we should not live to tell the tale. Davidka returned quietly and climbed into his place. "They say it is possible. Immediately," he remarked.

Then our chauffeur started his machine. A break in the procession occurred, and the two gendarmes drew closer to one another and spoke to the crowd between themselves and us. "Travelers," they said. "They must get through to the train. Make room." The crowd amiably, and without interest in us, parted. We slid up behind the two gendarmes. They then moved forward slowly, dividing the mob in two, and the latter stared at us in silence as we passed. I saw my husband feel his revolver, but he made no remark, and I was glad he was in the middle of the back seat and not driving as of old. It made him less noticeable. We crossed safely between two of the deputations taking part in the march. Then we pushed on behind our guard, into the audience on the opposite side street. There stood another Cuirassier, camouflaged as a gendarme. He saw us, recognized his regimental motor and his old commander, and he silently saluted, with a pleased look on his face. We reached the free street a moment after and left the danger behind, and we all of us sighed at once from sheer relief. Mme. Ivanov wiped her eyes. The poor little old lady was dreadfully upset, but she made no trouble. Cantacuzene now thanked our Cuirassier saviors. They, with broad grins, answered in voices gay and with the fashion of ancient days, "Your health, Highness! You are very welcome!" After that, we reached the station safely.

Biron had planned our capture of a compartment and had sent two sturdy agents to meet the train on its way north at a station outside Kiev. There they were to get on, and when the passengers left the cars in Kiev, they were to seize and hold a compartment until we could pile in.

As old Mme. Ivanov watched the wavering mob, she broke down. Trembling, she said she was too old to risk such conditions and that she preferred to remain in Kiev. We parted sadly, feeling we should probably never meet again. I keep a warm and grateful memory of her and her comfortable home. Her anxiety for our welfare was most touching, and her letters followed us on our wanderings for a long time.

Our train drew in. We had been placed, surrounded by our bodyguard, who held the small baggage, exactly on the right spot. As soon as the final incoming voyager had descended to the ground, we slid to the car steps, after which the crowding and pushing behind only helped us forward to our places. We found the compartment held by Biron's men, and we occupied it. I had kept Élène with us in order not to lose her, and we also retained for the moment all our four men until the first fight for seats should have subsided. Only Davidka left us, as he was going to travel in the baggage car in an attempt to defend our trunks from tampering or loss. In a compartment for two, consisting of one lower and one upper berth, both of them narrow benches, we were two women and five men; and thus we stayed for hours, until we had convinced various groups it was hopeless trying to accompany us. I knew from past experience that we could never keep the whole compartment for ourselves. I told Michael of this, and we decided when the second rush of passengers should come, we would at least choose our companions in misery and quickly and adroitly avoid, if possible, the dreadful dirty soldiers or refugees who might choose us. Soon our car was mobbed again, this time by a throng who came in on a train from the frontier military stations.

We saw in the front of the mass, entering the corridor, a Sister of Mercy, clean and in Red Cross uniform. "Quick, Sister, there is room for you here!" said Cantacuzene. One of our guardians slipped out of the compartment window while she pushed in through our door. I stored her with Élène on the top-berth, where they proposed to get on as best they could together. Below there was only my husband and myself and the rest of our guardians now. In a moment along came a huge, blond, amiable-looking creature, comparatively clean, well shaved, and dressed in the uniform of a colonel of our cavalry of the line. He had baggage that advertised three years and more of war service by its looks, and a tea kettle was slung on one bundle he carried; with him was a small, dark soldier, evidently his soldier servant, for they were talking with familiar gaiety, in old patriarchal fashion. We at once added this pair to our party. Then, feeling that those most desirous of entering our compartment would acknowledge it could hold no more, we sent off our last guardians and began to settle down. We closed the door and opened the windows so we six in our small space could breathe.

With Élène and the sister on the upper-berth, their baggage stored in the racks about them, the colonel and his soldier, Michael and I had the narrow lower berth and the floor-space to ourselves. The men gave me the seat nearest the window, and I rolled my cloak and furs behind me for a cushion, putting inside them my jewel-case and the bag containing our money and papers. In front of me more bags were piled to a great height, with the provision basket on top, where it was within reach. My husband sat next me, with a roll of plaids behind him; then came the enormous colonel, radiating cheerfulness and gratitude that he had been chosen, and saying with ready hospitality, "I can make you tea whenever you care for it. Ivan here will run for hot water at every station." Ivan squatted on the floor at his officer's feet and grinned at his luck in having escaped the roof through our invitation. He looked ready for anything in the way of service. Cantacuzene introduced himself, since in civilian clothes he could not be recognized. The colonel in turn gave his name and announced he had a leave, as had his Ivan also, and that they were going home for two months to Simferopol, the Crimean capital. We should, therefore, be making the entire trip together. I said I would feed the party, and since we could count on the colonel for tea and Ivan for errands, we should keep house most comfortably in our compartment. We were still in the yards, with soldiers settling on the roof and all the compartments packed. Our corridor had numerous people and much baggage piled in it.

But this was not all that was coming to us. After another hour of waiting, we were hitched to our locomotive and were dragged into the station, where a new set of what seemed lunatics tried to take us by storm. Secure in the fact that we were already like sardines in our compartment and could tempt no one, we sat quietly listening. The colonel laughed. "It is worse than the noise of battle. They are wild beasts, not men," he said.

A new wave surged into the corridor, and the roof above us creaked. Heads were stuck in at our window, eyes looked, and their owners were convinced at once; then the head drew out again. Our door was pounded and Ivan instantly opened it. "Two above, three below, one on the floor and also much baggage." And the intruders passed on. Now the corridor was so full none could sit down there, save a few who had come early and had perched on top of their bags. Our colonel peeped out and reported the toilet room was taken over by several soldiers and that we couldn't possibly reach it during the trip since it was more than one's life was worth to get through such a distance. Two wounded officers were raised over heads in the crowd. Word came along, "Wounded officers," and somehow they were carried or passed from hand to hand. Before they reached us, two charitable people had given up places to them. I am sure no one but

Russians could make a revolution in such a contradictory manner.

It was hot, stuffy, and frightfully uncomfortable, and
the stench from the corridor was unbearable. I was
persuaded by my companions it would be better if, in
spite of the November cold, we left our windows
open, and only this kept us alive.

At night we slept, sitting up on the hard, unmade
berth. There were neither cushions nor bedclothes,
which had long ago been stolen. We couldn't get at
our own, nor think of unpacking any of our bags. It
was impossible to move or change places either, and
equally impossible to stretch out. Above, the two
women were lying down, but they had no room for an
upright position, and it was hotter where they were.
The colonel and Cantacuzene risked taking off their
boots. Ivan curled up, and in the darkness it was impossible to make out how he managed to take so little
room. He was, I found, a Mohammedan Tatar soldier,
seemingly devoted to his master and anxious to please
and serve us.

Pitch-dark it was in the car, save for the moonlight
coming through my window, and very cold. The
colonel snored comfortably and reassuringly. My husband moaned in his sleep, with the pain of his wound
and worn nerves. Both women were quiet in their
berth above, and all through the car there was the
heavy weight of slumber.

I had fallen asleep toward dawn, but not for long. I
was too spoiled to rest well in such cramped quarters.

Fortunately I had plenty of reserve strength to draw on, and my desire at last fulfilled, to make this trip, helped me in spite of discomfort.

In the morning at our first stop, Ivan went through the window and fetched the colonel's kettle full of boiling water; then he and his master made us excellent tea, drawing the leaves from a newspaper scrap and some sugar lumps from a rag, all of which were packed together in an old flour sack they carried, tied with a string. I found cups and bread and butter in our provision basket, and we breakfasted contentedly enough. Then the men smoked and talked of their army experiences.

As long hours passed and we dozed or read or chatted, I appreciated our colonel more and more. He was a thoroughly Russian type, dignified and never familiar, though always friendly and helpful. His tea and sugar and his servant were entirely at our service. But he showed great hesitation in accepting any of our provisions for himself and Ivan. All his conversation was addressed to Cantacuzene, and he did not propose to light a cigarette, until I thought of telling him I did not object to smoke. He was as modest as to the space he and his bundles should take as it was possible to be, and was the most undisturbing traveling companion one could imagine. He saw how ill my husband was, and he went on from war topics to entertain Cantacuzene with anecdotes and stories.

Another long night, and we had still no possibility of moving from our places. I had not even taken off my gloves or veil for thirty-six hours. When we approached the station where we were to change trains for Simferopol, it was a serious question how we should get out of our prison. Nearly all the passengers were remaining on the cars and going toward the Caucasus. Impossible, therefore, to get through the corridor; and we were five people, and all those bags, which must be somehow removed. My husband was dreadfully perplexed. I had watched so many going in and out of windows, that though all these had been men, I felt I had learned their method and could follow it in spite of cloak, skirt, and furs. So I proposed this to Michael, saying it seemed to me infinitely preferable to the idea of traveling beyond our destination. The colonel, on the alert, had heard our talk, and he now intervened, "Ivan and I will go first, and pile our bags; then you and your maid shall come, Princess, and we will help you land; then the prince shall pass us your bags and follow himself." And so we did it.

As we drew into the station, it looked a vast hive of angry bees, and when the train stopped, the spry Ivan scrambled through the window and dropped lightly. The colonel threw him their bags, which made a soft mountainous cushion on the ground. Then the ponderous colonel himself passed, and I caught my breath, for I thought he had stuck in the narrow window. But he wriggled through somehow and fell down on his property with a mighty thud. Now was my turn. First, I scrambled up on our pile of bags. Reaching the window sill, I sat down, swinging my feet outside. Then I wrapped my cloak tightly around me so it could not catch or float, but held my skirts. With the jewel case tight in my arms and a bag of valuables in one hand, I gritted my teeth, shut my eyes, and jumped.

Élène dutifully followed. Having reached the windowsill she looked below and cried with a despairing voice, "I can't! Oh, I can't!" She looked fanatic and disheveled. "Jump at once!" I said. "You must." But Cantacuzene was more energetic. Without a word, he pushed her from behind. With a scream, she cleared the space and landed near me, where the colonel steadied her. Our bags followed. Then my husband unlocked the door into the corridor, and saying to the crowd in the hall, "There are five free places in here," he made a rush for the sill, stepped through the window, and dropped beside us, while the occupants of the corridor broke into our compartment with a howl.

We rushed into the station. I felt dazed and crippled by the long trip, with its fatigue of enforced immobility. Élène and I lost no time in reaching for dressing bags and hunting up the ladies' private rooms. Although there were fifty or more women as travel-stained as we, and the place was far from attractive, I enjoyed my first sight of soap and water for two days. Never had I greater pleasure than that given me by a sponge and a toothbrush and my rubber traveling-bowl filled with hot water, all laid out on a window sill of that dirty station room.

Our train did not leave until noon, and I drank bad

coffee without either cream or sugar. Then I slept soundly for two hours, with my head on my muff and jewel case, which were propped upon the restaurant table. Michael waked me in time to get on our next train, which was expected from Moscow. He was very anxious because he feared this part of our trip would be worse than the first chapter had been, since now we must get into a train already filled with travelers. He was wondering how we should ever negotiate the corridors! I reminded him we still had the bird along, by way of valuable help. Strong with our recent experience, I said Élène and I were not afraid of going through windows. We had hired two sturdy baggagemen and had promised each five rubles if they secured us places. In the crowd on the platform, our colonel saw us, and he and Ivan joined us at once. "Of course, there will be places," he answered. "I am the biggest and shall go in first as the train stops. You will be just behind me."

So we lined up and as the car stopped, a flying wedge went up its steps and in, all with the valiant colonel at the apex. He scolded, coaxed, joked, and apologized, as he shoved through, drawing our two sturdy baggagemen and myself along. My husband and Ivan, just behind us, brought up the rear. It was a complete triumph, largely because of our energetic action, but also because in this Moscow express there was slightly more room than in the other train and only a dozen or twenty occupants were in the corridor. I was shoved somehow into an empty seat in a compartment between a gentleman, very fat and very grumpy, and a neat, pleasant-looking officer. Beyond him sat a shy, miserable young woman with lovely black eyes, big turquoise earrings, and an untidy, dressy silk gown.

I slipped off my ulster and furs, and rolled them into a bundle to use as a cushion. Then I sat down with a sigh of real joy. Here was room enough, clean companions, and good air; and only twelve hours more of traveling! To cap the climax of our happiness, Davidka had managed to get the trunks off on another train, slower but ahead of us. The worst of our trip certainly was over, and though we were scattered about and I hadn't the vaguest idea what had become of our bags or provision basket, I hopefully left them to Élène's care and let myself go to solid enjoyment.

My fat neighbor on the other side continued silent, indignant he had so many traveling companions; yet he was in the best corner near the window and had two of the red velvet train cushions behind his back, while neither the officer nor I had even one. He protested when I entered that the compartment was "complete"; but ignoring him, I had sat down without a word. Now he wriggled, and moved a large pasteboard box, which probably contained his best costume. It stood between us. "It is very crowded," he said. At once, and without remark, I took hold of the big box and put it on a pile of luggage opposite me.

"That is my box," he said.

"So I suppose," I answered; "but it is large and

made me uncomfortable, and now you say you are so, too; consequently, we will remove it."

And I sat back much more at ease and turned again to join the conversation on my left.

My husband brought me a French newspaper to read, which contained the very latest war telegrams. "When you have finished that journal, Madame, would you allow me to look at it?" said my neighbor suddenly, in most humble tones. I felt I could afford to consent after the triumphs of having kept my seat and disposed of his box, so I passed him the paper after I had read it, and with my best smile, "Do you read French?" I asked. "It is in French." "Yes, Madame, I read that easily enough."

I felt very weary later on, and seeing me pushing my cloak about, the fat man said, with an evident desire to have his crimes forgiven, "Won't you have one of these cushions? I have two." I took it and it was luxurious. I slept some time, and on awaking I found my cross old neighbor had completely thawed. "May I be indiscreet, Madame, and ask your nationality?" he said. "You speak of Russia with good-will and affection even in these dark days; and yet you are obviously not Russian. You read French; yet you are not French, since you are not agitated, as are the Latins. You spoke English, but you are not British, I am sure, for you are more animated and more sociable than are they; and I have long been enquiring in my mind what you may be?" I laughed. "I am a Russian subject. My husband and children are all Russians, but I was born in America," I said.

I like odd types always, and the fat man became charming now. He left us that evening, but before going, he called in Michael to inherit his place and cushion for the night.

It was now three nights and two long days we had traveled, without once lying down or being really comfortable for a moment, and as we drew near Simferopol, I felt I should be able to stand no more. My husband was ghastly, and I began to wonder if he would not break down before we reached our destination. I counted we could get hot food at the station which I remembered as clean and gay in the summer. Then we would start at once in a good auto, on the trip of nearly eighty miles, across the mountains to my mother-in-law's villa at Simeiz on the southern coast.

The station I had looked forward to with such anticipation was a terrible disappointment; and because I had hoped for good air, seats, and breakfast, it seemed to me this was the worst experience of all. My tired eyes saw millions of men, in worn and dirty khaki, all pushing us or lying under our feet; and the stench was so dreadful that one could scarcely breathe. Twice I worked my way to the only open window, which was in the women's dressing room, for a breath of air, and this was already filled with a number of women, who had either fainted or were near it, like I was, from the crowd in the main room. The rest of the station, packed until there was hardly a corner with standing room, was only dimly lighted.

Since Sebastopol, which was where our railroad

line terminated, was closed to all passengers save its own inhabitants and the sailors who were on duty, this small station of Simferopol became the clearing-house for the whole Crimean coast; and it was the traveling terminus for the soldiery who came south as well. Half the crowd was made up of these deserters, all carrying huge bags, with food and other comforts for themselves. The other half seemed Tatars with their families, or Jews, or refugees and beggars. All had their bundles. I never conceived so much apparent misery and dirt as there was here. Eating was out of the question, and chairs we seized through luck, after more than an hour's waiting. Rest was impossible in such noise, and I proposed moving out to the platform for our long wait. But after inspection my husband refused, saying the crowd was greater there and even rougher than inside, that it was completely dark yet and seemed unsafe for Élène and me. So we resigned ourselves and remained suffocating where we were from four a.m. until after seven.

Men, women, children lay about us on the floors, asleep or half awake, unpacking, eating, dressing there without scruple. We had to watch our bags constantly, and two or three times we turned suspicious-looking people, whom we judged to be thieves, away from them.

It was really an anxious three hours to live through, and Michael felt and looked so ill, I was frightened for him; but at last daylight came, and the welcome sun appeared, also various motor-cars with their agents.

XXVI

The Crimea

WE LOST no time in renting one of the autos and in leaving Simferopol. As the fresh air struck my face, I realized the nightmare of our travels was over for this time. I was deeply grateful to the special providence which had guided us! We were safely out of Kiev and, I hoped, through with the worst of our experiences. Although we still had some discomforts and dangers ahead, I counted there would be no further subjection of my husband to particular pursuit, since from now on, we should be beyond the Ukraine provinces and out of reach of those who sought revenge. So for the moment we might put anxiety behind us and enjoy the soft springs of our conveyance and the utterly splendid Crimean scenery, which I most specially loved. My husband, suddenly feeling the strain on his nerves, relaxed and dozed off, and I had all the beauty of our wonderful drive to myself.

Down we wound, and the temperature changed so rapidly that within a short half-hour, I dragged off first my furs, then cloaks, and finally my sweater, and we opened all the car windows to let in the feast of fresh sea air and sun, soft to the touch. We stopped near a small restaurant on the quai in the first town we reached and were served quickly and with a smile by a pretty country girl, who recognized me from my last trip and asked after the children. Never in my life had coffee and rich cream, hot toast, and fruits tasted so good. Cantacuzene woke up and did full justice to his share of the food. He still looked haggard, but his spirits were answering to the charm of our surroundings. I hoped the Crimea would mend his health enough to make the long trip northward that must follow seem easier to him.

After breakfast our road skirted the coast, through woods and attractive watering places, where gay hotel guests in pretty clothes were shopping or strolling, and listening to music, as if wars and revolutions were far away indeed. By Yalta we passed, rich and luxurious still, and beyond it were "Livadia" and "Oreanda," with the Imperial palaces shining in the light. No wonder the ex-emperor had loved this, his private home, which did not belong to the state. I thought of the large family living now crowded into that small, far-away house, in a freezing Siberian town.[1] What a contrast to this!

Finally, we reached my mother-in-law's villa at Simeiz—simple but comfortable and pretty, all white, with a garden of roses in bloom and a view of mountains behind and sea before, and large enough to

[1]Tobolsk, in western Siberia, where Nicholas II and his family were exiled by Kerensky in August 1917. The Bolsheviks sent them back westward to Ekaterinburg in the Urals in April 1918. It was there, in the basement of the Ipatev house, that they were murdered on 17 July 1918.

The Cantacuzene villa on the Black Sea

Revolutionary Days

Princess Elizabeth Cantacuzene,
mother of Prince Michael

Courtesy Rodion Cantacuzene

house her group quite easily. There was great excitement over our arrival. She had not seen her son since she had been in Petrograd, where the princess and Cantacuzene had lived through the first days of the revolution together. I, also, had not met her since the spring. She was greatly distressed by my husband's evident bad health and glad we had left Kiev. Michael reported as to her business, and it seemed she and her household might consider themselves protected and comfortable for a year ahead at least by his financial arrangement.

Her only danger was from the motor-loads of Bolshevik soldiers or marines who made expeditions from Sebastopol all over the country expressly to steal and kill. My mother-in-law had entirely changed her feelings toward the revolution during the summer months, and from her immense enthusiasm, she had passed to an especial horror of those first revolutionaries who had established the provisional government. She could not find words strong enough to speak her anger and contempt, and she vowed that when she should be able to go beyond the frontier, she meant to live always away from Russia and never again have to do with any of our people. Her French soul and powers of expression served her well in the present condition of her mind!

Every Russian noble I saw was more sad about our action toward the war than about his own private distresses, and each one said "anything could be forgiven but the revolutionists' failure to keep faith with our allies." Some feared our defection might mean Germany's victory, and this thought caused the worst suffering. No one blamed the people much; instead, many thought the revolution in the long run would develop our nation. Of course without exception, these aristocrats deplored the passing of the old, beautiful traditions and the poetry of our country life with its patriarchal relations between proprietor and peasant; and undoubtedly these *had* disappeared for good. All spoke with pity of the poor emperor and of his danger and of the sad, imprisoned life of the Imperials here in the Crimea.

Two weeks passed all too quickly. To me saying good-bye was hard, and I didn't want to go, leaving all these associates of years behind. Yet the reasons for our departure made it seem imperative. If my husband was ever to regain health and strength, it could only be by going quite away from all these surroundings, with their tragic influences. There was nothing more he could do to serve the country now; and with means of communication cut, he and I should be but two more mouths to feed from the family supplies; whereas, beyond the frontiers we no longer depended on them.

It was infinitely difficult, we found, to get places and tickets to go north to Petrograd; but fortune served as usual, and a kind friend who was giving up her trip ceded us two compartments, which she had retained long ago. By an amazing miracle, the Soviet of Sebastopol Sailors replied to Cantacuzene's telegraphic request; they granted us permission to pass through their fortress city and to embark upon our journey from the railroad terminus there. Our family would not believe this permission possible, until we proved it to them by exhibiting our telegram. I was immensely grateful for this boon. Now it would be possible to settle ourselves and our belongings in the empty train, and we had some hope we might even hold the reserved places we paid for, since it was a direct express train we were taking.

The final good-byes were distressing, and I feared very much we might never see the family again. I hated leaving all the members to such danger. It was hard for the poor old princess to be going through such trials at seventy, after her easy and luxurious life. It was also too sad for my sisters-in-law and their children, all in fragile health and with despair in their hearts, to face the future. They made a tragic picture as we parted!

It was 5 December, and though we were leaving the southern coast bathed in sunshine and draped in flowers, our mood was not in tune. Numerous pessimistic friends foretold that our telegram from the Sebastopol Soviet was a trap, and they were not reassuring as to what would happen to us when we got into the Bolsheviks' fortified city. They felt sure we would be attacked or a least detained under arrest. Others, equally dismal, said this first part of our travels might turn out all right, but once embarked on the train, our troubles would certainly begin. And they told us the express trains were especially ill-treated. The Cossacks on the Don River were gathering under

Generals Kaledin[2] and Kornilov (who had now escaped from his prison during an uprising at staff headquarters and had managed to traverse half of Russia incognito, joining Kaledin at Novocherkasok). A battle was expected between them and the Bolshevik forces moving to meet them from Moscow, while the Ukrainians were also sending troops from Kiev and Poltava. No one knew on which side the latter would take part. We should undoubtedly be caught between two fires, we were told, and be killed in the scrimmage. We heard there was no food in Petrograd and that everyone was being assassinated, while permission to go beyond the frontier was always refused. The refrain of all conversations was the utter folly of our attempt!

My husband and I discussed with some hesitation what we should do, but we finally decided circumstances would not be improving for a long time and that if we wanted to go abroad, we must try to do so now. Going seemed a necessity because of Cantacuzene's health. From every point of view, we found it better to put our luck to the test, while we still had sufficient strength of nerve and money in plenty, and while communications seemed possible. We knew if the Cossacks' raiding cut the country in two, or if the

[2] General Alexei Maksimovich Kaledin (1861–1918), a Don Cossack, was one of the first generals to take up arms against the Bolsheviks in the south after the October revolution. He committed suicide in January 1918 in despair over the situation of anti-Bolshevik forces.

railroads broke down through strikes, we should be tied up in a bag in the Crimea, helpless to carry out our plan. Having once decided, we promised ourselves that whatever happened, we would not regret our present act and that we would leave no possible stone unturned to get through successfully. If from Petrograd we could not push on to foreign lands, we would simply gather what ready money we could from there and somehow manage to return, then establish ourselves near the family group for an indefinite stay. Meanwhile, we were ready to pay in coin and with all our resources to get through.

By way of beginning, my jewels were sewn into our traveling clothes, where they would attract less attention and be less encumbering than in the jewel case. We then divided our money, so each should carry half in case one or the other of us should be searched and robbed, or we became separated. In case of accident, we took 10,000 rubles in bills. We reduced our baggage, leaving two trunks to my mother-in-law. With our determination wound up for any emergency, we took the first step on our journey.

Davidka started ahead by some hours, driving our trunks in a cart harnessed with a troika of good horses. We followed by motor. He was to wait for us at the gates of Sebastapol, since my husband had the pass for us all on one paper. Cantacuzene was in civilian clothes, but our passports naturally gave our names and rank, and we were obliged to show them. I counted much on Davidka's soldier uniform to help.

We were too excited to talk during our long drive. Upward we climbed to the pass in the mountains and from there turned for a last silent look at the beautiful garden of paradise: the Crimean coast below. As we came out of the narrow Baidarsky Gateway in the rocks and faced northward, the bleak cold winds blew against us with a flurry of snow. Two or three hours we traveled onward through it, to the battlefield of Balaklava,[3] and we passed the monuments of French, English, and Russian soldiers who had died and been buried there where they had fallen, enemies in that great fight of long ago. Then we reached the outside fortifications of Sebastopol and were stopped at the guardhouse.

Davidka and his cart were already there. Instead of the amiable dapper officer of old régime days, two rough soldiers with sullen faces came to meet us. But they were neither untidy nor drunk, and they read our pass and then examined our passports with gruff but perfectly intelligent comments. They were not entirely pleased with Cantacuzene's passport and mine, and hesitated a moment, while of course my heart went down into my boots. My husband explained we were only going through the city, leaving by the night train for Petrograd, and the men finally acquiesced and said we might go in.

[3]Port city in the Crimea, site of a famous battle in the Crimean War in October 1854 (and in the Russo-Turkish War of the previous century, 1773). The memorials are to the victims of the Crimean War (1853–1856).

We went to the hotel, dined, and then had time to read a paper and to take a turn about the town. It had acquired an evil reputation lately with the inhabitants of those regions where we had been. Ever since late June, when Admiral Kolchak had been dismissed by his fleet, destruction and disorder had radiated from Sebastopol over the whole countryside. But now the place—though its sinister quiet and emptiness gave an oppressive atmosphere—was clean, and the most perfect order reigned.

However, at the hotel the director bewailed losses suffered through dearth of travelers and through constant requisition of his provisions. Some French officers were in the hotel, mainly young aviators; but they seemed on the eve of departure. Otherwise, the house was practically vacant. At the station it was the same— few travelers, no motley public at all, almost no soldiers, a sprinkling of smart sailors and naval officers with their families, everything clean, and business being run without confusion. We found our train easily and quickly, and our car, also. We paid twice the old prices or more, and we discovered that we had an entire trunk's weight more baggage than the very latest law allowed. We were ordered to leave the trunk, but this was so distressing that Cantacuzene gave Davidka unlimited power to act for us, knowing the influence of a soldier's position. Our man did his best, and after a half-hour he returned to say the trunk would not be confiscated. It might go along in spite of the recent rule. Only he had been obliged to buy an extra first-class ticket, all the way to Petrograd, and to spend fifty rubles in bribes because the ticket would not be used!

In the train we had two compartments adjoining and a dressing room; so if the "comrade soldiers" did not invade our premises, we might count on a very comfortable trip. At first, everyone had plenty of room. Two brawny sailors of the garrison got on our car, merely telling the conductor they "wished to do so," by way of excuse; but they promised, incidentally, to see that we had no other inconvenient guests. They were allowed to sleep in our corridor and had soon settled down chatting quite genially with Davidka. I had put Élène with Davidka and kept my husband with me, for the sake of protection, with the doors between the servants and ourselves all open, and we piled plaids and baskets, with our bags, against every window so the station mobs along the road would think our places crowded and would not be tempted in. There was no longer a pillow, blanket, or sheets left in any car. One of my windows was cracked from top to bottom and, of course, undressing was impossible. But it was much to be able to lie down and stretch out, even if at any moment an invasion might be expected. I shivered to think of the masses awaiting our train at Simferopol and elsewhere on our route! For the moment we could, however, count on a few hours of tranquil sleep; we hastened to seize that.

I slept soundly until about two a.m. Then in a panic I awoke and listened to howls and shrieks, thumps and bumps all about me. All this there was, while our sailors could be heard keeping their word to us, for no intruders invaded our car. A window crashed just beyond me, and then a heavy thing was thrown against one of our own. Fortunately, it held and this seemed to discourage the attacking party. There were insults and cries of "Capitalists!" "Bourgeois!" And I saw Michael feel for his revolver. We both sat up and waited in silence for what might come. Nothing happened, and the train drew out of Simferopol leaving a vociferating group of seething humanity behind.

I took courage from this first experience and went to sleep again. But we were told there would be other stations, where the crowd was worse than this had been, and we spent many anxious hours. Our sailor protectors were truly admirable. They were the greatest aid and comfort, fraternized with Davidka and Élène, and looked after our safety always. They admitted to the premises, during the two days and three nights to Petrograd, those who showed proper tickets for reserved places in our car and made exception only in favor of three wounded soldiers, for whom they begged our hospitality. One of these was shot through the lung and could scarcely breathe; another, with a stomach wound, lay on his back; and the third was lacking both legs. There were no Red Cross trains since the revolution to transport such misery, and the wounded depended on chance. These three had been fortunate, for our big sailors and Davidka helped the poor fellows as much as they could, while my husband often talked to them and saw to their comfort, and we gave them tea and biscuits from time to time.

Safely we passed through the Cossack country, and the city of Kharkov was one of our stops. When, the next day, we reached Moscow, we read in special telegrams sold in the station that there had just been a battle during the night at this same Kharkov and all communications were cut off with the south, our train having probably been the last to go through. Finally, after all our false alarms, we reached the capital, twenty-four hours late, but quite content even though our trip had cost nearly 2,000 rubles, when in old times 300 would have amply paid for it.

We thanked our protectors, the two sailors, for their good services, and we bade our wounded soldiers good-bye, while they with enthusiasm all wished us well. We had had warm relations with them, such as certainly could never have existed in any other country in a like situation. It takes Russians to be so unexpectedly simple in the midst of complications.

XXVII

Petrograd Under the Bolsheviki

PETROGRAD looked frightfully run down. The streets were lost in deep snow, frozen hard on them, but worn in ruts and holes, and the going was dreadful. The crowds were greater and more disorderly than ever. Hardly anyone ventured out at night without accident, which consisted generally in one's being stopped and relieved of money, furs, woolen clothes, and boots, then left to go one's way, almost naked in the cold. Misery stared out of every decent face. It was the dreadful soldiers who had now taken to selling every kind of stolen merchandise, and we bought on the street pavements several valuable editions of rare books for absurdly small prices. Evidently these came from some of the palaces that were being constantly looted.

Half the shops were closed, and many had been sacked, with their windows left broken, or they were boarded up against the street. Criminals infested the town; well-to-do people were feeling the pinch of actual hunger, while the honest poor were starving. The hideous Red Guards[1]—who looked like men I have seen depicted in old French paintings, representing

---

[1] The "workers' militia" organized by the Bolsheviks and so named in April 1917; they were to play a significant role in subsequent Bolshevik actions in the course of the year.

the Reign of Terror in Paris—were "keeping order" on all sides, dressed in rough clothes, with occasionally some fine garment in their make-up, evidently stolen. These men stalked about or sat at street corners, with excellent guns, drawn from our old reserves, loaded and slung across their shoulders by a rope, or hanging loosely over an arm, or even sometimes being used to bump along as a walking-stick. Naturally with such treatment, guns were always going off.

At the street corners fires were kept burning to warm these protectors of the new government, and I personally saw many a Red Guardsman use the barrel or the bayonet fixed to the barrel of his loaded gun to stir the blaze! Constantly also one heard machine guns firing in various quarters of the city, while occasionally passers-by would rush for shelter under doorways as the shooting approached. But no one stayed at home because of bullets, which had become a matter of constant recurrence. Prices of everything had soared to the sky, and people were obliged to pay, or to go unfed, unclothed, and unwarmed.

There is no word for the general depression; yet I saw all my old friends who were still in Petrograd, and I found them glad to talk of outside things or to laugh with sudden gay irony at some comic incident of their own plight, as they tried to forget their troubles for a little while. General Komarov was still in charge in the Winter Palace, and he told us of the horrible days when the great building had been taken and sacked by the mob. I myself saw its broken panes of glass and the walls riddled with bullets. From several eye-witnesses we heard details of the multitude's work. Strangely enough, the rabble had passed by furniture, paintings, porcelains, and bronzes of great value, and had even looked uncomprehendingly at a vitrine[2] full of ancient Greek jewelry wrought in pure gold. Saying disdainfully, "Those are toys," they had let them stand; and then they hustled one another to cut leather coverings off seats of modern chairs in anterooms and in the emperor's sitting room, and to knock down gilded plaster from the walls, sure it must be real gold. The great Malachite Hall was smashed beyond repair, and infinite damage was done to some of the apartments of ceremony. The cellars had been robbed, until all the crowd was dead drunk. All over the town the tragedy oppressed one, and the splendid capital seemed like some luxurious and renowned beauty, dying in the gutter, disfigured and disgraced.

On the street I heard German spoken constantly and openly; doubtful-looking men, with unmistakably German faces and clothes, went about with assurance. The deputies from the German government had arrived, Count Mirbach at their head, and Bronstein (alias Trotsky) was entertaining them.

Tatishchev I saw, and he described Trotsky's entry into the ministry after Tereshchenko's arrest. The assembled group of secretaries and officials, himself at their head, handed Trotsky the keys to all the cupboards and then, bowing themselves out, had left their

[2] A display case (French).

resignations piled on the center table. He pictured the new minister's surprise and his perplexity as to how he should get on without their services, his threat to publish all the secret treaties of Russia with her allies—a threat that was quite empty, though the creature did not know it. Long ago all important documents had been spirited away by loyal hands and could not now be traced.

Each day some part of the city was in darkness, and the water supply was constantly expected to break down. All other public service was erratic, and telephones and cabs were entirely accidental luxuries. Even in our well-organized hotel, where we had gone into my same old apartment, with almost a feeling of home-coming and of being protected, everything was more or less up in the air. We could not complain, however, as compared to those about us we lived in the lap of quiet luxury. By some miracle, we had the good will of the hotel servants, who gave us admirable care. Even when one day there was a strike belowstairs, and the other guests were without food, the waiter on our floor confided to me with his ever-ready grin, "Your Highness shall have your lunch and dinner as usual, served here in the salon, since we do not wish you to be inconvenienced." And so it was. Afterward I learned our party were the only people in the hotel who had had any meals! It was quite puzzling. My husband had accused me of being in league with the Bolsheviki; but I have never understood the real reasons for the curious protecting influence that hovered about us through all our stay in Petrograd, unless it came from the devotion of these servants, whom I had known and often talked with through the three years I had been occupying that same apartment for my brief visits to the capital. I had done some of them small favors but not enough to explain their present kindness.

The most mysterious proof of this care for us was an occurrence on the evening of our arrival. We had been warned by the hotel director on that first day of the constant visits the Bolsheviki made to our hotel to inspect and to requisition arms, which requisition amounted to their carrying off anything striking their fancy. In consequence of this, we had done up all our valuables at once, had carried them to my bank, confiding them there to an old acquaintance, the manager of the Credit Lyonnais—all except my string of pearls, of which I was particularly fond, and some earrings, rings, and pins I habitually wore. That evening we had dined, keeping with us a friend who dropped in casually, and when the latter left us, about ten, Cantacuzene finished smoking. We moved to our bedrooms to begin preparations for the night. My room and my husband's communicated, and they were between Davidka's room, on Cantacuzene's left, and the salon on my right, while my maid was placed alone, somewhat farther down the corridor. All our doors on the corridor were locked. In a dressing gown, I was seated at my mirror with clothes tossed on chairs and odds and ends spread on the dressing table, when a knock on the salon door attracted my attention. Too lazy to rise and open it, I called out, "That door is locked. Go to Number 15." Davidka slept there, and I spoke to my husband, asking him to tell Davidka to get whatever was being brought. Cantacuzene, himself always on the alert, went into his man's room, just as the latter answered the summons from the hall. In an instant my husband was back at our communicating door. "Quickly get ready! It is the Bolsheviki. I will hold them a minute or two in my room, but they will want to come in here." Then he disappeared, and I heard loud conversation approaching from Davidka's room into his own.

I seized my pearls and rings, and threw them high into my wardrobe, where they fell down behind the piles of lingerie there; then I hid my new slippers and my traveling boots behind the tub in the bathroom and the Fabergé bird went under a corner of the rug. There was nothing else I could put away, save my revolver, which I shoved into the lining of the empty traveling bag, as it stood open. Clothes, furs, and toilet silver must take their chances. I decided in order not to seem too busy, I would join Cantacuzene and his party. I entered his room and remained fixed on the threshold from sheer amazement, for our much-feared Bolsheviki were already going out. They were saluting my husband respectfully in military fashion, and were giving him his title of "General" and begging his pardon for having disturbed us! I could scarcely believe my eyes and ears! Cantacuzene answered them amiably, and as they retired, he closed the door and locked it, sending Davidka with the men to show them Élène's room. The twelve sailors making up the party were commanded by a young doctor, and they had simply examined our papers and then said politely that these were in perfect order and would pass. Two of the men had also remarked that they had known Cantacuzene since long before the revolution!

The following day our servants told us the sailors had left Davidka his revolver after some hesitation and had said they knew all about his master and that he was "ours." We have never comprehended to what we were indebted for such excellent treatment. Was it Cantacuzene's reputation since old times among his various commands as a liberal and an officer they respected and were fond of? Or was it sheer blind luck, and the influence of my Fabergé bird? At any rate we gratefully accepted the results, and for the time being eliminated the fear of Bolshevik inspection from our list of anxieties.

Toward the end of our stay in Petrograd, when conditions had grown worse, I received a telephone message from the manager of the Credit Lyonnais. He asked me to his office on urgent business, and naturally I lost no time in going. He received me with the news that by a mere chance he had been informed of the probability of all banks—foreign as well as Russian—being raided and closed within a few days.

Would I give him checks ahead on my account for any sum we needed to pay our traveling expenses?

He could pay me this money from funds he had in the management's private safe, and then he would replace it there later, when it became possible to cash my checks. He said I must accept this arrangement, as already the banks were not allowed by law to hand out to their clients more than a thousand rubles a day. Even this would soon be stopped, with the complete closing of the banks, after which no one could act. Cantacuzene's money, he knew, was in a Russian bank and could not be touched, and: "I want you and your husband to be able to leave the capital on the day fixed, so you must take my advice, Princess, now immediately. Also, today please carry your jewels home with you. If anything should happen to me, you could not get them, for I put your packages in my own private safe. One never knows, even if I am here, the Bolsheviki may take it into their heads to confiscate all such objects, and insurance can't be claimed."

After a little hesitation I did as Monsieur C. suggested. I made a rapid calculation of what we should need until our departure and for the trip, and I wrote him at his desk a series of checks for 1,000 rubles each, dated to follow one another on successive days; then he handed me the 10,000 or 11,000 rubles I required in bills. By way of recommendation he then added: "Buy as many 500-ruble bills from the old régime as you can find, even paying a premium for them, at your hotel and in any shops. On these you will get a good rate of exchange, even if our values here should drop still lower than now. The Germans are collecting them in Stockholm and in Copenhagen, and you mean to go that way, I understand? I have already given you all of those I have here."

Infinitely grateful, I tried vainly to put my thanks into words, and I asked with interest what he meant to do and what would become of him. He laughed. "I am waiting the Bolsheviki's orders," he said, "and we are quite expecting their invasion here. Our books are all prepared for inspection. I think they won't ill-treat us seriously, as we are a French institution, but accidentally some of us might be killed. I know I am taking chances."

I inquired if my checks and his payment of them would not perhaps augment his difficulties. "Don't think of that, please, Princess," he replied. "I believe the men who will come here cannot judge of any accounts they see. If they disapprove of this, it is a very small detail, as compared to all the other irregularities I have on my conscience. For months I have been running the bank to fit outside circumstances and the needs of our clients, taking care of the latter as best we could; and it has necessitated unconventional action constantly. If you hear I am killed, don't you and your husband reproach yourselves. I shall not die for you, most surely. Good-bye, Princess, and good luck, and if you find I can serve you, in case I have lived through all this racket, let me know."

One couldn't have rendered a more thoughtful service in a kinder manner! He had been correct in his information, for the very next morning the Bolsheviki took over, occupied, and closed every bank in town. All the directors were arrested and taken to "Smolnyi Institute,"[3] where the de facto government held high carnival in an orgy of confusion. Most of these gentlemen of finance were set at liberty soon after, on payment of high ransoms, but until we left Petrograd, the banks remained closed. Had it not been for the providential warning and help of Monsieur C., we should never have been able to leave Russia when we did.

After I brought my jewels back to our hotel, it became—in the constant uncertainly of life—a great question as to where we should keep them. We ended up tying them up in a bundle, together with our money, papers, and other valuables, and then wrapping the latter in a small white tablecloth. We kept this quaint object near the window of our salon. Outside this window was a small balcony, from which the deep snow was never cleared, and we decided should by chance our rooms be subjected to an unwelcome visit of Bolsheviki, or other thieves, it would only be the act of a moment to drop our precious bundle outside into the snow-drift; then we counted on the whiteness of the tablecloth not to attract attention from anyone who might look out casually.

It was quite dreadful to see the troubles of those

[3]The Smolnyi Institute was an aristocratic girls' school installed by Catherine the Great in the buildings of a nunnery (one of the outstanding ensembles of baroque architecture in Russia). In mid-1917, the Petrograd Soviet had moved here from the Tauride Palace, and in November, Smolnyi became the seat of the new Bolshevik government.

surrounding us, most of whom had not our hopes of getting away to lean upon. Estates were confiscated, and practically all factories were out of commission. Town property was paying nothing, either, since no one settled rent or taxes. In my own case I discovered why.

I had a large piece of city property, given me years before by my husband, which I managed myself. The intendant who looked after it informed me in September that none of the tenants—not even the municipality, which was the lessee of one apartment—had paid rent for six months, not in fact since the beginning of the revolution.

I gave orders that until 1 January the house expenses should be paid, and I left enough money with the intendant for this purpose; after which date he was to abandon the whole affair to take care of itself, and he was to pay no expenses or taxes until the inhabitants themselves should come to the rescue. At least it would not be a daily drain on me, and as proclamations announced that all city property would shortly be "nationalized," it seemed unnecessary to take care of it further. I found in questioning other proprietors that they were all going through my experiences and reaching my decisions.

It certainly looked bad for the future of the government's finances, as well as for our own, and it also seemed as if soon all the city-houses would be falling in ruins, since no repairs were being made and our climatic conditions are so bad. The dangers of poverty and disorder never seemed, however, to strike the demagogues in power. Trotsky made violent and blood-thirsty speeches, preaching anarchy and crime against the "counter-revolutionists," posing himself as the "protector of the people's revolution." I never could make out just what he and his government counted on for their continued popularity. Evidently they had no plans for saving Russia, or for doing anything rational.

The base of government upon which everything stood was "Smolnyi." In the old buildings of the Young Ladies' Institute, founded by Catherine the Great for the education of the daughters of her noblemen, there were held meetings (in continuous session) of disorganized groups of Bolsheviki. Somewhat on the model of the Ukraine's Rada it was, but those in Petrograd spent their whole time wrangling and struggling for power, while only giving out proclamations. Each man was doing business for himself alone, without rhyme or reason, and with no result, except the general augmentation of noise and confusion. There one must go, however, to ask for passports or for anything else, and it was the merest accident as to what reply, if any, one received.

Curiously, protection was given to certain people of the old régime, especially those who at court had belonged to the Occult party. Mme. Vyrubova was released and so well furnished with money that she established herself with more luxury than she ever knew in ancient days. She was, I heard, an intimate friend of

Trotsky-Bronstein. Also I was told we should have no difficulty in obtaining passports if we addressed ourselves to her. But we did not consider this to be a possible method!

Perhaps the most deplorable situation was that of the officers, both of the army and navy. They were degraded from their rank, and they walked about minus their epaulets, unpaid, and literally starving. One of the railroad stations wanted to engage a group of them as baggage porters; General Komarov tried to take another group to cut wood for the stoves in the public buildings. All this was not allowed. "They are intelligensia and can use their science, and work with reading and writing, which we cannot do. Let them then do that and not take the bread from us poor men" was the reply the rabble government gave in each case. Pensions were abolished for the old and weak and for retired government officials, for all officers both wounded and well, also for every man wearing the St. George's Cross, which decoration had till now carried a small pension with it. This last measure affected many soldiers, which made a beginning of discontent in their circles against the workmen Red Guards who were now on the top of the wave. As to the officers, they and their families were dying of want, when they were not being actually killed by mutinous troops. Some friends of ours picked up a starving officer, who when discovered unconscious on their doorstep had no underclothes beneath his uniform, and he had eaten no food for three days! He had simply tramped the streets looking for any kind of work until he fell. A charming little woman, whom I had known previously, came to me to ask for sewing. She told me her husband, decorated for bravery and twice wounded, was now without pay, pension, or work. Cases like these could be counted by the thousands, and stories of the torturing and murdering daily of officers on every side were too horrible to relate!

The foreigners were greatly worried. They were not allowed to count on protection in Russia or on permission to leave. Their situation was certainly most precarious. I heard from all those who met the French (both of the embassy and of the military mission) that they were loud in their complaints and accusations, and in their unconcealed anger against our country and its people of all classes. The British kept much cooler, though they were even more harassed than the French were because Sir George Buchanan,[4] with great dignity and continued determination, had refused to receive Trotsky or to have anything to do with him, and had refused also the Red Guards that were offered for the protection of the embassy. Now M. Noulens,[5] had, on the contrary, had an interview with Trotsky at the French Embassy and had also accepted

[4]Sir George William Buchanan (1854–1924), career diplomat, British ambassador to St. Petersburg, 1910–1918. See George Buchanan, *My Mission to Russia and Other Diplomatic Memories*, 2 vols. (Boston: Little, Brown, 1923).

[5]Joseph Noulens (1864–1939), ambassador of France (1917–18), former war and finance minister, senator. See Joseph Noulens, *Mon ambassade en Russie soviétique* (Paris: Plon, 1933).

from the actual government a guard, which I believe was composed of Polish troops.

The Italian ambassador had long ago fallen ill and had left Petrograd when the Bolsheviki came into power. Mr. Francis was as usual cheerful and amiable and deeply interested in the historical situation he lived in, and in a most difficult position, he seemed full of strength and resources. He hoped for the successful interference of the Cossacks, led by Kaledin and Kornilov, and though we were not converted by his optimism, we could not but admire the splendid spirit and fearlessness of the American ambassador. Once he admitted he was somewhat disappointed in the Russian people, or rather in the use they had made of their great boon of liberty, but this was merely in passing. It evidently never occurred to him to leave his post, whatever came, though he spoke quite frankly of the threats and dangers to which he was constantly subjected. He had refused the guards offered by the government for the embassy, while permitting General Judson, head of the military mission, to accept them for his offices. The ambassador and his secretaries were themselves keeping watch at the embassy night and day. The embassy staff equaled their chief in pluck and good spirits, and one was full of admiration for the little group.

In spite of everyone's predictions, we had obtained our passports suddenly. My husband, without trying any byways or protections, intrigues or bribes, had merely spoken with the hotel man who looked after such documents for those living in the house. They had ended by driving together to Smolnyi one morning to ask the permission necessary, before applying to the municipal police for passports to go beyond the frontier. At Smolnyi, where they had been scarcely noticed, a soldier had directed them to a large room, on the door of which they saw written "Passports." Here they had knocked, been admitted, and found themselves opposite a Jewess, who wrote out the application which Cantacuzene had signed. Then she had taken over all our papers of identification and our old passports, saying there would be a reply in three days. We waited five, of which the last two were spent in acute anxiety as to what answer would be given us.

Finally, the passport agent returned from Smolnyi on the fifth day and came to our rooms at once, saying with what seemed real pleasure, "See, Highness, your papers are all here and in order, and you are the only people to whom permission had been granted. These others are all refusals." And he showed a large sheaf of papers he carried. Needless to say, my husband gave the man a fat tip, but again we could not understand the mystery of our success in these circumstances.

XXVIII

Last Days in Russia

AFTER THIS we were still in Petrograd about two weeks until all the formalities of our passports had been gone through. These were most complicated. With Smolnyi's permission we claimed and received ordinary passports from the municipality police section. Then the general staff, because they did not recognize Smolnyi, gave us military passports. The fact that America did not recognize the Bolshevik government either made it necessary for the American embassy to give us still another set of documents for admission to the United States. Besides all this we had to obtain a visa from Swedish, Danish, and British legations and "control offices." These were finished at last, and we were able to turn to the question of tickets, which came to us through someone's giving up accommodations taken long before—the same luck we had had in the Crimea!

All these various arrangements progressed slowly. Quite frequently we were obliged to change details in our plans. Each time panic seized us, lest everything should fail, or lest, if we stayed too long, the railroad strike, which was daily threatened, should shut us in. My husband's health suffered extremely from the cold. He was on the verge of a nervous breakdown, and I was very weary of the struggle. But each day more than ever, I felt convinced we must and would go somehow, and I was less worried since our first success in obtaining passports.

We then gave up the trip we had planned through Siberia and Japan, on account of the cold and disorders on the railroads there. Also, we heard of violent outbreaks along the road in the big cities of the East. Besides, a three weeks' trip in such circumstances seemed impossible in my husband's ailing condition. When finally we were sure we should go by the Swedish route, I was greatly relieved. At the last moment the problem of what to do with my jewels became the worst of all, and I grew almost to hate the pretty things I had worn with such delight formerly.

Finally, Cantacuzene left the disposition and hiding of my jewelry to me. I sewed it into my furs and heavier clothes, scattering the latter about in different trunks, with a silent prayer that I was choosing places wisely, where rough soldier hands would not encounter weights or hard surfaces. I also sewed into various stiff collars (of dresses or of coats) a quantity of the old régime 500-ruble notes. My most valuable stones (pearls and diamonds) I fastened to the inside of my traveling muff and boa, between the fur, which was heavy and stiff, and the cotton stuffing of the linings, where except for a slight addition to the fur's weight, they could not be noticed. Some smaller things I put between my hat form and its ribbon trimmings.

With all these placed as they were, I could quite easily undress if necessary, without an appearance of having anything to hide and without calling attention to the valuables. Michael carried only the sum allowed and all our necessary papers, putting them quite visibly in his portfolio, while I had a little money in my purse, so we should not rouse suspicions by seeming too poor. Élène also carried money and some of my jewels scattered in her small trunk. Cantacuzene had the brilliant idea of calling in the hotel painter, who the day before we left, under our direction, covered over the crowns and monograms on our trunks and bags, with black or white paint, roughly splashed, and who made our belongings look as shabby and smeared as possible.

For the trip we wore the clothes that had served until now for hunting and winter sports in the country and which looked unpretentious, shapeless, and comfortable. We decided we would thus be quite inconspicuous in the crowd of travelers, and hoped for the best.

At the entrance to Finland Station, our passports fell into the hands of an officer who, by chance, had known Cantacuzene in the army and who took pains to be very polite and make us no trouble. Several other passengers were stopped and turned back to Petrograd from this station, in spite of their protests. That night in the train we were quiet and all the next day as well. We heard we were eight hours late, and we wondered what effect it would have on the feelings and the humors of the soldiers who awaited us at the custom house. As we approached the frontier, we noticed the general agitation. My husband grew feverish, while I felt very cold somehow. We saw the passengers around us destroying letters and papers, and we did the same, keeping only our most necessary documents of identification.

As we reached the station at Torneo, we realized our train had been very warm and comfortable, for outside in the dark night, the thermometer registered thirty-three degrees below freezing, and it was almost impossible to breathe. When we went into the station, a row of soldiers sat about behind a low counter, on which baggage must be examined. They were looking tired and sleepy, and were dully talking to one another. We preceded the crowd that entered. There among the men, I saw one drowsy, good-natured face that attracted my attention at once. I said to Cantacuzene, "Let us choose that man," and we instantly had our bags carried and laid upon the counter in front of him. He opened Élène's and, finding nothing of interest, passed on. I think he judged us poor and probably without anything worth confiscating in our baggage. We ourselves seemed so shabby. However, he opened one of my bags and fingered casually a blue serge costume, which he regarded with indifference. He never guessed that under his hand in its high, stiff collar, I had sewed 5,000 rubles. The other bags were even less exciting to him, though he did draw a time-table map of Russia from Cantacuzene's, saying if the latter

wished to take this with him abroad, he must go with
it to the censor. It was offered him as a present since
it had lost its use for us. We were leaving Russia, we
explained.

In one of my bags, the soldier found a few sheets of
white writing-paper with their envelopes, and he
opened each one of these, holding it to the light, to see
that nothing was written thereon. Then he captured a
sheet of black tissue paper Élène had laid on top of my
dressing gown. This he held up to the light also with
the greatest interest; but when I told him to keep it, he
put it back with a grunt. We were entirely patient and
encouraged him, saying how well it was to look carefully into everything. We made as if we would continue
opening bags and plaid shawl rolls until the fellow
said that it was enough. Then with my best smile, I
pointed out our trunks and asked when I should open
these. "You need not do that at all," he answered amiably enough. "You evidently have nothing of importance or which is forbidden. You are three people, and
there are but four trunks." With the weight of my
knowledge of all that lay in my trunks (I had jewels,
furs, laces, and cloths, also money and five ancient,
valuable oil-paintings—which were heirlooms I had
risked saving by rolling them at the bottom of one
trunk), I carried also on my heart a terror of these ruf-
fians and a fear they would arrest Cantacuzene. Now
since we had safely passed this ordeal of the custom-
house examination, I began to breathe more normally.

Just then someone spoke to us from behind, in a

cordial voice and giving my husband his title, which seemed perhaps a little risky in such circumstance. "Why, Prince, is it really you, and can I do anything to help you? Your passports have just been put into my hands, and I was so glad to get them. Will you present me to your wife?" We turned, and Cantacuzene recognized a young officer he had known at the front. Under fire they had formed a warm acquaintanceship and my husband was delighted to see the nice young fellow again. He presented him to me, and we were soon chatting casually, and as if in ordinary times, we gave him some news of Petrograd, while he told us he had already looked over and stamped our passports, adding: "Now if you are through here with these comrades, you can go on and make your declaration as to money, then continue to the restaurant and dine there, while the other travelers are struggling through their interrogations." He accompanied us, and we showed what visible money we had and made our declaration that we carried no gold coin, Russian or foreign. Then we passed into the dining room and ordered a hot supper.

I felt ravenous after the long train trip and the extreme tension of the last hours. The officer, whom we had invited to join us, came after a little, bringing a colleague, who had also met Cantacuzene somewhere at the front, and soon we were eating gaily and conversing. I noticed at the next table a group of five sailors listening to us with sinister expressions and extreme attention. One of them turned sidewise and sat almost touching Cantacuzene's chair, to hear better what the latter was saying of conditions and politics in the South. I signaled, and my husband at once understood and changed the course of his remarks. Instantly the interest of his hearer flagged.

I felt triumphant over our very successful passage through the custom house in spite of its dragons. I had always prided myself that no guilt of smuggling on any frontier was mine, but now I had no scruple with reference to the Bolshevik government, and enough was to my credit in that direction during past years to balance the debts of tonight. Besides, we were carrying nothing away of all Cantacuzene's fortune, which lay behind us, confiscated and smoking, an absolute loss.

Having finished supper, we gathered our effects together and put on our heavy coats. Then sending the baggage ahead in one big sleigh, we followed in a second. A low, deep affair it was, with a soft straw cushion, upon which we stretched out, while great carpets were warmly tucked about us. We pulled our furs high over our mouths to breathe the cold air through them. One young officer drove with us as far as the passport delivery at the frontier barrier, where a guard house stood and where we were told one must get out for a last identification before passing into Sweden.

As the sleigh slowed down, preparing to stop, the officer spoke. "You need not get out," he said. "Here are your passports, Prince, and they are in order. I separated them from the others at the station already and have kept them for you. Take them and drive on, right through the barrier-gate. I will answer for you." And he stepped off the back of our sleigh and saluted, while our driver whipped the three horses of his troika, and we dashed on over the soft snow, past the barrier, down the river bank and across the ice, climbing rapidly to the other side, with the lights of Haparanda just ahead.

We were in Sweden, and I turned back to look my last at the home-land we were leaving. Three or four hours before, when we had left our train at Torneo, the sky had been dark and threatening. Now there was a complete transformation. It was hung with millions of stars, while on the horizon rose high into the heavens the most splendid halo of a magnificent aurora-borealis. Perhaps it was a promise for the future of our unhappy country.

Mysterious as always, Russia stretched out her great plains toward the light, and that was all we could see of her.

Then I faced around again, and I saw the gay lamps of Haparanda station, which we were approaching; and I realized we were out of danger now, and free, though we were refugees in a strange kingdom.

Index

INDEX

Alekseev, Michael Vasilevich, 245n

Alexander II, xxix, xxx, 5n

Alexander III, xxix

Alexander Mikhailovich, Grand Duke, 265, 266

Alexandra Fedorovna, Empress, xx, xxxix, 74n, 75, 149, 150, 161–162, 172, 185–186, 203, 214, 216, 217–218, 219, 246, 277; after Stolypin assassination, 134–135; arrest of, 261–262; during February Revolution, 235–240, 242; problems with Russian society, 79; relationship with emperor, 117,148; relationship with Vyrubova and Rasputin, 144, 144n, 147, 170, 218

Anastasia of Montenegro, 108n, 139, 178, 265

Badmaev, Peter Aleksandrovich, 236n

Bark, Peter Lvorich, 202n, 204, 209, 214, 225, 237, 251, 285

Beliaev, Michael Alekseevich, 210n

Bezobrazov, Alexander Mikhailovich, 95n

Bloody Sunday, xxxii, 118–124, 118n, 124n

Bouromka, xviii, xxii, 58, 109,115, 124, 290, 324;

confiscation of, 364–365; family at, 61–69

Brusilov, Alexei Alekseevich, 344n

Brusilov offensive, xli, xlvii

Buchanan, Sir George, 424n

Buckner, Simon Bolivar, 17n

Cantacuzene, Bertha (Barbara)(daughter), lix, 106, 126, 166

Cantacuzene, Boris, 72, 107, 109n

Cantacuzene, Elizabeth, Princess, xxii–xxiii, lix, 62, 64–65, 67, 68, 70, 74, 90, 93, 109, 226, 237, 269, 290, 324, 367, 398–402

Cantacuzene, Irina, lix

Cantacuzene, John, xvii

Cantacuzene, Julia Grant, arrival in Russia, 57; assessment of her views, lx; attempt to return to Russia (1905), 125–131; audience with empress, 216–218; birth of, 7; birth of children, 72, 106, 139; death of father, 140, 143; death of grandfather, 23–25; debut at Austrian court, 34–37; debut in Newport, 42-43; divorce, blindness, lvi; during 1905 Revolution, 119–124; European tour (1898), 45–47, 51; European tour

437

Cantacuzene, Julia Grant *(cont'd)*
(1902 and 1903), 115;
European tour (1905),
124–125; family visit in
Russia (1901), 109–114;
importance of memoirs,
liv–lv; in new St. Petersburg
home, 173, 183; meeting
Michael, 46–52; problems
with Crown Prince Wilhelm,
83–90; publishing history,
lii–liv, lvn, lvi; Red Cross
work, 171–172, 191; return
to United States, lii–liii; trips
to Kiev, 284–287, 316–317;
trips to America, 137,139;
wedding, 52, 55–56; with
empress, 162–163; with
grandparents in Galena,
9–10; with grandparents in
N.Y.C., 10–11; with
Vyrubova, 147

Cantacuzene, Michael, xvii,
xx–xxii, lv–lvi, 46–52, 74,
115, 119, 123, 125, 129,
130, 152, 225–226, 237,
253, 255–258, 262–264,
286, 322–323, 351–352;
attending Crown Prince
Wilhelm, 80; commendation,
181; convalescing, 174–178,
181–183, 189–190; during
Kornilov affair, 346–349;
during October Revolution,
367–374, in Kiev, 289,
295–296; interview with
Nicholas II, 205–207; later
life, lvi; leaving for WWI,
166; named Commander of
Cuirassiers, 193; named to

staff of Nicholas Nikolaevich,
137; return to regiment
(1915), 189, 190; return to
regiment prior to WWI,
158–160; return to staff
position, 183; visit from
Dowager Empress, 181; visit
from emperor, 181–182;
wedding 52, 55–56;
wounded, 174

Cantacuzene, Michael (son),
lvi–lvii, 72, 92, 109, 126,
166, 176, 253, 258, 264,
268–271, 283, 284, 285

Cantacuzene, Michael
Rodionovich, xxii;

Cantacuzene, Rodion, lix

Cantacuzene, Rodion
Mateevich, xxii

Cantacuzene, Sergei
Mikhailovich, lix, 58, 93n,
94, 109

Cantacuzene, Zinaida (Ida)
(daughter), lix, 139, 166

Conkling, Roscoe, 18n, 42

Crimean War, xxiii, xxv

Cumberland, duchess of, 36,
37, 75, 79

Dolgoruky, Alexander, 80,
83–85, 165, 175, 176, 247

Draper, Jeanette, lvi

Fabergé owl, 353–354, 377,
392, 416, 417

Francis, David R., 250, 296,
303, 307, 311–312, 425

Franz Joseph, xix, 33, 36–37

Frederiks, Vladimir Borisovich,
243n

Goremykin, 135, 195, 204, 207
Grant, Frederick Dent, xvii, xviii, xviiin, xix, 3–16, 3n, 41–44, 137; as ambassador to Austria, 29–38; as commander on Governor's Island, 140; as military commander of Puerto Rico, 44; death, 140; finishing Grant's memoirs, 27, 28; funeral, 143; Grant & Ward, 10–12; in New York politics, 41–43; Philippines, 55–56, 109; Spanish-American War, 43–44; tour of Russia (1901) 109–114; wedding, 6–7
Grant, Ida Marie Honoré, xx, 10, 11, 44, 45, 71–72, 140, 143, 308; tour of Russia (1901), 109–114; in Vienna, 29–38; wedding, 6–7
Grant, Julia (Mrs. Ulysses S.), xxi, 7–12, 27, 30, 39, 56
Grant, Ulysses (brother of Julia Cantacuzene), 10, 33, 41, 55
Grant, Ulysses S. (president and general), xvii, 3–4, 3n, 7–16, 56; death, 23; decline of health, 15–16, 17–24; funeral, 25–27; Grant & Ward, 10–12; injured, 15; memoirs, 15–16; in Andirondacks, 19
Grant, Ulysses S., Jr., 12, 26
Grant & Ward, 10–12
Guchkov, Alexander Ivanovich, xlvii, 242n, 256, 266

Hanbury-Williams family, lix
Harrison, William Henry 29, 42

Honoré, Henry Hamilton, xx, 6n, 56
Hotel d'Europe, 270, 301

Imperial Alexandrine Lycée, xvii, 270–271
Imperial Manifesto, xxxv–xxxvi, xxxvin, 96n, 98n
Ito, Hirobumi, 104–105, 104n
Ivanov, Madame, 318, 377, 378, 380–384
Ivanov, Nicholas Iudovich, 233n, 235, 239

Kaledin, Alexei Maksimovich, 404n, 425
Kauschen, 173, 178, 189, 207
Kerensky, Alexander Fedorovich, xlvi, xlvii–l, lv, 196, 196n, 237, 238, 247, 248, 250, 251, 252, 273, 275, 287, 288, 293–294, 295, 307, 315, 342, 346, 347, 350, 367, 379, 398; fall of government, 341–344; involvement in Kornilov affair, 354–358
Khilkov, Michael Ivanovich, 106n
Knorring, Vladimir Romanovich, 284n, 285
Kochubei, Victor Sergeevich, 251n, 280
Kolchak, Alexander Vaselivich, lv–lvi, 299n, 407
Komarov, General, 412, 423
Kornilov, Lavr, xlviii, 343, 343n, 344, 345, 347, 348, 349, 350, 355, 404, 425
Kornilov affair, xlviii–xlix, liv, lv, 345, 346–350, 354–358

Krivoshein, Alexander
    Vasilevich, 132n, 204, 205
Krymov, Alexander
    Mikhailovich, 345n, 350;
    involvement in Kornilov
    affair, 346–350, 353–357
Ksheshinskaia, Matilda,
    309–310, 309n
Kurakin, Prince, 322, 375, 377,
    378
Kuropatkin, Aleksei
    Nikolaevich, 106n, 108, 163
Kyril Vladimirovich, Grand
    Duke, 48n, 214n, 215, 268,
    276–278

Lenin, Vladimir Ilich, xlvi, xlix,
    lii, 308n, 309–310, 313
Logan, John Alexander, 17n
Lüttwitz, Count, 81–82
Lvov, George Evgenevich,
    250n, 266, 307

Marie Fedorovna, Dowager
    Empress, 74n, 75, 79, 85, 86,
    181, 191–192, 200, 214, 215,
    265, 266–267, 268, 279–280,
    361; after son's abdication, 246
Maria Pavlovna, Grand
    Duchess, 109, 362, 362n
Marie, Grand Duchess, 74, 76
McKinley, William, 42, 55
Michael Aleksandrovich, Grand
    Duke, xliv, 83, 220, 227n,
    244, 244n, 249–250, 268
Mikhail Nikolaevich, Grand
    Duke, 5n, 81
Miliukov, Paul Nikolaevich, xli,
    xlvi–xlvii, liv, 213n, 250,
    275, 287

Nicholas II, xx, xxix, 118–119,
    133, 138n, 144, 149, 150,
    155–156, 158–160, 164,
    182, 184–185, 186, 187,
    214, 219, 277, 279, 398n;
    abdication, xliv, liv, 227–228,
    231–245, 249; after
    abdication, 245–248; after
    Stolypin assassination,
    134–135; as commander in
    chief in WWI, xxxix, 201,
    203; during declaration of
    war, 161–162; during Russo-
    Japanese War, 108; Imperial
    Manifesto, xxxv, xxxvin,
    xxxvii; interview with
    Michael, 205–207; reaction
    to Occult influences, 207;
    relationship with empress,
    117; visiting Michael in
    hospital, 181–182
Nicholas Mikhailovich, Grand
    Duke, 214n, 215, 222, 223,
    227, 268, 280
Nicholas Nikolaevich, Grand
    Duke, xxxvi, xxxix, lx, 108n,
    131, 137–138, 155,
    158–160, 163, 164n, 178,
    187n, 188, 189, 265, 267;
    opposing the Occult Party,
    184–187, 194; dismissal as
    commander, 200–201, 223
Nieroth, Daria Cantacuzene, lx,
    70–71, 165, 226
Nieroth, Theodore, lx, 70–71,
    165, 376, 377, 378

O'Beirne, Hugh James, 209n
Olga Fedorovna, Grand
    Duchess, 5–6

Order Number One, xlv, 259, 259n, 263, 272

Orlov, Princess, 119–124, 172, 265

Orlov, Vladimir Nikolaevich, 88n, 89, 90, 119, 135–136, 160, 186–187, 190, 201, 240, 265

Paget, Sir Arthur, 183

Palmer, Bertha Honoré, xvii, xix–xxi, liii, 10n, 39–40, 42, 44, 45–46, 115, 125, 126, 129, 137

Palmer, Potter, xix, 10n, 42, 44, 45–46, 115

Paskevich, Irene Ivanovna, 358–362

Peter the Great, xxv, 73, 73n, 95, 151, 192

Pilchau, Pilar von, 174

Pleve, Viacheslav, xxx, 101–104, 101n, 134, 134n; assassination of, 103–104

Poincaré, Raymond, 150n, 151

Polivanov, Aleksei Andreevich, 188n, 194, 195, 199, 200, 204, 210

Polovtsev, Peter Aleksandrovich, 310n, 312–313

Protopopov, Alexander Dmitrievich, xl, 209n, 211, 221–222, 233, 236, 239, 254

Raev, Nicholas Pavlovich, 210n

Rasputin, Grigory, xl, 144n, 147, 148, 149, 171, 187, 201, 219, 220–222, 236n, 247

Rein, George Ermolaevich, 210n

Rodzianko, Michael Vladimirovich, 195n, 211, 235, 238, 239–242, 249, 262, 280, 344

Root, Elihu, 42n, 300

Rudolf (Austrian Crown Prince), 32

Russo-Japanese War, xxx, xxxii, xxxv, 79n; description of, 106–109; defeat in, 109; outbreak of, 105

Russo-Turkish War, 106n, 406n

Ruszky, N.V., 228, 241–242

Sazonov, Sergei Dmitrievich, 155–158, 155n, 204, 209, 300

Serge Aleksandrovich, Grand Duke, xxx, 118n, 134, 134n, 219

Sheremetev, Dmitri Sergeevich, 182n

Sheridan, Philip H., 6–7, 6n, 9, 10

Sherman, William Tecumseh, 4, 17, 42

Shingarev, Andrei Ivanovich, 287, 287n

Shulgin, Vasily Vitalevich, 242n

Sipiagin, Dmitri Sergeevich, xxx, 134n

Skobelev, Michael Dmitrievich, 106n

Smith, Bruce, family, liv

Smolnyi Institute, 420, 420n, 422, 426, 427

Socialist-Revolutionary Combat Organization, 134nn.

Speransky, Michael, xvii, 65

Stackelberg, George Karlovich, 255, 255n

Stalin, Joseph, lii

Stolypin, Peter Arkadevich, xl, liv, 100, 100n, 132–133, after 1905 Revolution, 131; agrarian reform, xxxviii; assassination of, xxxi, 134, 134n; as PM, xxxvii, 131; description of 132; funeral 135

Stürmer, Boris, xl–xli, 207–208, 209, 211, 212, 213, 216

Sukhomlinov, Vladimir Aleksandrovich, 164n, 194, 201, 210; dismissal of, 188; problems with delivery of war supplies, 184–189

Tatishchev, Boris Alekseevich, 302n, 303, 307, 413

Tereshchenko, Michael Ivanovich, 250n, 287, 287n, 294, 413, involvement in the Kornilov affair, 355–357

Thomas, Albert, 208n, 274–275

Trepov, Dimitri Fedorovich, 131n, 214, 215, 216, 219

Trotsky, Leon, xlix, l, 90, 90n, 308, 313, 413, 423, 424

Twain, Mark, 18–19

Ukrainian nationalist movement, 290, 293–295, 320–324, 370

Victoria, Grand Duchess, 216, 276–278

Viviani, René, 151, 151n, 208

Voeikov, Vladimir Nikolaevich, 182, 182n, 185, 214, 239, 240–241, 243, 246

Vyrubova, Anna Aleksandrovna (Taneeva), 89n, 117–118, 135, 149, 172, 185, 201, 203, 207, 214, 215, 217, 218, 219, 221, 223, 236, 239, 422; description of, 169–170; personal background, 170–171; relationship with empress, 144, 147, 170; relationship with Rasputin, 144

West Point, 4, 41, 55, 109, 143

Wilhelm II, 80, 137, 138n, 164

Wilhelm, Crown Prince, 80–90

Witte, Madame, 97–98

Witte, Sergei Yulevich, xxv, xxvi, xxxvi, xxxvin, liv, 96, 96nn., 100n, 132, 138n; physical description of, 98–99; through Russo-Japanese War, 97–100

World's Columbian Exposition (Chicago) xx, 39–40, 39n

Xenia, Grand Duchess, 220, 225, 265

Yusupov, Felix Feliksovich, 144n, 220–221

Zolotnitsky, Peter Nikolaevich, 302n

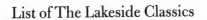

List of The Lakeside Classics

The Lakeside Classics

Number	Title	Year
1.	The Autobiography of Benjamin Franklin . . .	1903
2.	Inaugural Addresses of the Presidents of the United States from Washington to Lincoln . .	1904
3.	Inaugural Addresses of the Presidents of the United States from A. Johnson to T. Roosevelt .	1905
4.	Fruits of Solitude by William Penn	1906
5.	Memorable American Speeches I. The Colonial Period	1907
6.	Memorable American Speeches II. Democracy and Nationality	1908
7.	Memorable American Speeches III. Slavery	1909
8.	Memorable American Speeches IV. Secession, War, Reconstruction	1910
9.	The Autobiography of Gurdon Saltonstall Hubbard	1911
10.	Reminiscences of Early Chicago	1912
11.	Reminiscences of Chicago During the Forties and Fifties.	1913
12.	Reminiscences of Chicago During the Civil War .	1914
13.	Reminiscences of Chicago During the Great Fire.	1915
14.	Life of Black Hawk	1916
15.	The Indian Captivity of O. M. Spencer	1917
16.	Pictures of Illinois One Hundred Years Ago . .	1918
17.	A Woman's Story of Pioneer Illinois by Christiana Holmes Tillson	1919
18.	The Conquest of the Illinois by George Rogers Clark	1920

Number	Title	Year
19.	Alexander Henry's Travels and Adventures in the Years 1760-1776	1921
20.	John Long's Voyages and Travels in the Years 1768-1788	1922
21.	Adventures of the First Settlers on the Oregon or Columbia River by Alexander Ross	1923
22.	The Fur Hunters of the Far West by Alexander Ross	1924
23.	The Southwestern Expedition of Zebulon M. Pike	1925
24.	Commerce of the Prairies by Josiah Gregg	1926
25.	Death Valley in '49 by William L. Manly	1927
26.	Bidwell's Echoes of the Past—Steele's In Camp and Cabin.	1928
27.	Kendall's Texan Santa Fe Expedition	1929
28.	Pattie's Personal Narrative	1930
29.	Alexander Mackenzie's Voyage to the Pacific Ocean in 1793	1931
30.	Wau-Bun, The "Early Day" in the North-West by Mrs. John H. Kinzie.	1932
31.	Forty Years a Fur Trader by Charles Larpenteur	1933
32.	Narrative of the Adventures of Zenas Leonard.	1934
33.	Kit Carson's Autobiography	1935
34.	A True Picture of Emigration by Rebecca Burlend	1936
35.	The Bark Covered House by William Nowlin.	1937
36.	The Border and the Buffalo by John R. Cook.	1938
37.	Vanished Arizona by Martha Summerhayes	1939
38.	War on the Detroit by Thomas Verchères de Boucherville and James Foster	1940
39.	Army Life in Dakota by Philippe de Trobriand	1941

Number *Title* *Year*

40. The Early Day of Rock Island and Davenport
   by J. W. Spencer and J. M. D. Burrows   1942

41. Six Years with the Texas Rangers
   by James B. Gillett   1943

42. Growing Up with Southern Illinois
   by Daniel Harmon Brush   1944

43. A History of Illinois, I, by Gov. Thomas Ford . .   1945

44. A History of Illinois, II, by Gov. Thomas Ford .   1946

45. The Western Country in the 17th Century
   by Lamothe Cadillac and Pierre Liette   1947

46. Across the Plains in Forty-nine
   by Reuben Cole Shaw   1948

47. Pictures of Gold Rush California.   1949

48. Absaraka, Home of the Crows
   by Mrs. Margaret I. Carrington.   1950

49. The Truth about Geronimo by Britton Davis . .   1951

50. My Life on the Plains
   by General George A. Custer   1952

51. Three Years Among the Indians and Mexicans
   by General Thomas James   1953

52. A Voyage to the Northwest Coast of America
   by Gabriel Franchère   1954

53. War-Path and Bivouac by John F. Finerty . . .   1955

54. Milford's Memoir by Louis Leclerc de Milford .   1956

55. Uncle Dick Wootton by Howard Louis Conard .   1957

56. The Siege of Detroit in 1763   1958

57. Among the Indians by Henry A. Boller   1959

58. Hardtack and Coffee by John D. Billings. . . .   1960

59. Outlines from the Outpost by John Esten Cooke   1961

60. Colorado Volunteers in New Mexico, 1862
   by Ovando J. Hollister   1962

Number	Title	Year

61. Private Smith's Journal   1963

62. Two Views of Gettysburg by Sir. A. J. L.
    Fremantle and Frank Haskell   1964

63. Dakota War Whoop
    by Harriet E. Bishop McConkey   1965

64. Honolulu by Laura Fish Judd   1966

65. Three Years in the Klondike by Jeremiah Lynch .   1967

66. Two Years' Residence on the English Prairie
    of Illinois by John Woods   1968

67. John D. Young and the Colorado Gold Rush . .   1969

68. My Experiences in the West by John S. Collins   1970

69. Narratives of Colonial America, 1704-1765 . . .   1971

70. Pioneers by Noah Harris Letts
    and Thomas Allen Banning, 1825-1865. . . .   1972

71. Excursion Through America by Nicolaus Mohr .   1973

72. A Frenchman in Lincoln's America, Volume I,
    by Ernest Duvergier de Hauranne   1974

73. A Frenchman in Lincoln's America, Volume II,
    by Ernest Duvergier de Hauranne   1975

74. Narratives of the American Revolution   1976

75. Advocates and Adversaries by Robert R. Rose .   1977

76. Hell among the Yearlings by Edmund Randolph   1978

77. A Frontier Doctor by Henry F. Hoyt   1979

78. Mrs. Hill's Journal—Civil War Reminiscences
    by Sarah Jane Full Hill   1980

79. Skyward by Rear Admiral Richard E. Byrd. . .   1981

80. Helldorado by William M. Breakenridge. . . .   1982

81. Mark Twain's West   1983

82. Frontier Fighter by George W. Coe.   1984

83. Buckskin and Blanket Days
    by Thomas Henry Tibbles   1985

Number	*Title*	*Year*
84.	Autobiography of an English Soldier in the United States Army by George Ballentine.	1986
85.	Life of Tom Horn	1987
86.	Children of Ol' Man River by Billy Bryant	1988
87.	Westward Journeys by Jesse A. Applegate and Lavinia Honeyman Porter	1989
88.	Narrative of My Captivity among the Sioux Indians by Fanny Kelly	1990
89.	We Pointed Them North by E. C. "Teddy Blue" Abbott and Helena Huntington Smith	1991
90.	A Texas Ranger by N. A. Jennings	1992
91.	From Mexican Days to the Gold Rush by James W. Marshall and E. Gould Buffum	1993
92.	My Life East and West by William S. Hart	1994
93.	The Logbook of the Captain's Clerk by John S. Sewell	1995
94.	Arctic Explorations by Elisha Kent Kane, M.D., U.S.N.	1996
95.	Fighting the Flying Circus by Capt. Edward V. Rickenbacker	1997
96.	Behind the Scenes by Elizabeth Keckley	1998
97.	Revolutionary Days by Princess Julia Cantacuzene	1999

DESIGNED, TYPESET, PRINTED, BOUND, AND DISTRIBUTED BY
R.R. DONNELLEY & SONS COMPANY

COMPOSITION:
ALLENTOWN DIGITAL SERVICES,
ALLENTOWN, PENNSYLVANIA

SCANNING, COMPUTER TO PLATES, PRESSWORK, AND BINDING:
CRAWFORDSVILLE, INDIANA, BOOK MANUFACTURING DIVISION

IMAGE PROOFING (EASTMAN KODAK APPROVAL DIGITAL COLOR):
WARSAW, INDIANA, CATALOG MANUFACTURING DIVISION

MAPS:
MAPQUEST.COM, INC., LANCASTER, PENNSYLVANIA

WORLDWIDE DISTRIBUTION:
DONNELLEY LOGISTICS SERVICES

BODY TYPEFACE:
11/12 POINT BULMER

PAPER STOCK:
50-POUND WHITE LAKESIDE CLASSICS OPAQUE,
50-PERCENT RECYCLED SHEET, BY GLATFELTER

CLOTH:
ROXITE C VELLUM CHOCOLATE BROWN,
BY HOLLISTON MILLS, INC.